PATENTING LIVES

Intellectual Property, Theory, Culture

Series Editor: Johanna Gibson, Herchel Smith Professor of Intellectual Property
Law, Co-Director Queen Mary University of London, UK

This series presents theoretical and cultural examinations of intellectual property
laws, developments, and policy. Volumes in the series may be identified by their
innovative and critical analyses and their original contributions to international
debate. Interdisciplinary in approach, the series will be of interest to intellectual
property experts and stakeholders, policy advisors, and NGOs, as well as students
and researchers in the very critical areas of intellectual property law, anthropology,
and cultural studies.

Forthcoming titles in the series:

Intellectual Property Aspects of Medicine
Current Debates
Johanna Gibson
ISBN 978-0-7546-7218-0

Patenting Lives
Life Patents, Culture and Development

Edited by

JOHANNA GIBSON
Queen Mary University of London, UK

ASHGATE

Published by
Ashgate Publishing Limited
Gower House
Croft Road
Aldershot
Hampshire GU11 3HR
England

Ashgate Publishing Company
Suite 420
101 Cherry Street
Burlington, VT 05401-4405
USA

www.ashgate.com

British Library Cataloguing in Publication Data
Patenting lives : life patents, culture and development. -
    (Intellectual property, theory, culture)
    1. Life sciences - Patents
    I. Gibson, Johanna
    346'.0486

Library of Congress Cataloging-in-Publication Data
Patenting lives : life patents, culture and development / [edited] by Johanna Gibson.
    p. cm. -- (Intellectual property, theory, culture)
    Includes index.
    ISBN 978-0-7546-7104-6 (alk. paper)
    1. Biotechnology--Patents. 2. Biotechnology. I. Gibson, Johanna.

    K1519.B54P378 2008
    346.04'86--dc22
                                                                    2008009815
ISBN 978-0-7546-7104-6

Mixed Sources
Product group from well-managed
forests and other controlled sources
www.fsc.org Cert no. SGS-COC-2482
© 1996 Forest Stewardship Council
FSC

Printed and bound in Great Britain by
TJ International Ltd, Padstow, Cornwall

Contents

List of Contributors

Kathryn Garforth is the Legal Officer for the Biosafety division of the United Nations Secretariat of the Convention on Biological Diversity. Her chapter was written while she was working as an independent consultant.

Johanna Gibson is Herchel Smith Professor of Intellectual Property Law and Director of the Queen Mary Intellectual Property Research Institute, Queen Mary University of London, where she researches and teaches in intellectual property and traditional knowledge. Johanna was Director of the AHRC Patenting Lives Project and was an expert interviewee for the European Patent Office *Scenarios for the Future* Project.

Tony Howard graduated from Cambridge in Natural Sciences in 1976 and, following two years in industry, joined the Patent Office (now the UK-IPO) as an examiner in 1978. His assignments have included operational and policy work, including EU and domestic patent and other intellectual property law. Since May 2007, he has been an *inter partes* hearing officer and Divisional Director, with responsibilities taking in development of UK patent law and practice, as well as approximately one third of the patent examination function of the Office, including chemical, biotechnological and mechanical subject-matter areas.

Fred Håkon Johnsen is Associate Professor in the Department of International Environment and Development Studies (Noragric), Norwegian University of Life Sciences (UMB), Agricultural University of Norway NLH. His research interests include resource economics in development studies, project appraisal (cost benefit and cost effectiveness analysis) and smallholder farmer development.

Chika B. Onwuekwe, LL.B, LL.M, PhD, is a consultant and attorney-at-law (Canadian and Nigerian Bar). Dr Onwuekwe is an Associate at MacPherson Leslie & Tyerman LLP, a foremost Canadian law firm. He practises, consults and publishes in the areas of emerging and transformative technologies, intellectual property, business law, natural resources law, emerging democracies, governance and policy issues around resource allocation and intellectual property.

Adejoke Oyewunmi is a barrister and solicitor of the Supreme Court of Nigeria, as well as a senior lecturer in the Department of Commercial and Industrial Law, Faculty of Law, University of Lagos. She was formerly the Sub-Dean of the Faculty of Law, University of Lagos. Between January and December 2000, she was a World Intellectual Property (WIPO) Fellow at the Franklin Pierce Law Centre, Concord, New Hampshire USA, where she obtained a masters degree in intellectual property law (LLM IP). She also holds an inter-departmental masters degree (LLM) of the

University of Lagos (1991), and a bachelor of laws degree (LLB) of the Obafemi Awolowo University, Ile-Ife, Nigeria (1988), and was called to the Nigerian Bar in December 1989. In the course of her teaching and research experience, she has published papers in the area of intellectual property, labour law and other commercial and industrial law subjects.

Luigi Palombi, LL.B., B.Ec., PhD, has practised law for over twenty-five years and is a specialist in intellectual property, but particularly with regard to patents over biological materials and their application in human diagnostics, therapeutics and pharmaceuticals. He consults to and advises various international and governmental organisations and law firms on specific matters concerning intellectual property and lectures and writes on the subject. He is currently a member of the Centre for the Governance of Knowledge and Development at the Regulatory Institutions Network at The Australian National University where he is undertaking an Australian Research Council project on traditional knowledge and intellectual property, in collaboration with his colleague, Prof. Peter Drahos.

Diwakar Poudel's academic background is in natural resources management and agriculture. He holds an MSc (Norway) and is currently working in a national non-governmental organization, Local Initiatives for Biodiversity, Research and Development (LIBIRD), Nepal. He has been working as a socio-economist in the field of agrobiodiversity conservation for the past five years, where he has worked on economic valuation methods for the analysis of biodiversity, socio-economic studies on the management of biodiversity and its components, social network analysis for informal seed and information flow studies, and participatory research and development (PR & D). His research interests include biodiversity valuation, common-pool resources management, economic aspects of biodiversity, policy on agrobiodiversity, and the study of environmental benefits.

Dwijen Rangnekar is a Research Councils UK Senior Fellow at the University of Warwick – a post held jointly between the Centre for the Study of Globalisation and Regionalisation and the School of Law As an evolutionary economist. His research focuses on the innovation process, technical change, knowledge production, and appropriation strategies; of special interest is the role of intellectual property rights. The issues that are of interest include the transformation of the agro-food industries and the relationship between plant variety protection and patent law; biotechnology, the life science industries and patent law; intellectual property rights and plant genetic resources; the international politics of intellectual property rights; protection of traditional knowledge, rural development and the role of geographical indications and trade marks; and the impact of intellectual property rights on knowledge production. He teaches on the LLM program and is the course convenor for International Intellectual Property Rights and Policy. He has worked as a consultant for, inter alia, the UK Government's Commission on Intellectual Property Rights, the United Nations Conference on Trade and Development (UNCTAD), the International Centre for Trade and Sustainable Development (ICTSD), ActionAid, Oxfam, UK Food Group, Panos, and the World-Wide Fund for Nature.

Daniel Robinson has worked for several years on intellectual property, traditional knowledge and biodiversity issues, particularly in Asia. Dr Robinson is currently a lecturer in environment and geography at the Institute of Environmental Studies, the University of New South Wales (UNSW). He has had research affiliations with the Australian Mekong Resource Centre, the University of Sydney; the Intellectual Property Research Institute of Australia (IPRIA), Melbourne; and the National Human Rights Commission of Thailand. On intellectual property issues, Daniel has worked for, or consulted to, several organisations including the International Centre for Trade and Sustainable Development and United Nations Conference on Trade and Development (ICTSD-UNCTAD) joint project on intellectual property, the Pacific Forum Secretariat, and the United Nations Development Programme. Daniel has a PhD on *Traditional Knowledge in Thailand* from the University of Sydney, as well as degrees in environmental law and environmental science.

Angela A. Stanton PhD is Assistant Professor of Economics at the Argyros School of Business and Economics at Chapman University and a research scientist at the Center for Neuroeconomics Studies at Claremont Graduate University, both in California, USA. Her research interest is the understanding of the neural substrates of human decision-making. She runs economic decision-making experiments with the use of a variety of hormones that stimulate enhanced responses in decision-making in particular directions. Currently she is working on a variety of projects examining the function of trust, generosity, and spitefulness in human decision-making.

Acknowledgements

The Patenting Lives Research Project was funded by a research grant and dissemination grant awarded by Arts and Humanities Research Council (AHRC), United Kingdom and it is to the AHRC that the greatest gratitude must be acknowledged. The AHRC's generosity ensured that the diverse contributors to this volume could collaborate on this collection, considering the technical application of patents in their many cultural contexts. I also wish to thank the Queen Mary Intellectual Property Research Institute (QMIPRI) for its rich intellectual community and tremendous support, particularly that of Charlotte Knights, who was instrumental in the administration of the project, Sharon Watson, who provided tireless administrative support, and Malcolm Langley, for his excellent development of the Queen Mary Intellectual Property Archive. Above all, thanks to the foresight of inventor, Dr Herchel Smith (1925–2001), whose tremendous generosity established QMIPRI almost three decades ago.

The early stages in the project involved two expert meetings of key individuals from diverse backgrounds in order to decipher the "public interests" at stake in these debates. Great appreciation and respect is due to Michelle Childs (Knowledge Ecology International), Gail Evans (QMIPRI), Vera Franz (Open Society Institute), Frederick Friend (Joint Information Society Council), Andrés Guadamuz (AHRC Research Centre for Studies in Intellectual Property and Technology, University of Edinburgh), James Leach (University of Aberdeen), Paul Leonard (Intellectual Property Institute), Christopher May (Lancaster), Andrew Moutu (Cambridge), Paul Oldham (CESAGen, Lancaster) and Geoff Tansey (Independent Consultant).

To the many participants in the Conference, this collection has been enriched by their contributions, discussion and debate, including the significant input and interest of Shirin Elahi, Berthold Rutz and Guy Carmichael (European Patent Office), Jeremy deBeer (University of Ottawa), Ashish Gosain (Advocate, Supreme Court of India), Edson Béas Rodrigues (University of São Paolo), Reetu Sogani (AADHAR) and Sangeeta Udgaonkar (Advocate, Maharashtra). Finally, thank you to the authors in this volume. And a special thanks to Phillip Johnson, Sean Smith and Guido Westkamp for their organisation and help. What has been made possible by the AHRC is a collaboration of work from researchers and civil society organisations in developing countries that grounds this volume as a genuine expression of the 'public' in these significant legal, political and cultural debates.

Johanna Gibson
January 2008

Dedicated to our network

Introduction

Patent Publics, Patent Cultures

Johanna Gibson

> Now, who is better able than scientists to make the world speak, write, hold forth? Their work consists precisely in inventing, through the intermediary of instruments and the artifice of the laboratory, the *displacement of point of view* that is so indispensable to public life.[1]

1. Introduction

The social and cultural dimensions of intellectual property frameworks are significant subject matter of intellectual examination and investigation. Indeed, the economic impact of patents on development and local infrastructures is of particular concern. However, critical engagement with patent law, as an area of intellectual property law, is generally undertaken in ways that are somewhat in contrast to the emphases on communication and cultural life that we see in other areas of intellectual property debate, such as copyright. Indeed, what is suggested is a distinction between the creativity of 'cultural goods', protected by copyright, and the technical skill of utilitarian economic goods, protected by patents.[2] Copyright protection arises automatically (a flash of inspiration perhaps?). Patent protection requires registration and the satisfaction of various criteria – including utility or industrial application (a patent is protection for a solution to a technical problem – a useless invention cannot be an invention, by very definition).

In other words, rightly or wrongly, what is suggested is perhaps a lesser public engagement with this area of intellectual property law, possibly because of its perceived technical and utilitarian character, which appears to distance users from the debate. This is notwithstanding discussions regarding access to medicines, access to seed and other examples, but the distance persists in the way in which criticism and recommendations are constrained within the framework of encouraging and disseminating innovation as an economic activity. Why is a patent not part of our cultural life?

This difference in treatment at the level of public debate more widely somewhat obscures the cultural aspects of patents. Patents in biotechnology and gene-related inventions are in fact an important legal and analytical nexus for the use and consumption of patents (their cultural character) and the economic interpretations of the market created for such products. In other words, what is the role of users

---

1 B. Latour, *Politics of Nature: How to Bring the Sciences into Democracy*, C. Porter (trans) (Cambridge MA: Harvard UP 2004), 137–8.

2 For instance, see the discussion by D. Throsby, *Economics and Culture* (Cambridge 2001), 5.

in motivating innovation and influencing the development of patent law and its interpretation? Arguably, it is significant and timely to recognise the cultural character of patent law and the growing relevance of users of the system in the interpretation of the market and in the development of the law.

In order to contribute meaningfully to this debate, the objective of the Patenting Lives Project[3] was to generate a network of researchers from diverse disciplines and contexts in order to examine not only the broader impacts, but also the diverse 'publics' constituted and motivated by this debate.

2. The Two Cultures of Patent Law

> This polarisation is sheer loss to us all. To us as people, and to our society. It is at the same time practical and intellectual and creative loss, and I repeat that it is false to imagine that those three considerations are clearly separable.[4]

The notion of 'two cultures' was presented with subsequent controversy in a 1959 lecture by Lord Snow, scientist and one time assistant to the Minister of Technology in the government of Harold Wilson, and Rector of St Andrews in the early 1960s. In his 1959 Rede lecture, 'The Two Cultures and the Scientific Revolution',[5] Lord Snow's lecture indeed anticipated this emphasis on interdisciplinary research, and it seems appropriate to reiterate it here to contextualise the Patenting Lives Project and this subsequent collection of the contributors to that network. Lord Snow was very derisive in his lecture of each culture's ignorance of the other – not only the illiteracy of the sciences when it came to the arts, but also the ignorance of intellectuals when it came to the sciences. Arguably, this kind of mutual elitism continues today in the patent law debates. Scientific innovation is separated as an economic and utilitarian activity, with little in common with the cultural products 'defended' against other intellectual property frameworks. What is left is a kind of innovation/creativity dichotomy. That is, one is an accountable, utilitarian narrative – that of innovation. The other is by contrast unaccountable, automatically protected by copyright and indefinable – the wellspring of creativity. It is this deferral of creativity in invention that obscures significant traditions in scientific research, such as the cultures of collaboration and esteem lauded by noted contemporary scientific figures like Sir John Sulston (known for his role in the Human Genome Project and his efforts to keep the information in the public domain).

This cultural character of patent law may be traced to the very functioning of the system itself. For the purposes of intellectual property law, there is no protection for information alone – only once it is fixed in some way (a book for copyright; a patent specification that discloses a technical solution to a problem for patent protection). This makes sense – not only would it be unconscionable to try and create

---

3 The Patenting Lives Project was funded by an Arts and Humanities Research Council (UK) Research Grant (2004 2005) and Dissemination Scheme (2006–2007), awarded to Johanna Gibson, the Principal Investigator.
4 C.P. Snow, *The Two Cultures* (Cambridge: Cambridge University Press 1998), 11.
5 *Ibid*, 1–21.

a market purely in ideas, but also it would be arguably inconceivable. Information is inexhaustible. So the market is achieved, rather, by imposing an artificial scarcity on that information through the application of intellectual property restrictions on use. The patent is perceived as a kind of contract solution to the imperfect competition in information and the perceived incentive problem that goes with this. The very value of a patent pivots on this relationship to use.

3. What are Life Patents?

The Agreement on Trade Related Aspects of Intellectual Property (TRIPS) mandates that patent protection must be extended to all fields of technology (Article 27.1), including biotechnology. Such inventions might include inventions based on gene sequences or whole organisms – the so-called 'life patents'. In the European Union, the introduction of the Directive on the legal protection of biotechnological inventions[6] is noteworthy for its attempt to harmonise 'attention' to biotechnology inventions, keeping in mind that patent law effectively was at the time, and continues to be, the subject matter of national members or the European Patent Office. Arguably, the Directive was created in the context of an emerging and uncertain market. In clarifying the validity of biotechnology inventions, the Directive says more about use as invention and the relevance of the market to the development of the interpretation of patent law in the field of biotechnology. Strikingly, biotechnology and biotechnology patents suggest a critical episode in the role of the user in modern patent law.

The development of patent protection for inventions relating to gene sequences has provoked both much debate and a considerable amount of concern and indeed misunderstanding. But in so far as intellectual property protection is afforded to products in order to develop and sustain certain markets, any misunderstanding cannot be dismissed. This is the very 'use' of the patent system. What is very interesting about this debate, and what is informing the development of economic analyses of innovation, is the very nature of the intellectual property bargain with the public, the 'users'. Most recently, this bargain is such that the relationship with the consumer underpins the legitimacy of the law. Patent law has received less attention from this perspective, that is, from the perspective of consumer and market limits on innovation. How might this public of 'users' be constituted in the research context?

4. What is Patenting Lives?

The Patenting Lives Project has been concerned with looking at the impact of patent protection in various areas of biotechnology and, in particular, so-called 'life patents' (patents relating to plants and animals). In this respect, the Project was especially interested in the socio-economic and cultural aspects of patent protection in these areas of technology.

---

6 Directive 98/44/EC on the legal protection of biotechnology inventions.

In its initial stages, the Project involved a core interdisciplinary expert group of intellectual property lawyers, social and cultural anthropologists, political scientists, social scientists, agricultural consultants, and non-governmental organisations, which met for the first time in February 2005. This group set out to identify and articulate key issues and interests at stake in the complex interaction of legal, ethical, cultural, and socio-economic factors. Most significantly, the assembling of experts across diverse but related fields reflected the objectives of achieving a breadth and integrity of the collaboration in this respect, as well as the relevance of the research across the widest range of interested persons and groups. The strong interdisciplinarity of the expert group that initiated the foci of the project was in part an awareness of the need to address the wider context in which patent law is developed and is applied.

The Project was fundamentally concerned with the diverse impact of international harmonisation of patent protection with a view to achieving a further understanding of 'intellectual property', as a cultural institution as it were, particularly in the way in which this term is in circulation in public policy and intergovernmental debate. In this respect, the patent frameworks, as applied to these technologies, with other international frameworks, including biodiversity, the environment, and human rights comprise an organising principle not only of the research but also of this book. As well as identifying the critical factors informing policy making and public debate, the authors necessarily consider the appropriateness or otherwise of patent protection (and other forms of intellectual property protection) to the specific forms of technology and processes of innovation in question here. The primary question of the various groups invested, as it were, in these issues is whether patent protection is compatible with the facilitation of social, cultural, and economic development in the context of international principles of trade.

5. The Patent Public

The Patenting Lives Project was in particular an attempt to motivate diverse input into issues and questions of patent application in biotechnologies. Indeed, this is an essential aspect of broadening the debate on these issues in that interdisciplinary discussion is also a kind of recognition of the diversity and division within the so-called 'public,' a deceptively uniform term. Ordinarily, this 'public' is represented rather than known through the articulation of opinion, generalised and prompted by intellectual property frameworks rather than informing. One of the aims of the Project and of this collection is to drive developments from the 'public' by facilitating diverse contributions. So the Patenting Lives conference and this collection attempt also, in the broader structural sense, to consider how that opinion is generated and captures the focus of a 'public.' In other words, the anonymous public emerges as a collection of active rather than passive users, and the technical distance is somewhat recovered in these debates.

For such reasons, this collection is often divergent and unexpected in its approach to these issues, showcasing various responses to these questions, including what may be considered non-technical or other responses, NGO and activist activity, and so on. As an editor, it has been critical to preserve the dynamic nature of this discussion and to facilitate the sometimes 'disagreeable' public. Indeed, it is neither possible nor desirable to intrude upon what is arguably one of the key expressions of this collection – the patent publics themselves. Our very disagreements, as contributors to this volume, are integral to the richness of the collection.

6. The Structure of 'Patenting Lives'

Drawing upon those early meetings of the Project, the collection characterises four key areas of intersection with life patents. In Part 1 – Context – Tony Howard, UK Intellectual Property Office, provides an important legal context for the chapters that follow. In providing a legal background to the questions of availability and scope, Howard's chapter delimits the framework for use. Importantly, this chapter also shows the way in which international agreements are translated in a national context for national practices, namely those of the UK Intellectual Property Office.

The second part – Human Rights and Ethical Frameworks – brings together two often divergent perspectives on the ethical challenges posed by biotechnology patents. Kathryn Garforth presents a critical 'triptych', exploring the interaction of biotechnology, ethics and patent law. In particular, Garforth explores the impact of language in the debate, the mechanism by which these concepts are understood and deployed, and the mechanism facilitating what she argues is a specious and unethical inclusion of genetically modified organisms within the discourse of patent law. Adejoke Oyewunmi examines the way in which the market for certain technologies has re-focused the intellectual property debate between developed and developing countries. Oyewunmi explains the way in which investment has motivated developments in intellectual property particularly in the field of biotechnology. In doing so, she artfully demonstrates the relevance of the historical and traditional use of living material (particularly in the context of traditional farming methods) and the way in which commercial models of patent law may limit traditional methods of dealing with and innovating upon living material. Further, she notes that there is an important diversity within developing countries as well, very carefully outlining the issues beyond a polarised north-south debate, that is, the cultural diversity in patent application in these fields of technology.

In the third part – Medicine and Public Health – Luigi Palombi explores the very question of use with respect to the patentability of inventions related to gene sequence. In order to address innovation in the specific research context presented by gene sequences, Palombi proposes a *sui generis* right, which he calls the Genetic Sequence Right, and the banning of patent protection in this field of technology. Angela A. Stanton makes a radical re-interpretation of the infamous case of *Moore v Regents of the University of California*,[7] reasoning that the opportunity to work upon tissue removed from the body is a troubling distancing of the human medical subject from their own cells – the 'eminent domain'. Stanton argues that this significant case demonstrates a prioritising of private rights over public interest.

---

7 51 Cal.3d 120 (1990).

Chika B. Onwuekwe and Daniel Robinson contribute two very valuable chapters to the overall literature on traditional knowledge and biotechnology in the fourth section, Traditional Knowledge. Chika B. Onwuekwe considers the distinction between higher and lower life forms and the consequent complications for the proprietary issues accompanying plant genetic resources and the associated traditional knowledge. In doing so, he describes the potential inequity and inconsistency of proprietary models. Daniel Robinson examines the way in which regulatory systems for traditional knowledge attempt to control use through the governance of access, relying in particular on the case studies of ethnic minorities in Northern Thailand. Robinson notes that benefit sharing arrangements, a gesture towards proprietary-like recognition, do not necessarily translate into community governance of resources according to customary law and so play no role in facilitating and sustaining indigenous and traditional knowledge and custom associated with those resources. For instance, attempts to document traditional knowledge are merely static records and do nothing, he argues, to promote traditional knowledge and innovation. Instead, he argues for stronger community rights, that is, emphasis on the communities themselves and their living knowledge, rather than merely upon the static objects of documentation.

The final part, Agriculture, is arguably one of the most critical arenas in which the cultural and developmental differences are experienced in the field of biotechnology. Diwakar Poudel and Fred Håkon Johnsen have contributed the results and insightful analysis of research into the relationship between farming and conservation in Kaski Nepal. Poudel, working from the perspective of a national non-governmental organisation, and Johnsen, from a European academic context, collaborate on a significant contribution to the debate on agriculture and conservation. The study shows that farmers are instrumental in conservation projects and community gene banks in particular, for which they are willing to pay much higher amounts. Relevant to this willingness, however, are the surrounding socio-economic factors, including education and knowledge. Nevertheless, the overwhelming support for community gene banks, as distinct from government gene banks, is noteworthy. In the second paper in this section and the final paper in the collection, Dwijen Rangnekar importantly looks at the possibility of exceptions to patents in agriculture, as provided in Article 27.3(b), bringing together the concerns of economics, use and socio-political context that inform the papers throughout this collection.

7. Conclusion

The objective of the Patenting Lives Project and of this collection is to try and facilitate public responses to life patents and to understand the relationship between public perceptions, the creation of the market, and environmental questions. If nothing else, the debates and inevitable disagreements in this book must remind us that technology is cultural, and that those with the greatest means, and those with the authority over the means of production, will have a significant role in the cultural life of citizens. It is this interaction that is of particular interest to the work of the Patenting Lives Project and will, I hope, be especially visible throughout this book.

PART 1
Context

Chapter 1

The Legal Framework Surrounding Patents for Living Materials

Tony Howard[1]

1. Introduction

With recent scientific and technical advances, particularly in biotechnology, knowledge has become, to an even greater degree than before, a key competitive advantage for both companies and countries. Intellectual property (IP) is a form of knowledge which some societies have decided can be assigned specific property rights, rights which have some resemblance to ownership rights over physical property or land. These IP rights are awarded by society to individuals or organisations principally over creative works i.e. inventions, literary and artistic works, and symbols, names, images and designs used in commerce, and give the creator the right to prevent others from making unauthorised use of their property for a limited period. IP is categorised as Industrial Property (Patents, Industrial Designs, Trademarks, Geographical Indications and Trade Secrets) and Artistic and Literary Property (Copyright) but, since current technological developments are, to some extent, blurring this distinction, some hybrid *sui generis* systems have emerged (e.g. Plant Breeders' Rights, Database Protection).

2. Patents and Patent Law

Patent law throughout Europe was, by and large, set by the European Patent Convention (EPC) in the 1970s and led to important harmonisation of the requirements for patentability among the EPC contracting States, as well as the establishment of the European Patent Office (EPO). The EPC (currently in force in 32 countries) is a multilateral treaty that provides a legal framework for the granting of European patents, via a single, harmonised procedure before the EPO. A patent in a European country which is a member of the EPC can be obtained either by applying to the national office in that country or by filing an application at the EPO. The effect of a patent awarded by the EPO is to create, for the Contracting States designated by the applicant, a series of parallel national patents, which are treated as

---

1 This text is part derived from a Study by the Intellectual Property Institute (IPI) on behalf of the DTI on *Patents for Genetic Sequences: The Competitiveness of Current UK Law and Practice* (May 2004) and the Report of the Commission on Intellectual Property Rights on *Integrating Intellectual Property Rights and Development Policy* (September 2002).

if they had been granted by each national patent office of each designated state. In 2000 the Convention was revised to integrate in the EPC, amongst other things, new developments in international law, especially those of the TRIPs Agreement and of the Patent Law Treaty. The revised Convention (EPC 2000) has entered into force on the 13th December 2007.

Patent practice in the UK grew up on the back of precedent cases in the UK courts and the Boards of Appeal of the EPO. Throughout the 1980s and early 1990s practice relating to biotechnological inventions in patent offices across Europe was not always in agreement over what was patentable or what was the appropriate breadth of patent claims and further harmonisation became a desirable objective. The existing patent law could not cope with biotech inventions, designed as it was for inventions which were far removed from those at the forefront of the biotech revolution. So, in an attempt to achieve harmonisation, an initiative for a European Directive was launched in 1988. Following rejection of the first proposal, primarily on ethical grounds, the EC Commission introduced a revised proposal which was finally adopted in 1998 as the European Directive on the Legal Protection of Biotechnological Inventions[2] (the Directive). The Directive has been incorporated, in so far as it is relevant to pre-grant proceedings, into the EPC by amendment of the Implementing Regulations to the Convention. Although the EPO is not bound by the provisions of the Directive (since it is not a member of the European Union) in 1999 the Administrative Council of the EPO amended the Rules of the EPC to include a new chapter on biotechnological inventions.[3] The Directive now clarifies how patenting applies to biotech inventions and concerns maintaining and encouraging investment in the field of biotechnology, addressing differences in the legal protection of biotechnological inventions, providing effective and harmonised protection across the European Community and balancing ethical considerations.

In 2000 the UK began to amend its patent law in order to implement the Directive. Articles 1 to 11 of the Directive were implemented by the Patents Regulations 2000;[4] Articles 13 to 14 were implemented by the Patents (Amendment) Rules 2001;[5] and Article 12 was implemented as the Patents and Plant Variety Rights (Compulsory Licensing) Regulations in 2002.[6] The Directive confirmed and clarified that inventions concerning biotechnological material, including gene sequences, may legitimately be the subject of patent protection and that such inventions are to be regarded from the same perspective as other inventions. Recital 8 of the Directive emphasises that a separate body of law is not required for the protection of biotechnological inventions and that the rules of national law remain the basis for such protection. A number of Member States were significantly late in implementing the Directive. An important reason for this was the uncertainty surrounding the bioethical and moral aspects of the law contained within the Directive, and concerns that it might, for example,

---

2 Directive 98/44/EC.

3 Implementing Regulations of the EPC, r. 23b-23e.

4 SI 2000/2037.

5 SI 2001/1412. The rules have now been consolidated in the Patents Rules 2007 (SI 2007/3291).

6 SI 2002/247.

run counter to the principles set down in the Council of Europe's Co
Human Rights and Biomedicine.[7] The unease with which these Member
regarded the Directive is mirrored in sections of the wider European pub
Commission has acknowledged the ongoing potential for conflict over con........uus
issues.[8]

Patents

Patents are exclusive rights granted for a limited period of time by states to prevent
others from exploiting the patent proprietor's invention. A patent is granted for
inventions which involve a novel advance over the prior art. In achieving protection
for this advance the applicant must also demonstrate, via the patent specification, that
it was not an obvious advance on the state of the art, that the invention is complete
(and does not require further development) and also that the inventive concept is
supported by the description provided. A patent will not be granted if the technical
advance was known or obvious at the date at which the patent application was filed.
It is necessary to examine every application to ensure that the public interest is served
by granting monopolies only where there is clear evidence that these are justified and
also to protect the interests of the patent holder and third parties.

Owners of patents will often exploit commercially the in patented inventions
themselves, but possession of a patent alone does not require this. It is possible
to have a patent but not to use or enforce it. Many patents are also licensed by the
owner to other parties for commercial use. A common misconception is that a patent
gives an inventor a right to exploit their invention: it does not. Exploitation will
depend on whether others have patents that overlap with the subject matter of the
invention, and will be subject to other laws, such as for example those concerning
health and safety.

3. Patentability of Biotechnological Inventions

The first attempts to secure intellectual property rights on living material can be
traced back to the nineteenth century. Article 1(3) of the Paris Convention on Industry
Property Rights states that 'Industrial property shall be understood in the broadest
sense and shall apply not only to industry and commerce proper, but likewise to
agricultural and extractive industries and to all manufactured or natural products,
for example wines, grain, tobacco leaf, fruit, cattle, minerals, mineral waters, beer,
flowers and flour'. This document does not state that living material or material
derived from living material should not be the subject of intellectual property rights

---

7 Convention for the Protection of Human Rights and Dignity of the Human Being
with regard to the Application of Biology and Medicine: Convention on Human Rights and
Biomedicine (October 1997).

8 Commission Staff Working Paper, *Results of the Public Consultation: Towards a
Strategic Vision of Life Sciences and Biotechnology*, SEC (2002), 630, 29 May 2002, Pt II.C.

and, indeed, there are many examples of patents granted on isolated natural products including Louis Pasteur's 1873 patent[9] for yeast.

The Directive confirms that biological material which has been isolated from its natural environment, or produced by means of a technical process, may, all other things being equal, be the subject of an invention even if it previously occurred in nature provided that the resulting biotechnological invention meets the usual threshold for protection. Article 3(1) of the Directive[10] states that:

> ... inventions which are new, which involve an inventive step and which are susceptible of industrial application shall be patentable even if they concern a product consisting of or containing biological material or a process by means of which biological material is produced, processes or used.

Novelty

Section 2 of the Patents Act 1977 concerns the novelty requirement in the UK:

> (1) An invention shall be taken to be new if it does not form part of the state of the art.
> (2) The state of the art shall be taken to comprise all matter which has at any time before the priority date been made available to the public...

The general patent law requirement for novelty is that an invention must not have been made available previously, in any document or by any action disclosed in such a way as to make it part of the state of the art, prior to the patent application being filed. A novelty destroying disclosure must also be 'enabling' if what is disclosed is to be regarded as being 'made available to the public'.

This principle has been established in the context of a number of biotechnology cases[11] and on this basis a disclosure only destroys the novelty of a later invention if the information it contains, when understood by a person skilled in the art, is sufficient to allow reproduction of the invention. The novelty requirement under UK law and the EPC is the same.[12]

The application of the novelty test to biotechnological inventions deserves special consideration not least because many biotech inventions are based on natural material. In this respect it is important not to confuse the objection that an invention involving biological material lacks novelty with the objection that the invention is unpatentable because it is merely a discovery. Article 3(2) of the Directive[13] states that:

---

9 US Patent No. 141072.

10 Which corresponds to the Patents Act 1977, Sch A2, para 1.

11 *Asahi's Application* [1991] RPC 485; *Synthon BV v SmithKline Beecham Plc (No.2)* [2006] RPC 10; T81/87 *Collaborative / Preprorennin* (1990) OJEPO 250; *Genentech's (Human Growth Hormone) Patent* [1989] RPC 613.

12 *Kirin-Amgen Inc v. Roche Diagnostics GmbH* [2002] RPC 1.

13 Patents Act 1977, Sch A2, par 2.

Biological material which is isolated from its natural environment or produced by means of a technical process may be the subject of an invention even if it previously occurred in nature.

Furthermore, and of specific relevance to gene patents, Article 5(2) of the Directive[14] states that:

An element isolated from the human body or otherwise produced by means of a technical process, including the sequence or partial sequence of a gene, may constitute a patentable invention even if the structure of that element is identical to that of a natural element.

For example, where genetic material has been isolated from a natural source for the first time then it will not lack novelty simply because it previously existed in nature.

In respect of gene sequences, relevance must be given to the context within which a sequence has been published, in order to assess whether an earlier publication will destroy the novelty of the sequence being claimed. Where the prior publication did not cover the sequence in the context which is the subject-matter of the patent (e.g. if a new application has been identified), then a claim to the sequence for that application is likely to be novel. The practice of recognising novelty for a natural substance which has been isolated for the first time and which had no previously recognised existence was established by a decision of the Opposition Division of the EPO in the *Relaxin* case.[15]

Inventive Step

The inventive step requirement in the UK is covered by section 3 of the Patents Act 1977:

An invention shall be taken to involve an inventive step if it is not obvious to a person skilled in the art, having regard to any matter which forms part of the state of the art by virtue of only section 2(2) above …

It is generally agreed, and is particularly relevant in the field of biotechnology, that a patent should not be granted merely because the applicant has been involved in laborious and costly effort. If the goal is known, and sufficient of the theory and practice is known for the applicant to know where he is going, without there being an original step, then an invention is likely to be regarded as being obvious. This reasoning was partly behind the rejection by the Court of Appeal in *Wellcome*[16] and is also considered in *Chiron*[17] and *Biogen*.[18] Where there is a reasonable expectation of success then the fact of attempting may not be sufficient to demonstrate that it was inventive.

---

14 Patents Act 1977, Sch A2, par 3(a), 5 and 6.
15 V8/94 *Howard Florey Institute's Application / Relaxin* (1995) OJEPO 388.
16 *Wellcome Foundation v. Genentech* [1989] RPC 147.
17 *Chiron v. Organon (No.3)* [1994] FSR 202.
18 *Biogen v Medeva plc* [1993] RPC 475; [1995] RPC 25 (CA); and [1997] RPC 1 (HL).

In relation to biotech inventions specifically it is considered obvious to (i) identify previously unknown members of a known gene/protein family if only arbitrary selection without a surprising result is involved; (ii) identify a gene in a database based on known structural information about the corresponding protein and (iii) assign a function to a gene by homology comparison with genes of known function. Therefore, with the elucidation of the human genome and the genomes of other animal species, together with the growth of bioinformatic techniques to achieve automated comparison of gene functions between species, it becomes increasingly hard to characterise much of this work as anything other than routine and consequently it is increasingly difficult to demonstrate an inventive step.

Industrial Application

All patentable inventions must be capable of industrial application: section 1(1) of the Patents Act 1977 states that:

> A patent may be granted only for an invention in respect of which the following conditions are satisfied, that is to say ... it is capable of industrial application.

This should be read in conjunction with section 4(1):

> ... an invention shall be taken to be capable of industrial application if it can be made or used in any kind of industry, including agriculture.

As defined in the EPC this objection has proved difficult to apply to biotech inventions because the requirement is that an invention must be 'capable of' industrial application. Taken at face value almost all biotech inventions are, in some respects, capable of industrial application. The bigger question is what needs to be specifically demonstrated in a patent application to prove that an invention is industrially applicable?

Where the invention resides in a sequence or partial sequence of a gene then Article 5(3) of the Directive[19] requires that the application must disclose the industrial application of the sequence or partial sequence of a gene and that this must be disclosed in the patent application. The UK Intellectual Property Office (UKIPO) has sought to address the issue of the extent to which an applicant must demonstrate industrial application within the specification. In keeping with the decided policy of the US Patents and Trademark Office (USPTO) and general practice of the EPO,[20] the UKIPO has introduced a requirement that the industrial application of the invention must be shown to be specific, substantial and credible. Taking an often repeated example of a gene sequence as a 'probe', this may be credible in a generic sense but, in the absence of further data, it is not specific enough or substantial enough to overcome an objection to lack of industrial application. However, it should be noted that this examination practice has yet to be tested in the courts.

---

19 Patents Act 1977, Sch A2, para 6.
20 EPO Examination Guidelines (C–IV, 4.6).

It is also common to find biotechnological inventions claimed in terms of methods of treatment of the human or animal body by surgery or therapy or diagnosis practised on the body. However, by virtue of section 4A of the Patents Act 1977 such methods are excluded from patentablity.

Sufficiency

A patent application is required to provide a technical description of the invention and disclose the invention, and the claims relating to it, in sufficient detail to enable a person skilled in the art to perform it. The level of sufficiency of the disclosure can vary and in some instances not every product or process covered by the invention has to be disclosed.[21] *Genentech*[22] was the first significant EPO decision dealing with sufficiency in a biotech context. In the view of the Technical Board of Appeal in this case an invention is sufficiently disclosed if at least one way is clearly indicated enabling the person skilled in the art to carry out the invention. However, it is now the case that only the disclosure of several ways to perform the invention will be required to justify a broad claim. *Mycogen*[23] sets out the interrelationship between sufficiency and the scope of the claims. Essentially, claims of broad scope are not allowable if the skilled person, after reading the description, is not able to readily perform the invention over the whole area claimed without undue burden and without needing inventive skill.

Plant and Animal Varieties

The EPC has conventionally regarded plant and animal varieties as non-patentable subject matter. This exclusion carried over into the Directive in Article 4(1) and (2):[24]

> (1) The following shall not be patentable:
>   (a) plant and animal varieties;
> (2) Inventions which concern plants or animals shall be patentable if the technical feasibility of the invention is not confined to a particular plant or animal variety ...

Patent protection was not considered to be a particularly effective system for the protection of plant varieties and these are protected under the Plant Varieties Act 1997. Both the 1997 Act and the separate European Community Regime[25] are based on the 1991 International Convention on the Protection of New Plant Varieties (UPOV). The system for granting plant variety rights differs substantially from the patent system and to gain protection a sample of the variety must be submitted to the Plant Variety Rights (PVR) Office where it is grown and tested for distinctiveness. However, patent claims may relate to plant genera or species but not individual

---

21 See n. 10 above.
22 T292/85 *Genentech 1 / Polypeptide expression* (1989) OJEPO 275.
23 T694/92 *Mycogen / Modifying plant cells* (1997) OJEPO 408.
24 Patents Act 1977, Sch A2, pars 3(f) and 4.
25 Council Regulation (EC) No 2100 of 1994.

varieties and claims to transgenic plants are acceptable unless expressed in plant variety terms and the invention is not confined to modifying a particular plant variety.

Novartis[26] concerned a patent containing claims to transgenic plants comprising in their genomes specific foreign genes the expression of which resulted in the production of antipathologically active substances, and to methods of preparing such plants. The EPO initially denied grant, supported by the Technical Board of Appeal, on the grounds that the invention could embrace plant varieties. However, the Enlarged Board of Appeal indicated that it would favour the application because, in substance, it did not involve an application for a plant variety. It was noted that in the case of a PVR an applicant had to develop a plant variety, fulfilling the particular requirements of homogeneity and stability, whereas in the case of a genetic engineering invention, a tool was provided whereby a desired property could be bestowed on plants by inserting a gene into the genome of a plant: development of specific varieties was not necessarily the objective of inventors involved in genetic engineering.

The EPC excludes the patenting of animal varieties but not of animals in general and the same reasoning is applied to patents to animals as to patents for plants. There is however no separate system for the protection of animal varieties so there is no established view of what constitutes an animal variety. The Directive allows the patenting of animals and the test case in Europe is the *OncoMouse*[27] application. This application concerns a technique for inserting a gene into the DNA of animal cells which increases sensitivity to cancer. This enables laboratory test animals to be cloned that are useful for testing and identifying potential cancer-causing chemicals. The EPO Examining Division and Board of Appeal accepted the case for grant. The application includes claims to the technique and also to non-human animals produced by the technique. Following opposition to the patent on ethical/moral grounds the Opposition Division of the EPO decided to maintain the granted patent with the claims restricted in scope to cover the invention carried out in rodents only. However, this decision was also appealed and in 2004 the Appeal Board decided to uphold the patent in a further restricted form that only covers transgenic mice.

Essential Biological Processes

Article 4(1)(b) of the Directive repeats the bar contained in the EPC on patenting 'essentially biological processes for the production of plants or animals' and has gone further by stating, in Article 2(2), that 'a process for the production of plants or animals is essentially biological if it consists entirely of natural phenomena such as crossing or selection'. These definitions therefore prevent the patenting of natural reproductive processes or non-technical processes such as selective breeding. For example a method comprising mating a bull from one cattle breed with a cow from another cattle breed to produce a cross-bred calf would not be allowable.

---

26 G01/98 *Novartis / Transgenic plant* (2000) OJEPO 111.
27 *Harvard / Onco-mouse* (1990) OJEPO 476, (1992) OJEPO 588.

Microbiological Processes

Article 4(3) of the Directive expressly states that microbiological processes and products thereof are not excluded from patentability by the prohibition on the patenting of 'essentially biological processes'. Viruses and bacteria are therefore patentable *per se*, as the products of microbiological processes. Because of the complexity of such organisms, it is unlikely that a patent could disclose their entire structure, properties and behaviour, possibly leading to uncertainties in assessing novelty, enablement and infringement. These difficulties can however be alleviated to some degree by the allowance of disclosure by deposition.[28]

The TRIPs Agreement also states that Members may not exclude micro-organisms from patentability.[29] 'Micro-biological or other technical processes' should be construed widely and include selective culturing or cross-breeding of micro-organisms including sub micro-organisms and should not be restricted to essentially chemical manufacturing processes in which micro-organisms are used. This so-called patenting of life has been strongly opposed by some developing countries[30] and still features as an agenda item in the TRIPs Council. However, the TRIPs agreement has not yet been amended and many believe that this issue will not be resolved for some time.[31]

It should also be noted that cells, even those derived from multicellular plants or animals, are the products of microbiological processes for the purposes of patentability and thus cell lines are patentable as such. As noted above, the Directive does not allow patenting of the human body and the discovery of one of its elements. However, when isolated by technical means the same elements may constitute a patentable invention. Since cell cultures and cell lines need to be isolated by a technical means this prohibition does not affect the patentability of human-derived cell lines.

'Ordre Public' and Morality

Article 6 of the Directive[32] states that biological inventions shall be considered unpatentable where their commercial exploitation would be contrary to *ordre public* or morality and, specifically, where they take the form of processes for cloning human beings, processes for modifying the germ-line genetic identity of human beings, uses of human embryos for industrial or commercial purposes and processes for modifying the genetic identity of animals which are likely to cause them suffering without any substantial medical benefit to man or animal.

---

28 See below.

29 TRIPS, Art. 27(3)(b).

30 UNCTAD, *Protecting and Promoting Traditional Knowledge: Systems, National Experiences and International Dimensions* (2004), 93; See also Third World Network (TWN) intervention at the Eighth Session of the WIPO IGC document (WIPO/GRTKF/IC/8/15), 93.

31 Developing countries are currently more interested in the relationship between TRIPs and CBD than Article 27.

32 Patents Act 1977, Sch A2, par. 3 (b)-(e).

Whilst the Directive does not contain any specific references to the patenting of human embryonic stem cells (hESC), there are some provisions which have been interpreted as having an indirect effect on whether these cells can be patented. In particular, the patenting of 'use of human embryos for industrial or commercial purposes' is prohibited. However, the scope of this exclusion has been interpreted differently by different patent offices. At the EPO this provision excludes from patentability hESC, cell lines derived from them and materials derived from such cell lines. This interpretation was given by the Opposition Division of the EPO in the *Edinburgh patent.*[33] The patent owner filed an appeal against the decision, but this was recently withdrawn.[34] The UKIPO has not followed the line taken by the EPO. In a practice notice issued in April 2003 it was confirmed that the UK Patent Office (now UKIPO) will not grant patents for processes for obtaining stem cells from human embryos nor for human totipotent cells as these have the potential to develop into an entire human body (such cells are not patentable because the human body at the various stages of its formation and development is excluded from patentability). However, since human embryonic pluripotent stem cells, which arise from further division of totipotent cells, do not have the potential to develop into an entire human body, the notice states that the commercial exploitation of inventions concerning such cells would not be contrary to public policy morality and are therefore patentable.

The number of times that morality issues occur in patent applications is relatively few and whether an application satisfies the morality requirement or not is obviously a difficult matter since the whole issue is subjective and patent examiners do not necessarily have a specific insight compared to other members of the public. Indeed, some quarters have questioned whether patent offices are the proper bodies to adjudicate the application of moral and ethical issues to the patent system[35]. In the area of cloning, further guidelines produced by the Human Fertilisation and Embryology Authority and the Human Genetic Commission can provide assistance. For example, the patents relating to the nuclear transfer technique used to clone a ewe from an adult sheep cell at the Roslin Institute in Scotland (the 'Dolly' applications)[36] were only granted after careful consideration of the information from these agencies and correspondence about them between the UKIPO and the applicant.

Exceptions/Limitations to Grant

Patent legislation in EPC countries now contains limitations allowing both private, non-commercial use and experimental use of patented inventions known as the 'research exemption'.[37] The scope of the research exemption is uncertain: whilst it

---

33 EPO Opposition Division, July 2003 against EP 94913174.2.

34 The appeal was withdrawn on 20 November 2007. The question relating to embryonic stem cell research is being referred to the Enlarged Board of Appeal in relating to *Primate Embryonic Stem Cells* (EP1640448).

35 Ford, R. 'The morality of biotech patents: Differing legal obligations in Europe?' *European Intellectual Property Review* (1997), 19 (6): 315–19.

36 GB 2318578 and 2331751.

37 See Patents Act 1977 s. 60(5)(b).

is reasonably clear that it may now apply to research which is commercially funded, it is only in Germany that the senior court has indicated that research can include clinical trials on a fairly broad scale. In the past, most European countries restricted their research exemption to non-commercial activity, i.e. typically to work carried out in universities and public institutions without industrial backing. Courts across Europe have been divided on the willingness to treat experimental research as exempt from patent infringement when the acts are for commercial purposes.

Under this experimental use exemption it is possible to conduct research which may modify or improve the patented invention and, in Germany at least, this includes providing further information about the properties of the invention, for example through clinical trials. One major ambiguity about the experimental use exemption concerns how far clinical tests can be considered experimental, since treatment and the continuing search for further genetic knowledge often go hand in hand. The exemption must also cover experiments to discover whether the invention can be made from its description in the specification (essential if the patent is to be challenged).

However, the exemption does not include research using a patented tool which is not itself the subject of further experiments (e.g. as where PCR is used to amplify genetic material). Nor does it cover tests which merely replicate the invention, for example where a generic drug company is seeking evidence for permission from a medicines authority to market its version of a drug once the patent on it expires.

The issue of access to protected material for research purposes is pertinent where attempts are made to develop alternative forms of genetic testing kits. Where an alternative to a kit supplied by a patentee is developed in-house and routinely used in clinical work this appears *not* to be experimental use nor private non-commercial use. Accordingly, without a licence the kit or its use may infringe the patent.

The exemption for experimental purposes concerns its restriction to research which builds upon the knowledge provided by the patent, and aims to discover something unknown about the subject-matter of the patent or to test a hypothesis about it.[38] This does not cover any use without a licence of a patented research tool or medium which is need for the research but is not being experimented upon for its own sake. The classic example in genetics is provided by *Hoffmann-La Roche's patent on PCR*. Work to provide an improved PCR would count as experimental use, but not work which simply used PCR as a standard procedural step.

The 'bolar' exemption overcomes infringement risk for generic producers of medicines by exempting studies, tests and trials necessary to gain regulatory approval, from constituting patent infringement. The 'bolar' exemption was a small part of a comprehensive reform of the current EU pharmaceutical legislation proposed by the European Commission in July 2001. Within the two Directives on medicinal products are proposals to allow the 'bolar' exemption which state:

Conducting the necessary studies and trials with a view to the application of paragraphs 1, 2, 3 and 4 (paragraphs 1–5 on the Veterinary Medicinal Products Directive) and the

---

38 *Auchinloss v. Agricultural & Veterinary Supplies* [1999] RPC 397.

consequential practical requirements shall not be regarded as contrary to patent rights or to supplementary protection certificates for medicinal products.

Agreement on the two Directives was reached on 18 December 2003, which were then adopted in March 2004. The deadline for implementation was the end of October 2005 and the UK implementing legislation came into force on the 30th October 2005 amending sections 60(5) and 60(7) of the Patents Act 1977.[39]

Compulsory Licences

Article 12 of the Directive provides for compulsory licensing of plant breeders' rights and patent rights where the existence of one right hinders the acquisition or exploitation of the other right. In order to succeed, applicants for these compulsory licences must show that they have applied unsuccessfully to the rights holder for a contractual licence and, more importantly, that the plant variety or the invention for which the licence is required constitutes significant technical progress of considerable economic interest compared with the invention claimed in the patent or the protected plant variety.

Deposit of Biological Material

One of the consequences of applications relating to biological material is that it may not be possible to define such material in the conventional manner i.e. by means of a written description. It has therefore long been realised that in some instances the description of a specification may only be regarded as sufficient if biological material mentioned therein is made available by depositing it in a recognised depository institution from which an interested third party may secure a sample. Articles 13 and 14 of the Directive relate to the deposit and access of biological material and by and large reproduce rules prevailing in the EPC and are common to the rules of many Member States.

Extent of Protection

Articles 8 and 9 of the Directive deal with the extent of patent protection of biotechnological inventions. By virtue of Article 8, the protection given by biological patents for products and processes is specifically extended to include material derived by propagation or multiplication and which posses the same characteristics as the initial invention. The patented process does not itself have to have been used to produce the further material: the only relevant factor is that the future derived material has a causal connection to the process by possessing the same characteristics as the initial invention produced using the protected process. Similarly, Article 9 specifically provides that protection given by a patent to a product containing or consisting of genetic information shall extend to all material in which the product

---

39 See The Medicines (Marketing Authorisations etc.) Amendment Regulations reg. 3 (SI 2005/2759).

is incorporated and in which the genetic information is contained and performs its function (subject to the exclusions of the human body under Article 5(1)). Article 9 therefore extends patent protection to any material within which the protected invention is placed (e.g. a gene within a plant) where that invention performs the function for which the protection was granted.

Protection does not, however, extend to biological material obtained from the propagation or multiplication of biological material placed on the market by the owner of the patent or with his consent, where the multiplication or propagation necessarily results from the application for which the biological material was marketed, provided that the material obtained is not subsequently used for other propagation or multiplication.[40] For example where patented plant material, such as seeds have been bought and sown then the first resulting plants will not be a violation of the rights of the patent holder. However, any further multiplication or replication would constitute an infringing act. A farmer who has bought seeds can therefore grow plants from them and harvest the plants but cannot retain any seeds from the plants for the purpose of further multiplication or propagation or sell any products from the second set of plants. The Farmers' Privilege, set out in Article 11 of the Directive, allows in certain instances, for the retention for one year to the next reproductive material obtained from a patented plant. This right is restricted to certain categories of plant material and the farmer must pay an equitable remuneration sensibly lower than the amount originally charged.

4. Traditional Knowledge, Genetic Resources and Biopiracy

Only recently has the international community sought to recognise and protect traditional knowledge (TK). In 1982, WIPO and UNESCO adopted a model law on folklore.[41] In 1989 the concept of farmers' rights was introduced by the Food and Agricultural Organisation (FAO) into its International Undertaking on Plant Genetic Resources and in 1992 the Convention on Biological Diversity (CBD) highlighted the need to promote and preserve TK. A number of cases relating to TK have attracted international attention and involve what is often referred to as 'biopiracy'. Although there is no accepted definition of biopiracy, the following, relating to patents, have been described as such:

(a) The granting of 'wrong' patents. These are patents granted for inventions that are either not novel or inventive having regard to TK already in the public domain. Such patents may be granted due either to oversights during the examination or simply because the examiner did not have access to the knowledge. This may be because it is written down but not accessible using the tools available or because it is unwritten knowledge.

(b) The granting of 'right' patents. Patents may be correctly granted according to national law on inventions derived from a community's TK or genetic resources but (i) patenting standards are too low e.g. national patent regimes may not recognise some forms of public

---

40 Directive, Art 10.

41 Model Provisions for National Laws on the Protection of Expressions of Folklore Against Illicit Exploitation and other Prejudicial Actions.

disclosure of TK as prior art or (ii) no arrangements may have been made to obtain prior informed consent of the community providing the knowledge or resource and for sharing benefits of commercialisation.

The *Neem* case[42] illustrates the issues that can arise when patent protection is granted to inventions relating to TK which is already in the public domain. In this case an invalid patent was issued because the patent examiner was not aware of the relevant TK. In 1999 the EPO determined that according to the evidence 'all features of the present claim have been disclosed to the public prior to the patent application … and [the patent] was not considered to involve an inventive step.' The patent was revoked by the EPO in 2000.

Use of Existing IP Rights to Protect TK

Examples are emerging which illustrate how current IP systems can be utilised to commercialise TK or prevent its misuse. For example aboriginal and Torres Strait islanders in Australia have obtained a trade mark to help promote the marketing of their art and cultural products and deter sales of products falsely claiming to be of aboriginal origin.[43] Other examples of protection of TK and folklore include the use of copyright in Canada to protect tradition-based creations such as masks, totem poles and sound recordings of aboriginal artists and the use of industrial designs to protect the external appearance of head-dresses and carpets in Kazakhstan. Other IP rights, especially those requiring some form of novelty or those with fairly limited periods of protection, seem less appropriate for protecting TK.[44]

Disclosure of Origin

The Convention on Biological Diversity seeks to ensure that countries benefit from the use of their genetic resources. Given the role of patents in providing financial rewards to innovators, the international patent system is seen by many, but not all (most notably the United States), as providing a suitable means of enabling countries to be recompensed for such use through imposing an obligation to disclose the country of origin of the material in any patent specification relating to that material. In this way, it would be easier for the 'source' country or countries to ensure that they benefit from the material used. Although no obligation to do so has been imposed by the CBD, many countries have amended their patent legislation to require such a disclosure.

Even among those countries who hold to such a view, there is, however, no consensus concerning the sanctions to be taken in the event of a failure to disclose the country of origin. In general the developed countries favour a weak requirement where failure to comply does not affect the granting of the patent and therefore

---

42 EP 0436257.

43 C. Correa, *Protection and Promotion of Traditional Medicine - Implications for Public Health in Developing Countries* (Geneva: South Centre 2002), 59.

44 See A. Jenner, *Are Intellectual Property Based Systems Able to Protect Local/ Indigenous Community Medicinal Traditional Knowledge* (2005).

recital 27 of the Biotech Directive states that 'the patent application should, where appropriate, include information on the geographical origin of such material, if known'. Developing countries such as Brazil and India favour strong sanctions such as revocation or transferral of the patent if the country of origin is not disclosed and they wish to have the TRIPS agreement amended to include such sanctions.

There are many practical difficulties surrounding disclosure of origin such as difficulties in determining the source country or countries and difficulties in proving what has been taken and the extent to which the source material(s) have contributed to the invention hence it is likely to be a source of debate in international fora for a long time to come.[45]

Farmers' Rights

Farmers' rights do not fit comfortably into an intellectual property context. IP rights are, generally speaking, concerned with the stimulation of innovation by providing the incentive of prospective monopoly rights as a reward for innovation.[46] Farmers' rights are a retrospective reward, of unlimited duration, for the conservation of plant genetic resources. It has been pointed out that since the concept of farmers' rights was originated as a counterbalance to the intellectual property system, it would be illogical to incorporate those rights within the intellectual property system.[47]

5. Examination Guidelines for Patent Applications Relating to Biotechnological Inventions in the UK Intellectual Property Office

Despite the guidance provided by the Directive, patent offices in Europe face a continuing challenge when examining patent applications for biotech inventions. It is easy to focus on the contentious issues surrounding biotechnology patenting, such as the criteria for patenting plants and animals, gene sequences and morality issues and to forget that the majority of biotech applications will be decided on the basis of novelty, inventive step and industrial applicability as well as support and sufficiency. The Manual of Patent Practice (MOPP) is the examiners' main source of information regarding current practice in the Patent Office under the Patents Act 1977, but Examination Guidelines have been produced to supplement the guidance given by MOPP. The guidelines help by looking at how the basic issue of protecting biotechnology have been applied in the past but also at how they should be applied subject to guidance from the courts and the EPO Boards of Appeal.

---

45 Queen Mary Intellectual Property Research Institute, *Report on Disclosure of Origin in Patent Applications* (2004) for the European Commission (DG-Trade).

46 The UK made a Declaration upon ratification that clarified Article 12.3.d of the Treaty on Plant Genetic Resources for Food and Agriculture, by recognising that plant genetic or their genetic parts or components which have undergone *innovation* may be the subject of intellectual property rights provided that the criteria relating to such rights are met.

47 C. Correa 'Options for the Implementation of Farmers' Rights at the National Level'. *Trade-Related Agenda, Development and Equity (T.R.A.D.E.) Working Paper 8.*

6. Concluding Remarks

The Directive and its incorporation into the EPC has created a new and important source of law in the field of biotechnology patents which is distinct from both national and EPO case law. It has also created a new set of rules at the level of Member States for biotech patent protection and the assesment of infringement. As a result, there is a new clarity in the legislative framework and a legal predictability and certainty – predictability in knowing what can be patented and what the parameters of that protection are, and certainty that rights, once granted, are not overly vulnerable to challenge. The legal protection it provides, together with the monopoly risks arising from excessive protection and the damage to commercial research resulting from insufficient protection, all serve to underscore the need for it to be implemented properly and uniformly.

It is clear that there are few problems with the notion of patenting genes, animals and plants, provided that the granting criteria are properly applied. The reality is that patent protection has been extended to these materials, and this extension has been sanctioned at the EU, EPO and UK political levels. Whilst public opinion has become much better informed over the last ten years, resulting in greater scrutiny of the behaviour of scientists, lawyers, government and business in the broad area of biotechnology, it is unlikely that the policy underlying the new legislative position will change to any great extent. Evidence of this can be found in the UKIPO Examination Guidelines where it is stated that the Patent Regulations that implement the Directive establish 'beyond doubt the legitimacy of biotechnology patents in the UK'. The view is that the test of protectability lies in the ability to meet appropriately determined granting criteria rather than on any special quality attached to the material involved; a view supported by the European Commission's report which makes the additional point that the language used in the Directive permits flexibility at the national level in applying the granting criteria.

PART 2
Human Rights and Ethical Frameworks

Chapter 2

Life as Chemistry or Life as Biology? An Ethic of Patents on Genetically Modified Organisms

Kathryn Garforth

The vitalist principle may indeed not explain much, but it is at least a sort of label affixed to our ignorance, so as to remind us of this occasionally, while mechanism invites us to ignore that ignorance[1]

1. Introduction

During the Middle Ages and the Renaissance, artists were frequently commissioned to create triptychs: painted altarpieces set in three panels. One purpose of these altarpieces was 'to instruct in the faith, with images serving as "the books of the unlettered"'.[2] Seen together, the panels of a triptych were not just paintings but also usually told a Biblical story. The metaphor of the triptych is illustrative here because we too will be examining a group of three: ethics, biotechnology, and patent law. Individually they may be theories, facts, policies or arguments. Together, they tell a story.

The centre panel of a triptych was traditionally the most important section as it drew the eye to the main figure of the story.[3] In our case, the centre of the triptych contains the science of biotechnology. Both ethics and patent law hinge on the particular way life is understood and represented by genetics and corporate science. The panel on ethics will focus on the debate between materialist and vitalist understandings of life. The former believes life to be explicable through its components, the latter does not, or at least warns that we have not been able to do so yet. Life is complex and this suggests we should respect its autonomy, uniqueness and sanctity rather than treat it as something that is under our control and is fungible and violable like any other commodity. The last panel of the triptych represents patent law. The interaction of patent law and biotechnology illustrates a gradual expansion of the former to include a broader number of aspects of the latter. In order for this to occur, however, the law

---

1 Henri Bergson, *Creative Evolution* (1907) (Barnes and Noble Publishing 2005), 34.

2 Kemp, M 'Introduction: The Altarpiece in the Renaissance: A Taxonomic Approach' in P. Humfrey and M. Kemp (eds), *The Altarpiece in the Renaissance* (Cambridge: Cambridge University Press, 1990), 1, 7.

3 R. Mayer, *A Dictionary of Art Terms and Techniques* (New York: Thomas Y. Crowell Company, 1969), 404.

has had to rely on the simplistic picture of biotechnology in the centre of the triptych and the materialist ethic of the opposite panel.

Viewing the three panels together leads to a conflict – the complexity in the ethics of life clashes with the forced simplicity of patent law. While the structure of the law may allow us to create legal fictions and ignore the complexity, in real life this complexity does not disappear. Ignoring it in one area of the law simply forces it to reappear in another. This is exactly what is beginning to happen and it creates consequences beyond the confines of the triptych.

Following this introduction, sections 2 to 4 of the chapter explore the individual panels of the triptych – the science of biotechnology, an ethical framework for examining patents on life, and key concepts from patent law. Sections 5 and 6 draw the panels together to tell their story. Section 5 delves into the case law to explore the basis on which patents have been granted on life forms. Section 6 returns to the ethical framework from section 3 to examine the problems with patenting life. Finally, section 7 offers some concluding remarks.

2. Scientific Background and Definitions

The science of modern biotechnology forms the subject of the central panel of the triptych. In the early 1970s, scientists developed techniques to remove a section of DNA from one organism and insert it into the genetic sequence of another.[4] Recombinant DNA (rDNA) techniques were the result and it is the modern applications of these methods that will be the focus of here. An understanding of the science of biotechnology is critical in order to follow the reasoning used to extend patent protection to living organisms.

Despite the sometimes daunting terminology for non-scientists, the structure of DNA is elegantly simple. DNA is actually an abbreviation for deoxyribonucleic acid which is one of the chemicals found within the cell nucleus. DNA, in turn, consists of four nitrogen-containing bases, adenine, thymine, guanine, and cytosine (usually referred to as A, T, G, and C respectively) as well as sugar and phosphate.[5] These components combine to form a nucleotide, with each nucleotide consisting of a molecule of phosphate, a molecule of sugar, and a molecule of one of the nitrogen bases.[6] The nucleotides are joined together in a chain to form a polynucleotide. The base of each nucleotide bonds with a complementary base (adenine with thymine and guanine with cytosine) to form base pairs, drawing two chains of polynucleotides together and forming the double helix structure of DNA (see Figure 2.1).[7] It is the bases, the order in which they occur and the near infinite number of ways they can be organized that create what we refer to as genes.

---

4 E.S. Grace, *Biotechnology Unzipped: Promises & Realities* (Washington, DC: Joseph Henry Press, 1997), 41–2.

5 *Ibid*, 15.

6 Industry Canada, *Bio Building Blocks* (Ottawa: Industry Canada, 1999).

7 *Ibid.*

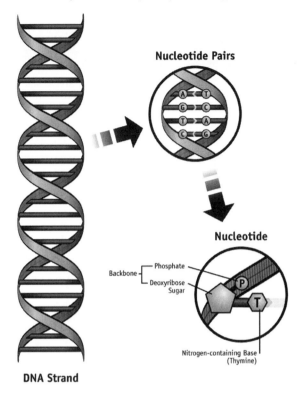

DNA Strand

Figure 2.1 The structure of DNA

The cell uses the sequence of bases in genes to build proteins. Protein construction is a two-step process involving transcription of the DNA and translation into amino acids.[8] In transcription, an enzyme 'reads' the code in one section of nucleotides and creates a complementary strand of messenger RNA (mRNA).[9] This new mRNA molecule then moves out of the nucleus into the cytoplasm of the cell where translation takes place.[10]

The process of translation converts the information encoded in the mRNA sequence into a sequence of amino acids, which will then fold up to become a protein.[11] Translation employs the cell's ribosomes which move along the mRNA 'reading' its bases in triplets or codons.[12] Another type of RNA, known as transfer RNA (tRNA), is used to build the amino acid. One side of tRNA consists of an

---

8 Grace, n. 4, 29.

9 S.R. Barnum, *Biotechnology: An Introduction* (Chicago: Cole Publishing Company, 1998), 34.

10 *Ibid*, 34, 40.

11 *Ibid*, 40.

12 *Ibid*, 39.

anticodon that is complementary to a codon in the mRNA.[13] Attached to the opposite side of the tRNA is a specific amino acid, so each anticodon corresponds to one amino acid. When the codon of the mRNA exposed in the ribosome is complementary to the anticodon of the tRNA, the latter moves into position, an enzyme unhooks the amino acid from the tRNA and joins it to the chain of amino acids that has already been created (see Figure 2.2).[14] The process continues until the mRNA has been completely translated.

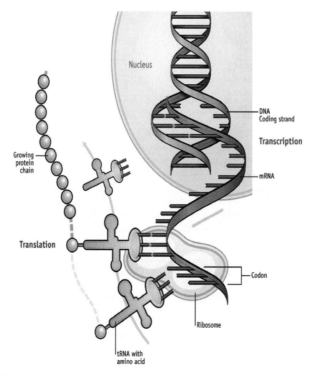

Figure 2.2 The process of protein construction: transcription and translation

The simplicity of DNA is also what allows genetic engineering to work. The chemical composition of deoxyribonucleic acid – sugar, phosphate, and the four bases – is the same whether the DNA is in an insect, a plant, or an animal, human beings included.[15] This compatibility in chemistry makes it possible to recombine genes from different organisms and different species.

---

13 S. Aldridge, *The Thread of Life: The Story of Genes and Genetic Engineering* (Cambridge: Cambridge University Press, 1996), 39.

14 *Ibid*, 40.

15 The genetic code of DNA is nearly universal with only a few exceptions: *ibid*, 35.

3. An Ethical Framework for Examining Patents on Life

The panel containing the ethical story in our triptych is hinged to one side of the science picture. The background on ethics and philosophy serves to provide a vocabulary for the discussion in section 5 of the case law that has led to the patenting of life. The ethical background will also aid in tying the three panels of the triptych together and determining how the science and the law should interact with ethics – our goal in section 6. For now, we will focus on the debate between two groups of figures: the materialists and the vitalists.

Materialism and Vitalism

Materialism and vitalism provide a useful starting point for understanding how life can be conceptualised as a human invention and thus subject to patent law, and whether the patenting of life is ethically acceptable. Traditionally, the positions are as follows: vitalists believe that there is some sort of vital force running through living beings and that life is due to this force. The force is immaterial and cannot be explained by biology, chemistry, or physics.[16] Materialists, on the other hand, dismiss notions of vital forces and believe that everything, life included, can ultimately be explained by the sciences.[17]

The current clash between the two perspectives is just the latest in a centuries-old debate in the West over whether there is something exceptional in living beings, and if so, what it might be. Materialism was a very successful perspective for locating and describing DNA as the hereditary material by which characteristics are passed on through the generations, as achieved by Watson and Crick in 1953. Since then, the focus has shifted to exploring the functioning of DNA. Materialism has still been at the forefront of this quest, but to date, its record has not been as spectacular.

The apparent simplicity and straightforwardness of the functioning of DNA led Francis Crick to publish his theory of the central dogma in 1958.[18] The central dogma consists of two hypotheses. First is the sequence hypothesis, which links the structure of DNA, the linear sequence of nucleotides, to its function, the transcription and translation of proteins. Secondly is the central dogma hypothesis (although this term is now usually applied to the theory as a whole). This hypothesis holds that 'once (sequential) information has passed into protein it cannot get out again'.[19] The central dogma was quickly accepted as just that – dogma.[20]

Almost as soon as the theory of the central dogma was published, new discoveries about genes began to undermine its tenets. In 1959, François Jacob and Jacques Monod distinguished between 'structural genes' and 'regulator genes'. The former code for the amino acids needed to make a protein while the latter regulate the rate

---

16 M. Hunt, *The Story of Psychology* (New York: Doubleday, 1993), 115–16.

17 Aldridge, n. 13, 243–5.

18 F.H.C. Crick, 'On Protein Synthesis' in *Symposium of the Society for Experimental Biology XII* (New York: Academic Press, 1958) 153.

19 *Ibid.*

20 E.F. Keller, *The Century of the Gene* (Cambridge, MA: Harvard University Press, 2000), 54.

at which the structural genes are transcribed.[21] The variety of types of genes has proliferated in the intervening years and now includes promoter and terminator sequences, leader sequences, and activator elements, amongst others.[22]

In the 1970s, Richard Roberts and Phillip Sharp discovered split genes.[23] In higher organisms, many of the structural genes are not continuous but fragmented with coding sections of DNA (exons) alternating with regions of non-coding DNA (introns). When these stretches of DNA are transcribed into mRNA, the non-coding sections must be removed before protein synthesis can continue.[24] This introduces a new stage between the two-step chronology of transcription and translation described in section 2. Furthermore, once the intron sections are excised, the remaining exons can be reassembled in a variety of ways thus leading to the creation of different proteins from a single stretch of DNA.[25] Also, exons from two different transcripts may be spliced together or an edited transcript may 'be modified by insertion of foreign bases or by the replacement of one base by another, thereby giving rise to proteins for which no corresponding coding sequence exists in the DNA'.[26] Known as alternative splicing, this process introduces further variability to the DNA–RNA–protein pathway.

The completion of the first draft sequence of the human genome in 2000 also offered a surprise. Going into the project, scientists had estimated that the human body produces approximately 100,000 different proteins. The human genome was thus predicted to consist of approximately 100,000 genes.[27] Once the sequencing was complete, however, the final tally was only about 30,000 genes,[28] reinforcing the lack of a one-to-one correlation between genes and proteins. Indeed, the Human Genome Project was a lesson in humility as the number of genes in human beings was found to be not much greater than the number in some types of plants.[29]

This brief timeline suggests that genes by themselves, or at least our current comprehension of genes, cannot explain the complexity of life. Since it was first proposed in 1958, the central dogma has suffered a series of setbacks that point to life not being as straightforward as Crick initially suggested. Enter the vitalists.

The notion of life containing a vital force is the classical definition of vitalism but as a school of thought, it has moved through a number of stages. Aristotle was an early vitalist, particularly in his conception of the soul. He argued that the soul causes and controls the growth of an organism as well as the development of its

---

21 *Ibid*, 55.

22 *Ibid*, 58.

23 *Ibid*, 59.

24 *Ibid*, 60.

25 *Ibid*.

26 *Ibid*, 61–2.

27 A. Lippman, 'Led (Astray) by Genetic Maps: The Cartography of the Human Genome and Health Care' (1992) 35 *Social Science and Medicine*, 1469.

28 M. Morange 'Century of the Gene' (2001), *Isuma* 22, 25.

29 B. Commoner, 'Unraveling the DNA Myth' *Harper's Magazine* (February 2002) 39, 42.

parts.[30] Another Greek, Galen, devised a system of three spirits that were produced in the body and were necessary for health.[31] The three spirits – natural, vital and animal – were increasingly non-material and reflected a belief 'that man and animals at least were beings utterly outside the reign of whatever laws controlled phenomena in the non-living portions of nature.'[32] Galen's theories on physiology held sway for over 1000 years.

From the mid-1600s to mid-1800s, scientists such as Georg Stahl, Paul-Josef Barthez, Jacob Berzelius and Xavier Bichat believed there was a distinction between mind and matter, animate and inanimate.[33] The former were governed by vital forces that were irreducible to physical laws and did not apply to the inanimate or purely material. The end of this sort of vitalism began with the synthesis of urea by Friedrich Wöhler. This was a stunning development as it illustrated 'that inorganic materials could be made into organic substances' and that living and non-living things were not so different after all.[34]

Since the mid-1800s, most vitalist thinking has centred on evolution and Darwinism. Jean Lamarck's theory of acquired characteristics is sometimes referred to as a form of vitalism although Lamarck himself was a materialist. Lamarckism suggests that animals respond to changing circumstances and needs, producing new habits which can, in turn, alter the animal's physiology and will thus be passed on to offspring.[35] Twentieth-century vitalist philosophers include Henri Bergson and Arthur Koestler. Bergson accepted the fact of evolution but not the mechanisms by which it was proposed to occur.[36] He looked to metaphysics for an answer and believed that intuition 'gives us a consciousness of a vital impulse (*élan vital*) within us. ... Accordingly, the history of life is to be understood as a process of creative evolution which has resulted from this primordial impulse'.[37] More recently, Arthur Koestler has questioned the simplicity of the central dogma, particularly its tenet of the one-way flow of information.[38] Science has also offered support for this

---

30 L. Richmond Wheeler, *Vitalism: Its History and Validity* (London: H.F. & G. Witherby Ltd., 1939), 4.

31 *Ibid*, 10.

32 *Ibid*, 12.

33 L. King, 'Stahl, Georg Ernst' in C.C. Gillispie (ed.), *Dictionary of Scientific Biography,* vol. 12 (New York: Charles Scribner's Sons, 1970), 599; R. Cowan, 'Barthez, Paul-Joseph' in C.C. Gillispie (ed.), *Dictionary of Scientific Biography,* vol. 1 (New York: Charles Scribner's Sons, 1970), 478; G. Canguilhem, 'Bichat, Marie-François Xavier' in C.C. Gillispie (ed), *Dictionary of Scientific Biography,* vol. 2 (New York: Charles Scribner's Sons, 1970), 122.

34 E. Kelly, 'Energy Metabolism in Animals and Plants' in N. Schlager (ed.), *Science and Its Times: Understanding the Social Significance of Scientific Discovery*, vol. 5 (Detroit: The Gale Group 2000), 122, 123.

35 L. Burlingame, 'Lamarck, Jean Baptiste Pierre Antoine de Monet de' in C.C. Gillispie (ed), *Dictionary of Scientific Biography,* vol. 7 (New York: Charles Scribner's Sons, 1973) 584, 589–90.

36 T.A. Goudge, 'Bergson, Henri Louis' in *Dictionary of Scientific Biography,* vol. 2 (Detroit, MI: The Gale Group, 2000), 8 at 10.

37 *Ibid*, 11.

38 A. Koestler, *The Ghost in the Machine* (New York: The Macmillan Company, 1967).

perspective, primarily through research on prions which suggest that some proteins may have the ability to change the characteristics of other proteins.[39] Current theories of intelligent design – i.e. that evolution and the current physical form of organisms are too improbable to be just a product of chance and so are being conducted by God – can also be understood as a form of vitalism.

Currently, vitalism is also often linked to complexity and this connection will be the focus here. The idea of vitalism as complexity is not intended to revive theories of animating forces or to surreptitiously support proponents of intelligent design but to offer an alternative to the reductionist, rationalist and materialist notions that typically prevail. Vitalism as complexity recognizes that we have not yet been able to explain life in purely chemical or purely physical terms. What we have uncovered engenders awe and wonder at its 'precocious simplicity';[40] what we do not know must be acknowledged and respected.

The Ethical Framework

Vitalism and materialism suggest a series of antonyms:

- Autonomy and control;
- Uniqueness and fungibility;
- Sanctity and violability.

Below we will assert why the complexity of life forms means they belong in the left-hand category; why autonomy, uniqueness and sanctity should be our ethical position. We will return to these antonyms in section 6 to tie together the three panels of the triptych – ethics, science and law – and examine the justifications for an ethic of complexity.

I. Autonomy and Control

The right-hand side of this antonym sees the genetic destiny of other creatures as being under human control. The simplicity of the central dogma and the reductionism of patent law (discussed below) imply that we already have a materialist explanation for life. These two approaches suggest that we can give a complete chemical description of not only the structure of DNA but also its functioning – how the translation and transcription of DNA leads to certain characteristics. This alleged materialist explanation also leads us to believe that we are able to control life and manipulate its genetic composition in a straightforward and predictable manner. In contrast, the left-hand side of the antonym sees the holes in our knowledge being ignored and the autonomy of other creatures denied. The complexity of life on the left-hand side is assumed away on the right through a simplistic approach to science and inadequate legal theories.

---

39 Aldridge, n. 13, 45–6.
40 Keller, n. 20, 54.

Autonomy reflects a vitalism of complexity because autonomy stems in part from complexity. As complex individuals (human or otherwise), we are unpredictable. We are not simply the product of stimulus-response. The complexity and autonomy of life defy true control because they are larger than any one of us. We were created through this complexity rather than the other way around:

> Remembering that the genes of different species are being mapped in parallel raises the question of the close relationship between ourselves and other species. Approximately one per cent difference in DNA between us and our mammal neighbours, such as the chimpanzee and the mouse has led to language and consciousness – the abilities needed to develop genetic engineering and all the other DNA technologies. Powerful as it is, it is unlikely that DNA alone can explain why we have discovered its secrets and their potential to meet human needs.[41]

We have already begun to lose sight of this complexity by allowing patents on living organisms.

The rationality and concrete nature of materialism leaves little room for the unpredictability of autonomous organisms. If life must be explicable in physical and chemical terms, there can be no role for what we do not know. Just as you 'can't manage what you can't measure', neither can you control what you do not understand. Attempts to circumvent this lack of knowledge and thereby circumvent the autonomy of other organisms in order to gain some manner of control is a key aspect of the role of patent law in biotechnology.

II. Uniqueness and Fungibility

The second set of antonyms derives somewhat from the first in that denying the complexity and thus the autonomy of life forms is a requirement for considering them as fungible. By fungible, we mean that life forms are no longer unique, rather they are 'freely exchangeable or replaceable for another of like nature or kind'.[42] In criticizing the decision of the U.S. Patent and Trademark Office (PTO) to allow the patenting of higher life forms, Jeremy Rifkin wrote that: '[l]iving beings are to be considered no differently than chemical products or automobiles or tennis balls'.[43] The legal fiction that assumes away the complexity of life to allow the patenting of organisms also suggests that these organisms are fungible with the other types of things patented under the statute.

Living organisms must be made 'pseudo-inanimate' to fit under patent law – seemingly inanimate but still, in fact, living. By its very nature this lifelessness denies the unique characteristics of life. Instead of legal fictions, we need to recognize the unique nature of living organisms. Unlike other patented things, living creatures can grow, reproduce and evolve, all without human intervention. They are the outcome of the same complexity that led to our existence. We ignore this at our own peril.

---

41 Aldridge, n. 13, 251.

42 *Random House Dictionary*, revised ed., *s.v.* 'fungible'.

43 K. Schneider, 'New Animal Forms will be Patented' *The New York Times* (17 April 1987): A1.

What is disturbing about making an organism a fungible object 'is the notion that a subject, a moral agent with autonomy and dignity, is being treated as if it can be used as an instrument for the needs or desires of others without giving rise to ethical objections'.[44] What should these ethical objections be? That living organisms are not merely instruments like other tools we have created for meeting our needs. That a living being is entirely different from manufactured goods. Forcing life forms into the patent law ignores these ethical concerns.

III. Sanctity and Violability

The third set of antonyms is, in turn, derived from the second. As life increasingly becomes a thing and becomes exchangeable and interchangeable with other things, we lose any reason to bar anyone from doing anything to life forms. Just as life is interchangeable, it is also violable. We come full circle – with violation comes loss of autonomy.

This third set of antonyms is different from the first two. It does not have the language of patent law or the sciences to help make its point. Its premise rests on the question of whether the limits of what is ethical and right are equal to what is legal and can be legally enforced.[45] By arguing that some things should remain sacred and not be violated, we are answering this question with a firm 'no'.

The very use of the word sanctity will lead to squeamishness on the part of some readers and critics. Its inherently religious connotations suggest that this vitalism of complexity is simply theories of animating forces or intelligent design in disguise. Let me reiterate that this is not the case. Leaving these theories behind does not mean that we must also leave behind all ethical restrictions on what we may do to life.

Various scholars have made a similar argument – that there are or should be ethical restrictions in the law or even that there are ethical restrictions above the law. So Somerville uses the concept of the 'secular sacred' to define the two fundamental ethical values that we should not breach: profound respect for life and protection of the human spirit, 'that deeply intuitive sense of relatedness or connectedness to the world and the universe in which we live'.[46] The term allows us to set fundamental principles without relying on religion, which is no longer a uniform feature in our modern multicultural society. These fundamental principles should guide our use of new medical technologies whether or not they are reflected in law.

In the area of property law, Joseph Singer is similarly attempting to reinvigorate the social norms and obligations he believes are already a part of the institution. He argues that there is continuity between moral obligations and legal institutions and

---

44 T. Schrecker *et al.*, *Ethical Issues Associated with the Patenting of Higher Life Forms* (Ottawa: Industry Canada, 1997), online: Industry Canada: http://strategis.ic.gc.ca/epic/site/ippd-dppi.nsf/en/ip00095e.html (date accessed: 20 January 2008), 62.

45 M. Somerville, 'Making Health, Not War – Musings on Global Disparities in Health and Human Rights: A Critical Commentary by Solomon R. Benatar' (1998) *American Journal of Public Health* 295.

46 M. Somerville, *The Ethical Canary: Science, Society and the Human Spirit* (Toronto: Penguin Books, 2001), xiv.

that 'our core rules of property law contain multiple duties to limit property use so that it will not impinge on the legitimate interests of others.'[47] Similar arguments can be made for limitations on the scope of patent law and what is patentable subject matter.

In sum, violability is both a product of control and fungibility as well as a contributor to their perspectives. In order to remain cognisant of the complexity of life – of which we are a part – we must recognise the autonomy, uniqueness and sanctity of life forms. Returning to our triptych metaphor, we see that the representation of ethics consists of opposing figures. At present, the materialists occupy the foreground and the vitalists have been forced to the back. The time has come for a vitalism of complexity to join materialism and inform science and the law.

4. Key Concepts from Patent Law

The Standards in Patent Legislation

This panel of our triptych presents the key concepts from patent law – and Canadian and American patent law in particular – that are necessary to understand how judges and lawyers have attempted to expand patent law to include living organisms.

The Canadian Patent Act[48] sets out certain requirements that must be met in order to obtain a patent. First of all, the thing to be patented must be an invention. According to section 2 of the Act, '"invention" means any new and useful art, process, machine, manufacture or composition of matter, or any new and useful improvement' thereof.[49] This is commonly expressed as meaning an invention must be novel, must have utility, and must be patentable subject matter. The definition of invention in the American legislation is almost exactly the same[50] whereas the United Kingdom Patents Act 1977[51] does not attempt to list the categories of things that can constitute an invention. Instead, as new technologies have been developed over the years, it has been left to the courts to interpret whether an invention is patentable.[52] Section 28.3 of the Canadian Patent Act also requires that an invention be non-obvious in order to receive a patent. Mere discoveries and products of nature

---

47 J. Singer, *The Edges of the Field: Lessons on the Obligations of Ownership* (Boston, MA: Beacon Press, 2000), 16.

48 Patent Act, R.S.C. 1985, c. P-4 (Ca).

49 *Ibid*, section 2.

50 35 USC 101: §101. Inventions patentable. Whoever invents or discovers any new and useful process, machine, manufacture, or composition of matter, or any new and useful improvement thereof, may obtain a patent therefor, subject to the conditions and requirements of this title.

51 Patents Act 1977 (c. 37) (UK).

52 E. Armitage 'Two Hundred Years of English Patent Law' in *200 Years of English and American Patent, Trademark and Copyright Law* (Chicago, IL: American Bar Center, 1977) 4.9; Patents Act 1977 s. 1.

are not inventions as they lack the requisite novelty.[53] What constitutes a product of nature has, however, been construed quite narrowly.

Finally, even if the matter claimed in a patent application is deemed to be an invention, the applicant must still meet certain application requirements under section 27 of the Canadian Patent Act in order to be granted a patent. Of particular relevance here is the fact that the application must contain a specification of the invention (section 27(2)) and,

> [t]he specification of an invention must (a) correctly and fully describe the invention and its operation or use as contemplated by the inventor; (b) set out clearly the various steps in a process, or the method of constructing, making, compounding or using a machine, manufacture or composition of matter, in such full, clear, concise and exact terms as to enable any person skilled in the art or science to which it pertains, or with which it is most closely connected, to make, construct, compound or use it.[54]

We will return to the importance of the written specification in section 4.

The Canadian Patent Act used to contain a provision prohibiting patents on inventions that had 'an illicit object in view' (formerly s. 27(3)) but this was removed in 1993. The prohibition was similar to a provision in the European Patent Convention that limits the patentability of inventions that are contrary to morality or *ordre public*.[55] The European provision has been used to challenge the patentability of genetically engineered organisms with varying degrees of success.[56]

Once a patent is granted, the patentee receives 'the exclusive right, privilege and liberty of making, constructing and using the invention and selling it to others to be used subject to adjudication in respect thereof before any court of competent jurisdiction'.[57] While expressed positively in the Act, this section has actually been interpreted as meaning that the patentee has a negative right to prevent others from making, constructing and using the invention, not a positive right to do so itself. The ability of the patentee to use the invention is limited by other potential legal requirements such as the need for health, safety and efficacy testing in the case of new drugs. The exclusive right conferred by a patent is twenty years in duration commencing from the date of application.[58]

---

53 *Pioneer Hi-Bred Ltd. v. Canada* (Commissioner of Patents), [1989] 1 S.C.R. 1623; Canadian Intellectual Property Office, *Manual of Patent Office Procedure* (Ottawa-Hull, 1998), online: Industry Canada: http://strategis.gc.ca/sc_mrksv/cipo/patents/mopop/mopop-e.pdf (date accessed: 1 August 2007).

54 Patent Act s. 27(3) (Ca).

55 European Patent Convention, Art. 53(a).

56 For example the European Patent Office opposition division decided to limit Harvard's oncomouse patent to 'transgenic rodents containing an additional cancer gene' on the grounds that the suffering of the other onco-mammals outweighed the possible medical benefits, 'European Patent Office Limits Harvard's 'Oncomouse' Patent' (7 November 2001), online: European Patent Office: http://www.epo.org/about-us/press/releases/archive/2001/07112001. html (date accessed: 20th January 2008). The scope of the patent has subsequently been limited further to cover only onco-mice.

57 Patent Act s. 42 (Ca).

58 Patent Act s. 44 (Ca).

These standards are not unique to Canada, the US or the UK. The final agreement from the Uruguay Round of trade negotiations under the General Agreement on Tariffs and Trade included the formation of the Word Trade Organisation (WTO) and the Agreement on Trade-Related Aspects of Intellectual Property Rights (TRIPS). In particular, TRIPS embodies novelty, non-obviousness and utility as the standard for obtaining a patent, a standard that must be implemented by all of the Members of the WTO. Article 27(3) allows Members to exclude plants and animals from patentability but they must provide some form of intellectual property protection for plant varieties either through patents, some form of *sui generis* system, or both. It is into this regime of patent protection that inventors have tried to fit their biotechnological inventions.

Patent Case Law and Biotechnology

A steady progression of case law marks the way by which patent protection has been expanded to include living organisms. A brief timeline of first US case law and secondly, Canadian case law is presented here while the next section explores more specifically the arguments used to facilitate this expansion.

While formal patent law is about 500 years old, it is only in the past 130 years that it has begun to enter the area of biotechnology. The first step in the expansion of patent law turned out to be something of a false start. In 1873, Louis Pasteur received US patent number 141,072 which included a claim to a '[y]east, free from organic germs of disease, as an article of manufacture'.[59] This was the first patent on a micro-organism and the first patent on a living organism. It took over 100 years for the next patent on a microorganism to be granted.

In 1980, the US Supreme Court ruled in *Diamond v. Chakrabarty*[60] that living organisms are patentable so long as they fit within the definition of 'invention' in the patent legislation. Chakrabarty's application for a patent on a genetically modified microorganism had been rejected by the US PTO on the grounds that living organisms were not patentable.[61] Ultimately, the US Supreme Court, in a 5/4 split decision, reversed this policy and found that 'anything under the Sun made by man' is patentable.[62] In its decision, the Court adopted expansive interpretations of the terms 'manufacture' and 'composition of matter' in the definition of invention.

The next step involved expanding the terms 'manufacture' and 'composition of matter' to so-called 'higher life forms', namely plants and animals. In *Ex parte Hibberd*,[63] the Board of Patent Appeals and Interferences allowed a patent on a variety of maize which had initially been rejected on the grounds that the claimed subject matter was beyond the bounds of 35 USC §101 and should be protected by

---

59 US 141,072, claim 2.

60 *Diamond v Chakrabarty*, 444 US 1028 (1980).

61 *Ibid*, par. 2.

62 *Ibid*, par. 10.

63 *Ex parte Hibberd*, 227 U.S.P.Q. (BNA) 443 (1985).

the provisions of the Plant Patent Act[64] (PPA) and the Plant Variety Protection Act[65] (PVPA).[66] The Board relied upon the *Chakrabarty* decision to find that the definition of invention in 35 USC §101 does not exclude living organisms nor does it exclude plants, seeds or tissue cultures by virtue of the enactment of the PPA and PVPA.[67] Plants were thus patentable as well.

In 1987, the Board of Patent Appeals and Interferences reversed another US PTO policy and said that multicellular organisms are patentable subject matter. The case was *In re Allen*[68] and the decision held that claims to an oyster fell within the bounds of patentable subject matter. Four days after the *Allen* decision, the US PTO issued a statement including the declaration that '[t]he Patent and Trademark Office now considers nonnaturally occurring non-human multicellular living organisms, including animals, to be patentable subject matter within the scope of 35 U.S.C. 101'.[69] When Harvard applied for a patent on a genetically engineered mouse, the patent was granted without any litigation whatsoever.

The most recent American case on point is *J.E.M. Ag Supply, Inc. v. Pioneer Hi-Bred International*.[70] In this case, the Supreme Court upheld the validity of Pioneer's patent on a variety of hybrid corn thus affirming the patentability of sexually reproducing hybrid plants, whether they are genetically modified or not.

The interaction of IP law and biotechnology has a markedly different history in Canada than it has in the United States. Canada had no early intellectual property protection for plant breeders comparable to the PPA or PVPA in the US. It was only in 1990 that the country enacted the Plant Breeders' Rights Act[71] bringing it into conformity with the 1978 version of the UPOV Convention[72] and it became a member of the Convention on 4 March 1991. The country has twice made moves to join UPOV 1991 but has not done so to date.[73]

---

64 Plant Patent Act, 35 U.S.C. §161.

65 Plant Variety Protection Act, 7 U.S.C. §2321.

66 The Plant Patent Act and the Plant Variety Protection Act were two early forms of intellectual property protection available to plant breeders. The PPA was enacted in 1930 and allowed plant patents on varieties of asexually reproducing plants (plant patents are the same as regular patents except that the utility requirement in US patent law is replaced by a distinctness requirement, 35 U.S.C. §161, and a plant patent cannot be declared invalid if its description is as complete as reasonably possible, 35 U.S.C. §162). The PVPA was enacted in 1970. It creates a *sui generis* type of intellectual property protection for any type of plant variety so long as it is new, distinct, uniform and stable.

67 *Hibberd*, 227 U.S.P.Q. (BNA) 443 (1985), 4-5, 8-9.

68 *In re Allen*, 2 U.S.P.Q. (2d) 1425 (1987).

69 1077 Official Gazette 24 (21 April 1987).

70 534 U.S. 124 (2001).

71 Plant Breeders' Rights Act, S.C. 1990, c. 20.

72 The UPOV Convention, or *International Convention for the Protection of New Varieties of Plants*, was negotiated by a group of European countries and agreed to in 1961. There have been two subsequent versions of the Convention, from 1978 and 1991, and membership has been opened to non-European states.

73 The first move was in 1999 when a bill to amend the Plant Breeders' Rights Act died on the Order Paper, V. Duy, *A Brief History of the Canadian Patent System* (Canadian Biotechnology Advisory Committee, 2001): http://strategis.ic.gc.ca/epic/site/cbac-cccb.

The judicial interpretation of the Canadian Patent Act has also not had the same relatively smooth progression as has occurred in the US. A case similar to *Chakrabarty* came before the Canadian Patent Appeal Board in 1982. In *Re Application of Abitibi Co.*,[74] the company's patent claims to a microbial culture had been rejected by the patent examiner on the grounds that living matter is not patentable. The Patent Appeal Board reviewed recent decisions in other jurisdictions, including the *Chakrabarty* case, and found that even without changes to legislation, courts had been broadening their understanding of patentable subject matter in order to include living organisms, particularly micro-organisms.[75] The Appeal Board followed suit and granted the Abitibi Company a patent on the microbial culture.[76]

In 1987, the Federal Court of Appeal heard the case of *Pioneer Hi-Bred v. Canada (Commissioner of Patents)*.[77] Pioneer Hi-Bred had used traditional cross-breeding to develop a variety of soybean. The court ruled that a cross-bred variety did not come under the scope of the definitions of 'manufacture' and 'composition of matter', even as defined in *Chakrabarty*.[78] The case was appealed to the Supreme Court, which refused to rule on the patentability of living matter, rejecting the claim instead on the grounds that the specification was not complete.[79]

For the next 13 years, the patentability of higher life forms in Canada hung in limbo. The Canadian Intellectual Property Office maintained its policy that higher life forms are not patentable[80] but this was challenged in *Harvard College v. Canada (Commissioner of Patents)*.[81] In 1985, Harvard University applied for a Canadian patent on its genetically engineered mouse.[82] The patent examiner, the Commissioner of Patents, and the Federal Court Trial Division all rejected the patent claims to the mouse itself.[83] In its decision on 3rd August, 2000, however, the Federal Court of Appeal essentially adopted the definitions and approach from *Chakrabarty* and granted Harvard the patent.[84] The case was appealed to the Supreme Court, which overturned the Federal Court of Appeal's decision, and in a 5/4 split, rejected the patentability of higher life forms.

Most recently, in 2003, the Supreme Court issued its decision in *Monsanto Canada Inc. v. Schmeiser.*[85] Percy Schmeiser is a Saskatchewan farmer who discovered

---

nsf/vwapj/Duy_CdnPatents_e.pdf/$FILE/Duy_CdnPatents_e.pdf (date accessed: 1st August 2007) at 26. The second move consisted of public consultations in 2004–2005 on whether the country should join UPOV 1991. The idea proved controversial and has again been dropped.

74 *Re Application of Abitibi Co.* (1982) 62 C.P.R. (2d) 81, 83.

75 *Ibid*, 84–90.

76 *Ibid*, 90.

77 *Pioneer Hi Bred v. Canada (Commissioner of Patents)* (1987) 14 C.P.R. (3d) 491.

78 *Ibid*, 495–6.

79 *Diamond v Chakrabarty*, 444 US 1028 (1980), par. 18 and 34.

80 Manual of Patent Office Practice, n. 53, s.16.05. This section does allow the patenting of lower life forms.

81 *Harvard College v Canada (Commissioner of Patents)* [2002] 4 S.C.R. 45.

82 *Ibid*, par. 121.

83 *Ibid*, par. 123.

84 *Harvard College v Canada (Commissioner of Patents)* [2000] 4 F.C. 528.

85 *Monsanto Canada Inc v Schmeiser* [2004] 1 S.C.R. 902.

Monsanto's Roundup Ready canola growing in his fields despite the fact that he had never purchased or planted the seed. He saved the seeds from his fields and replanted them the following year at which point Monsanto sued him for patent infringement. In Canada, Monsanto does not have a patent on the Roundup Ready plant itself, only on the gene that confers resistance to the Roundup herbicide and cells that contain the gene. Schmeiser never actually used the invention for the purpose for which it was patented as he never sprayed his crop with Roundup. Nonetheless, a majority of the Court ruled that Schmeiser had infringed the patent by relying on the 'stand-by' value of the invention, i.e. he could have sprayed his crop with Roundup if he wanted to. The outcome from *Schmeiser* is to effectively nullify the decision from Harvard. Patentees can now do indirectly what they cannot do directly, they can gain exclusionary rights over higher life forms by patenting components of these organisms.

5. Blurring the Lines Between Chemistry and Biology

Now that we have described individually the three panels of the triptych, it is time to look at them together as a whole. We will begin in this section by going beneath the simple decisions in the case law to examine the basis on which these decisions have been made. The starting point is a blurring of chemistry and biology.

At the molecular level, chemistry and biology are essentially the same. As discussed in section 2 of this chapter, DNA is simply a combination of various chemicals and these chemicals are largely the same in all species. As stated, this similarity is what makes recombinant DNA technology possible. The discussion of the materialists in section 3 illustrated, however, that, at increasing levels of complexity, the simple relationship between chemistry and biology becomes less and less true. While organisms have the same chemicals in DNA, somehow these chemicals are organized and activated differently in order to create a plant rather than an insect, for example. The chemistry may all be the same, the biology is not.

Delving a little deeper into the case law outlined in section 4, we find a muddling of the language; the distinction between chemistry and biology is being blurred. As the courts in the US and Canada have sought to expand the scope of patent law to include living organisms, the primary difficulty they have encountered is that living organisms are not usually conceived of as 'manufactures' or 'compositions of matter' within the definition of 'invention'. In order to circumvent this problem, courts began to conceive of living organisms as akin to chemicals.

While not described in section 4 for the sake of brevity, one of the first cases concerning the patentability of living organisms was *Re Bergy*,[86] a case decided by the US Court of Customs and Patent Appeals in 1977. The patent examiner had rejected a claim to a biologically pure culture of a micro-organism on the grounds that it was a product of nature and thus not patentable subject matter.[87] The Court of Customs and Patent Appeals found that the fact that the micro-organism is alive does

---

86 *Re Bergy*, 563 F. 2d 1031 (CCPA 1977), vacated, 438 US 902 (1978).
87 *Ibid*, 1032.

not remove it from the statutory subject matter of §101.[88] In determining that micro-organisms are patentable, the majority had this to say: 'The nature and commercial uses of biologically pure cultures of microorganisms like the one defined in claim 5 are much more akin to inanimate chemical compositions such as reactants, reagents, and catalysts than they are to horses and honeybees or raspberries and roses'.[89] In dismissing the slippery slope argument that deciding this microorganism was patentable would lead to all life forms being patentable, they wrote: 'As for the board's fears that our holding will of necessity, or 'logically,' make all new, useful, and unobvious species of plants, animals, and insects created by man patentable, we think the fear is far-fetched.'[90] The Court was very careful to limit its decision to micro-organisms, finding that the patentability of other living organisms should be decided on a case-by-case basis.[91]

An amendment to the patent application at issue in *Re Bergy* ultimately rendered the case moot leaving the US Supreme Court to consider *Chakrabarty*.[92] In the latter case, the lawyer for General Electric (where Chakrabarty worked) adopted the approach of equating the modified bacteria with chemicals in arguing that the bacteria should be patentable.[93] The majority of the court agreed resulting in a situation where, 'By treating the microorganism as a natural chemical substance into which a useful new characteristic had been introduced and thereby rendered unnatural, the court found that it was patentable in accordance with long-established practice with respect to chemical products that allowed a natural chemical to be the basis for an invention as long as it was modified'.[94] The court is less explicit in blurring the line between chemistry and biology but ultimately it treats the bacteria as something that has become 'unnatural' by virtue of its modification by Chakrabarty. By this logic, it is no longer a product of nature but has become a manufacture and a composition of matter.

Re Bergy appears to have been quite influential in similar Canadian jurisprudence. In *Re Abitibi*, the Canadian Patent Appeal Board used similar reasoning to the US Court of Customs and Patent Appeals to grant a patent on an engineered micro-organism:

> Certainly this decision will extend to all micro-organisms, yeasts, moulds, fungi, bacteria, actinomycetes, unicellular algae, cell lines, viruses or protozoa; in fact to all new life forms which are produced en masse as chemical compounds are prepared, and are formed

---

88 *Ibid*, 1035.

89 *Ibid*, 1038.

90 *Ibid.*

91 *Ibid*, 1036.

92 D.J. Kevles, 'A History of Patenting Life in the United States with Comparative Attention to Europe and Canada' (Report to the European Group on Ethics in Science and New Technologies, 12 January 2002), online: European Group on Ethics in Science and New Technologies: http://ec.europa.eu/european_group_ethics/publications/docs/study_kevles_en.pdf (date accessed: 20 January 2008), 29.

93 *Ibid*, 15.

94 G. Dutfield, *Intellectual Property Rights and the Life Sciences Industries: A Twentieth Century History* (Aldershot: Ashgate, 2003), 155.

in such large numbers that any measurable quantity will possess uniform properties and characteristics. ... Whether it reaches up to higher life forms – Plants (in the popular sense) or animals – is more debatable.[95]

Adopting the chemical approach allowed the Board to grant Abitibi a patent on the microbial culture.

While the US Supreme Court acknowledged few potential limits on patentability posed by the terms 'manufacture' or 'composition of matter', the Canadian courts have generally been much more aware of the distinction between chemistry and biology. In 1987, when the Federal Court of Appeal heard *Pioneer Hi-Bred*, it refused to accept that the definitions from *Chakrabarty* applied to a cross-bred plant variety:

> Such a plant cannot really be said, other than on the most metaphorical level, to have been produced from raw materials or to be a combination of two or more substances united by chemical or mechanical means. It seems to me that the common ordinary meaning of the words 'manufacture' and 'composition of matter' would be distorted if a unique but simple variety of soybean were to be included within their scope.[96]

The US has had no qualms about applying patents on plant varieties obtained through cross-breeding as held in the recent *J.E.M. Ag Supply* decision.

Next, in December 2002, the Supreme Court of Canada denied the patentability of higher life forms in its decision in *Harvard*. The written opinions of both the majority and dissent reflect the linguistics of chemistry and biology and are also a microcosm of the materialist versus vitalist debate. The decision turned on whether higher life forms came under the definition of invention in the Patent Act and particularly whether a mouse genetically engineered to be susceptible to cancer could be considered a manufacture or composition of matter. Justice Bastarache, writing for the majority, found that it could not. In construing the word 'manufacture', Bastarache, J. concluded that 'while a mouse may be analogized to a 'manufacture' when it is produced in an industrial setting, the word in its vernacular sense does not include a higher life form. ... In my opinion, a complex life form such as a mouse or a chimpanzee cannot easily be characterized as "something made by the hands of man"'.[97] Moving on to composition, Bastarache, J. was willing to concede that the genetically altered 'onco-egg' could be considered a composition of matter.

> However, it does not thereby follow that the oncomouse itself can be understood in such terms. ... The body of the mouse is composed of various ingredients or substances, but it does not consist of ingredients or substances that have been combined or mixed together by a person. Thus, I am not satisfied that the phrase 'composition of matter' includes a higher life form whose genetic code has been altered in this manner.

95 *Re Abitibi* (1982) 62 C.P.R. (2d) 81, 89.

96 *Pioneer Hi-Bred* (1987) 14 C.P.R. (3d) 491, 496. As discussed in section 4 of this chapter, the Supreme Court on appeal refused to grant the patent but on different grounds from those of the Federal Court of Appeal.

97 *Harvard* [2002] 4 S.C.R. 45, par 159.

It is also significant that the word 'matter' captures but one aspect of a higher life form. ... Higher life forms are generally regarded as possessing qualities and characteristics that transcend the particular genetic material of which they are composed. ... [This] makes it difficult to conceptualize higher life forms as mere 'composition[s] of matter'. It is a phrase that seems inadequate as a description of a higher life form.[98]

Justice Bastarache did not fall into the trap of muddling chemistry with biology. Instead, he recognized that a life form is much more complex than the sum of its parts.

The distinction between chemistry and biology was also raised by the majority in its consideration of whether it is defensible to draw a line between lower life forms and higher life forms and allow patents on the former but not the latter. In its first reason why the line-drawing was defensible (and the most relevant here), the court cited *Re Abitibi* and *Re Bergy* to make the point that 'it is far easier to analogize a micro-organism to a chemical compound or other inanimate object than it is to analogize a plant or an animal to an inanimate object'.[99]

Turning to the dissent, Justice Binnie explicitly adopts a materialist perspective in his decision on the dispute. This is most evident in his discussion of whether the oncomouse can be considered a composition of matter:

The Court's mandate is to approach this issue as a matter ... of law, not murine metaphysics. In the absence of any evidence or expert assistance, the Commissioner now asks the Court to take judicial notice of the oncomouse, if I may use Arthur Koestler's phrase, as a 'ghost in a machine' but this pushes the scope of judicial notice too far. With respect, this sort of literary metaphor (or its dictionary equivalent) is an inadequate basis on which to narrow the scope of the Patent Act, and thus to narrow the patentability of scientific invention at the dawn of the Third Millennium.[100]

The consequences of this approach are particularly evident at two points in his decision. The first is in his characterisation of the claims in the patent application. He adopts the description of the invention used by the majority – 'the genetic matter of which [the oncomouse] is composed'[101] and writes that: 'I believe that the extraordinary scientific achievement of altering every single cell in the body of an animal which does not in this altered form exist in nature, by human modification of "the genetic material of which it is composed", is an inventive "composition of matter" within the meaning of s. 2 of the Patent Act'.[102] The problem is, Justice Binnie is confusing the mouse with its genetic material. Altering the genetic material of which the mouse is composed may be an inventive composition of matter and the Patent Office granted Harvard a patent on the oncogene, its insertion into the genetic code and even the cells that contain the gene. The last part of Justice Binnie's sentence can be considered correct. But the entire sentence suggests that if an inventive genetic code is a composition of matter, the entire mouse must be as well.

---

98 *Ibid*, par. 162–3.
99 *Ibid*, par. 203.
100 *Ibid*, par. 45.
101 *Ibid*, par. 7.
102 *Ibid*, par. 8.

The second point is during his discussion of whether granting a patent on the mouse would give Harvard ownership of a form of life. Binnie, J. dismisses this argument: 'Harvard did not construct the mouse from scratch, nor did it create "life". What it did was to modify the genome of the oncomouse so that every cell in its body contained a modified gene.'[103] Justice Binnie's reasoning again falls prey to the blurring of chemistry and biology. If what Harvard did was modify the genome then it should get a patent on the genome.[104] But extending patentability to the entire mouse conflates the genome with the organism when the two are not one and the same.

The final case to be considered is *Schmeiser*. The *Schmeiser* decision is somewhat different inasmuch as the primary question considered by the Supreme Court was not whether a life form was patentable but whether Schmeiser had infringed a patent that had already been granted. The blurring of chemistry and biology is less obvious but is still there. Again, the two groups of judges adopt different ethical perspectives on the case except this time the materialists are in the majority.

The difference between the majority and the dissent in *Schmeiser* rests on differing constructions of the scope of the patent claims. Both sides are quite clear that Monsanto does not have a patent on the genetically modified canola plant, that it only has a patent on a chimeric plant gene and the cells that contain it. The modified gene and cells, however, are commonly located within a plant. The crux of the interpretation is whether the patent on the gene and cells should also give rights over the plants that contain them. The majority said yes, the dissent said no.

In order to find that Schmeiser had infringed the patent, the majority conflated the modified gene and cells with the entire plant: 'the patented genes and cells are not merely a "part" of the plant; rather, the patented genes are present throughout the genetically modified plant and the patented cells compose its entire physical structure.'[105] The dissent disagreed and felt that the majority's approach, by effectively extending patent rights to the plant as a whole, contravened the decision from *Harvard*. Instead, in construing the claims, the dissent largely maintained the distinction between chemistry and biology: 'In order to avoid the claim extending to the whole plant, the plant cell claim cannot extend past the point where the genetically modified cell begins to multiply and differentiate into plant tissues, at which point the claim would be for every cell in the plant, i.e. for the plant itself.'[106] If the patent claims were extended beyond the gene and the cell in this isolated laboratory form then the biology of the plant becomes muddled with the chemistry of the gene and the biology of the cell.

Thus concludes the first part of the story in the triptych. The net result of the case law is that an initial blurring of chemistry and biology has paved the way for much broader patent claims on multicellular organisms. Characterising micro-organisms as akin to inanimate chemicals in order to allow patents on them has created the slippery slope dismissed by the court in *Re Bergy*. More generally, bringing together

---

103 *Harvard* [2002] 4 S.C.R. 45, par. 68.
104 Notwithstanding other controversies surrounding the patentability of genes.
105 *Ibid*, par. 42 and par. 69.
106 *Ibid*, 138.

the three panels of the triptych illustrates how the initial use of a materialist ethic in equating biology with chemistry led to a greater generalisation of genes and genomes with life. Our final task is to return to the antonyms from section 3 to see how our ethical framework can inform this relationship between science and law.

4 Materialism, Vitalism and an Ethic of Patenting Life

To complete the story told by the triptych, we must return to ethics and our antonyms – autonomy and control, uniqueness and fungibility, sanctity and violability – to fully understand the problems with patenting life. If autonomy, uniqueness and sanctity are to be our ethical framework then there are certain things that this perspective does not allow. The patenting of life forms is one of them.

False Impressions of Control

Under Canadian patent law, a patentee has the right to exclude others from making, selling or using the invention covered by the patent. Indeed, patent claims are often described as a series of fences that delineate the invention from other patents and the public domain.[107] Patent law thus gives the impression that the inventor has control over the invention. Describing patents as intellectual *property* reinforces this impression even further. This may, however, be a false impression in the case of living organisms. Simply put, there is a divide between the actual and the effective exclusionary rights as they relate to patents on life. There are two aspects to this divide, the first serves to narrow the effect of the patent somewhat while the second serves to broaden it.

In the first aspect, the patent assumes that the patentee is *capable* of excluding others. Also, these 'others' to be excluded only extends to human beings. So, for example, with its patent on a chimeric plant gene and glyphosate resistant plant cell,[108] Monsanto cannot exclude other canola plants from using the patented gene. This has important implications for how the patent is enforced, as illustrated below. In the second case, patents in Canada have primarily only issued for the novel gene and the cell that contains it, not the entire creature.[109] In most of their uses, these genes and cells are obviously contained within an organism. The right to exclude others from using the invention means effectively that the patent holder can prevent others from using the entire organism even though this is not what is stated in the patent claims.

These divides are best explained by way of an example: the *Schmeiser* case. In this context, the key is that canola is a living organism that can spread and interact with other canola plants without human intervention but it does not have standing in courts of law. In order to enforce its patent rights, therefore, Monsanto must go after the farmer as it cannot go after the canola. Monsanto's effective exclusionary rights

---

107 *Free World Trust* v. *Électro Santé Inc.* (2000), 9 C.P.R. (4th) 168 (S.C.C.), par. 14-15.

108 Canadian Intellectual Property Office, 'Glyphosate-Resistant Plants', No. 1,313,830.

109 The exception being patents on micro-organisms.

are narrower than the actual exclusionary rights implied by the patent because the company cannot exclude canola plants from using the patented gene and cell.

This case illustrates that the law is only one part of a larger picture when it comes to biotechnology. Just because a life form is considered under an inventor's control for the purpose of patent law does not mean that the inventor has biological control over the life form as well. If the law recognised the true autonomy of living organisms, then perhaps the canola infringed Monsanto's patent but Schmeiser did not. To the extent that patent law ignores the autonomy of life forms, in this instance by finding a farmer liable for uncontrolled patented genes and cells, it is unethical.

Schmeiser also illustrates the second aspect to the divide between actual and effective monopolies. While Monsanto only has a patent on the altered gene and the cells that contain it, because these are both further contained in a canola plant the company can effectively exclude others from using the entire plant. According to the dissent in *Schmeiser*, 'a person skilled in the art, upon filing of Monsanto's patent, would not reasonably have expected that the exclusive rights for gene, cell, vector, and method claims extended exclusive rights over unpatentable plants and their offspring.'[110] The result of the majority's decision in the case is a broadening of the patent beyond what is stated in the patent claims.

Returning to our antonyms, the canola example illustrates that the alleged control of an inventor over its living invention is, in fact, a legal fiction. The biological reality demonstrates that these organisms continue to act autonomously. They cross-breed with one another in a way that cannot be controlled by the companies that own the patents. The genetic drift occurring on the Prairies illustrates the extent of this fiction and how we must remember the autonomy of living beings if we are to remain on a solid ethical footing.

Uniqueness verse Fungibility

There are two means by which patent law has evolved to deny the uniqueness of living organisms. The first, more obvious method is to force life forms into the same patent system that protects all other inventions. The second, somewhat paradoxically, is special rules to circumvent the specification requirements of patent law.

In the first instance, we have already highlighted how some of the characteristics of living organisms make them unlike inanimate inventions. Ironically, it is the dissent from the Supreme Court's decision in *Harvard* that makes this point quite clearly. Justice Binnie describes the Harvard mouse as one with a modified gene in every cell in its body. He adds that this achievement 'is not like adding a new and useful propeller to a ship'.[111] If this is the case, however, then why is Justice Binnie trying to force the modified mouse into the same system that protects the propeller? Why must the mouse be made fungible with the propeller? The majority in *Harvard* as well as the dissent in *Schmeiser* both recognised that life forms are unique in comparison to non-living inventions protected by the Patent Act.[112] Instead of trying

---

110 *Schmeiser* [2004] 1 S.C.R. 902, par. 128.

111 *Harvard* [2002] 4 S.C.R. 45, par. 68.

112 *Schmeiser* [2004] 1 S.C.R. 902, par. 156; *Harvard* [2002] 4 S.C.R. 45, par. 167.

to fit a round peg into a square hole, the law must consistently acknowledge life forms as unique.

The second difference between living organisms and inanimate inventions focuses on the specification requirements of patent law. In *Pioneer Hi-Bred*, the Supreme Court of Canada found that the specification for the soybean was insufficient and so a patent could not be issued. The question remains whether a specification for a living organism can, given the state of our knowledge, ever be complete:

> Unfortunately, it is the degree with which these constituent materials can be described that is limiting as well as the length of time it would take to perfectly reproduce the conditions. Such limitations are, presently, intrinsic to biological materials:

> That the description of a biotechnological invention must ultimately focus on a modification of existing complexity, rather than on the creation of complexity 'from scratch', is in part an artifact of man's still rudimentary understanding of living matter *per se*. Our ability to implement and redirect the biological information stored in the living matter may someday advance to a point where fungible protoplasm can be totally reformed at will to create any desired plant, animal, or microorganism. At that point, in a manner analogous to the way inanimate inventions are described according to the classical model, the description of all biotechnological inventions will be grounded on the basic organizational principles of living matter, the vague outline of which we only now begin to recognize.[113]

This quote begs the question of why, if it is not currently possible to completely describe the 'constituent materials' of life forms, it should be possible to obtain patent protection for these life forms? We do not have fungible protoplasm that can be used to create any type of life form so why should life forms and their inadequate descriptions be fungible with the way 'inanimate inventions are described according to the classical model'?

To circumvent the problem of the specification, at least in part, many states have joined the Budapest Treaty, the purpose of which is to recognise the physical deposit of a sample of a micro-organism as disclosure of an invention for the purpose of patent protection. While the patent application still requires some form of specification, the deposit system means the specification does not need to be as complete as it would be in the absence of such a system. Essentially, it is the creation of another legal fiction whereby the deposit stands in lieu of a full specification.

The preceding quote recognises the complexity of life forms and the impossibility of full description. Unfortunately, it fails to take the next step and say that this should preclude patents on life. By circumventing the specification requirement, we allow living organisms to be fungible with other inventions. It allows us to ignore that the creation of life forms cannot be described through a step-by-step process. In other words, it allows us to ignore that life forms are unique and unlike the other things protected by the Patent Act.

---

113 J.R. Rudolph, 'Biotechnology, Pioneer Hi-Bred and Patent Law: Judicial Expertise Missing?' (1990) 7 *Canadian Intellectual Property Review* 69, 75: quoting S.A. Bent *et al.*, *Intellectual Property Rights in Biotechnology Worldwide* (New York: M. Stockton Press, 1987), 7.

Is Nothing Sacred?

The previous two sections have argued that patents on life are unethical because they do not reflect reality. Patents on life are coming back to haunt us as legal fiction runs headlong into biological reality. This section is different. We cannot use biology to show that life is sacred and that the law is leading to a violation of this sanctity. Instead, we asserted sanctity in section 3 of this chapter and now must use the information of the intervening discussion to argue why life should be considered sacred – or secular sacred – and that patenting life is a violation of this norm.

One argument for the sanctity of life is to look at the alternative – violability. As already discussed, violability is the next step after control and fungibility. It is easier to violate something that is not autonomous and is just another object like any other. What is more, violability also leads to loss of autonomy and uniqueness. For something to be violated, it must be brought under someone else's control and it involves denying the moral standing of the thing in question. In essence, allowing the violation of life through patenting will perpetuate the unethical conduct of control and fungibility disavowed in the previous two sections.

Another rationale for establishing the sanctity of life is the lack of understanding of the consequences of our actions. Notwithstanding Louis Pasteur's patent, the patenting of entire varieties of life forms is a new phenomenon. As genetic engineering continues to advance, the patenting of new types of life forms and new aspects of life will become possible. Is this really in our best interests? An analogy to the precautionary principle is possible here. This principle is an ethical position itself. As articulated in Article 15 of the Rio Declaration on Environment and Development, it holds that: 'Where there are threats of serious or irreversible damage, lack of full scientific certainty shall not be used as a reason for postponing cost-effective measures to prevent environmental degradation.' So the principle presents an ethic of precaution in the face of scientific uncertainty. Is it also possible to have precautionary ethics whereby in the face of threats of serious or irreversible damage, lack of full certainty should not bar measures to prevent ethical degradation? Should we not move cautiously across dangerous ethical terrain rather than proceeding full steam ahead?[114]

As discussed in section 3, various authors are attempting to invigorate or reinvigorate ethical limitations to law. Others are rediscovering historical norms and comparing them to the current state of the law. Carol Rose, for example, uses Roman law to examine 'Traditions of Public Property in The Information Age', i.e. 'nonexclusive property under the Roman law – its applications and limitations in the realm of tangible things, and the analogies and contrasts that might be drawn in the realm of intellectual achievements'.[115] The final category of Roman law in her discussion is *res divini juris*. It included religious objects such as temples and tombs

---

114 Somerville, n. 45, 21.

115 C. Rose, 'Romans, Roads, And Romantic Creators: Traditions of Public Property in The Information Age' (2001) *Conference on the Public Domain*, online: Conference on the Public Domain: http://www.law.duke.edu/pd/papers/rose.pdf (date accessed: 1 August 2007), 4.

which 'were considered to belong to no one because they were in the service of the gods, or because an offense to them was offensive to the gods'.[116]

Rose makes an analogy between this category of Roman property law and modern notions of wilderness:

> Such places suggest to the visitor the majesty of creation, the vastness of space, the untamed-ness of something outside human capacity to grasp. … Of course, it is physically possible to cut down trees in such places or to drill for oil in them or to race around in noisy wide-tire vehicles, but the argument against such behavior is chiefly one that sounds in the quasi-religious terms of travesty and sacrilege: such lands should be open to all, but each visitor should treat them with the appropriate attitude of awe. However, no bolt from heaven strikes down the logger, the oil well-driller, or the dune-buggy driver. The divine wildness of the wide open spaces is in the end metaphoric; the organized public, after all, has to protect them and invest in them if these spaces are to last.[117]

In the intellectual realm, Rose describes the classics, be they in art, literature or music, as fulfilling the equivalent role. No matter how they are appropriated for other purposes, they cannot be owned.[118] She also uses the language of wildness to make her point: 'it is the canon, the classics, the ancient works whose long life has contributed to their status as rare, extraordinary – and also a little wild, never quite capable of domestication even by the most erudite pedant'.[119] Her metaphor is also applicable here.

As we have seen, the law that attempts to turn life and living beings into intellectual property can only do so by simplifying them. The law pretends to capture the entire organism but this is simply not possible. If we are honest with ourselves, the patented creature in fact remains wild – uncontrolled and autonomous. Following Rose's logic it should thus not be appropriated and its sanctity should be protected. In the modern context of patenting life that barrier need not be based on the divine, as it was in Roman law, but it may be an ethic of the secular sacred as part of a larger set of principles acknowledging the complexity of life.

It is fitting to end our triptych story with a secular conclusion. We have now seen how the law – our third triptych panel – relies on only parts of the rest of the picture – the central dogma from the science centerpiece and the materialist ethic from the opposing panel – to extend patent protection to living organisms. Examining the full story of the triptych reveals this approach to be both misleading and unethical. The law needs to broaden its perspective and incorporate a vitalism of complexity in order to tell the full story.

7. Conclusion

The story of our triptych is now complete. We have examined the science, the ethics and the law relating to biotechnology as distinct panels and brought them together

---

116 *Ibid*, 21.
117 *Ibid*, 21.
118 *Ibid*, 22.
119 *Ibid*, 22.

to illustrate a larger message. The message is that the language of patent law is not suitable for living organisms. It requires their animate nature to be reduced to chemical descriptions in order to be squeezed into the categories of patentable subject matter. These chemical descriptions are misleading, however, because they suggest we have a complete materialist explanation of life when in fact, we are not even close. The patenting of life created by these simplistic representations of living organisms is unethical because it denies the true nature of life and life forms, namely their autonomy, uniqueness and sanctity. — vitalism

The question remains whether these ethical arguments are in vain. Have we gone too far in granting patents on life to turn back now? Certainly in both Canada and the US it will require acts of government to overturn the judicial precedents that have been set, acts that seem highly unlikely. The potential consequences of continuing along this route, however, will affect not just the science, ethics and patent law we have discussed but other areas outside the story in the triptych. These include impacts on property rights, seed saving, biodiversity and food security to name a few. Perhaps the most fundamental fallout, though may be an undermining of human respect for the complexity of life. Given the ignorance of which Henri Bergson wrote, we would do well to curtail our hubris and reconsider our current trajectory.

Chapter 3

The Right to Development, African Countries and the Patenting of Living Organisms: A Human Rights Dilemma

Adejoke Oyewunmi

So far, the development of intellectual property policy and law has been dominated by an epistemic community comprised largely of technically minded lawyers ... No legislature, no policy maker can, in the quest for efficient property rights, afford to rely on a narrowly constituted epistemic community. The stakes are too high ... Ideally the human rights community and the intellectual property community should begin a dialogue. The two communities have a great deal to learn from each other. Viewing intellectual property through the prism of human rights discourse will encourage us to think about ways in which the property mechanism might be reshaped to include interests and needs that it currently does not.[1]

1. Introduction

The last few decades have witnessed a knowledge revolution, resulting in the emergence of new technologies in the global marketplace. The shift in technological paradigm is particularly felt in the field of biotechnology, where the historical exploitation of living matter through traditional fermentation, cross planting and cross breeding has evolved into a more sophisticated system involving the sequencing of genes and proteins, recombinant DNA technology, cell fusion techniques and protein engineering.[2]

This development has changed the focus of intellectual property (IP) protection debate between the developed and developing countries. Due to higher expenditures on a much wider scope of research and development (R&D) mainly by the developed North, international discussion on IP has become dominated by demands from the North to strengthen intellectual property rights, and particularly, patents, worldwide. The extension of patent rights to the biotechnology sector, however, has critical impacts in the economic, social, and political spheres, with significant human rights implications in the health, food and agricultural sectors: areas which are critical to the actualisation of the right to development of a largely underdeveloped south.

---

1 P. Drahos, 'The Universality of Intellectual Property Rights: Origins and Development', in *Intellectual Property and Human Rights* (WIPO Publication No 762(E)) (1999), 34.

2 The emergence of the second, and most recently, third generation biotechnology: see R. Acharaya, *The Emergence and Growth of Biotechnology: Experiences in Industrialized and Developing Countries* (Cheltenham, Edward Elgar 1999), 16.

The possible implications for Africa, in particular, deserve special attention, given the realities of poor infrastructures, inadequate R&D and industrial capacities, and pathetic socio-economic conditions confronting the Continent.[3]

This chapter seeks to highlight the imperative of factoring in human rights considerations into the patenting lives discourse, consistently with the obligations of diverse international human rights instruments, such as the Universal Declaration of Human Rights, (UDHR), the International Covenant on Economic, Social and Cultural Rights (ICESCR), and the African Charter on Human and Peoples Rights (ACHPR), among others. The relatively recent emergence of a new category of rights – the human right to development, more effectively situates the discourse in the international human rights framework.

2. The Human Right to Development: Meaning, Evolution and Challenges

In its most basic form, the concept of development aims at the constant improvement of the well-being of the entire population and of all individuals on the basis of their active, free and meaningful participation in development and in the fair distribution of benefits resulting there from.[4] The right to development on its part confers on every human person and all peoples the right to participate in, contribute to, and enjoy economic, social, cultural, and political development.[5] The actualisation of the right to development contemplates the enhancement of 'the capabilities or freedom of individuals to improve their well-being, and to realise what they value',[6] while the process of development would result in the constant improvement of the well-being of the entire population and of all individuals, on the basis of *their active, free and meaningful participation* in development and in *the fair distribution of benefits* resulting *there from* [emphasis added].'[7]

The common thread running through the descriptions of the right to development is the emphasis on the participatory nature of the right. It is not externally imposed, and neither is it exclusive, but an inclusive process, which is not only acceptable to the peoples concerned, but is also beneficial to them.

The right to development was formally recognised following the almost unanimous adoption of the Declaration on the Right to Development (DRD) by the United Nations General Assembly on the 4 December 1986. Prior to 1986, certain

---

3 The Human Poverty Index of the United Nations Development Programme (UNDP) *Human Development Report* (2005) indicates that African countries are in the lead of the world's poorest countries, with Nigeria, Mali, Niger, Gambia, Zambia and the Central African Republic having more than 60 per cent of their populations living below the United Nations' specified poverty line of US $1 a day. See also S. Chen and M. Ravallion, 'How Have the World's Poorest Fared Since the Early 1980s' (2004) 19 *World Bank Research Observer* 141.

4 See Preamble to the Declaration on the Right to Development (DRD), adopted by the United Nations General Assembly on the 4 of December 1986.

5 Article 1 of the DRD.

6 See A. Sengupta, 'The Human Right to Development' (2004) 32(2) *Oxford Development Studies* 179.

7 Article 2.3 of the DRD.

human rights instruments, notably the Universal Declaration of Human Rights (UDHR),[8] had accorded the status of human rights to civil and political rights, as well as economic, social, and cultural rights.[9] The UDHR, which was adopted in the aftermath of the devastating effects of the Second World War, represented a consensus by the community of nations to provide an idealist framework for the promotion of human rights and fundamental freedoms for all. Beyond entrenching the notions of freedom and justice, the UDHR was also a commitment to the improvement of the economic and social well being of the individual.

Though not enforceable as legal rights, the ideals enunciated in the UDHR were, however, strengthened with the adoption in 1966 of two United Nations Covenants – the International Covenant on Civil and Political Rights (ICCPR) and the International Covenant on Economic, Social and Cultural Rights (ICESCR).[10]

Two decades after the adoption of the ICCPR and the ICESCR, the world community reached a consensus on the need for a specific and comprehensive instrument formally embodying both levels of human rights and incorporating them within the broader framework of a comprehensive 'right to development'. This resulted in the adoption of the DRD in 1986.

As a follow-up to the DRD, the Vienna Declaration and Platform for Action was adopted,[11] which reaffirmed the right to development as a universal and inalienable right and an integral part of fundamental human rights. A further step was taken with the decision of the Economic and Social Council of the United Nations to establish a two-fold mechanism to explore more effective ways of actualising the provisions of the Declaration.[12] Thus, an Independent Expert was appointed and an open-ended

---

8 The Universal Declaration of Human Rights was adopted by UN General Assembly Resolution 217 (A) II on 10 December 1948.

9 Traditionally classified as 'first generation' and 'second generation' rights respectively, notwithstanding that the trend now is to regard all human rights as universal, indivisible and interdependent and interrelated: see Article 5 of the Vienna Declaration and Programme of Action 1993. Former American First Lady (Eleanor Roosevelt) as head of the US delegation during the drafting of the Universal Declaration, had contributed to the process through her now famous statement 'one of the most important rights is the opportunity for development See M. Glen Johnson, 'The Contributions of Eleanor and Franklin Roosevelt to the Development of International Protection for Human Rights,' (1987) 9(1) *Human Rights Quarterly* 19.

10 Adopted on the 16 December 1966. Even though the two classes of rights were secured in separate Conventions, the concomitant adoption of the instruments lends credence to the interconnection and mutual interdependence between political and economic rights, and a confirmation that neither could be meaningful without the existence of the other. To the extent however, that there was a departure from the UDHR which incorporated both sets of rights in one instrument, the adoption of separate instruments may be viewed as a set back in the recognition of a comprehensive, unified human right to development.

11 See Vienna Declaration and Programme of Action, June 1993, which further describes the right as encompassing a number of other rights such as full sovereignty over natural resources, self-determination, popular participation in development, equality of opportunity, and the creation of favorable conditions for the enjoyment of other civil, political, economic, social and cultural rights. (Pars. 10, 11, 72 and 73.)

12 Decision 1998/269, endorsing the recommendation contained in Commission on Human Rights Resolution 1998/72.

Working Group set up. One to carry out studies on the current state of progress in the implementation of the right to development and the other to monitor and review the progress of the Independent Expert and report back to the Commission. Both bodies function alongside the High Commissioner for Human Rights, whose role includes promoting and protecting the realisation of the right to development and enhancing support from relevant bodies of the United Nation system for that purpose.[13]

Thus, there is now in place not only a formal framework for recognition of the right to development, but also what one may, for want of a better description, describe as the administrative machinery to explore, analyse and generally bring to light the issues concerned.

However, while a great deal of theoretical and academic expositions have been carried out with a view to the articulation of the right, the full acceptance, assimilation and practical implementation of the lofty ideals enunciated in the DRD have remained largely problematic, and little more than empty words for the unfortunate victims of underdevelopment, poverty and want. According to Professor Stephen Marks 'the right to development ... has not yet entered the practical realm of development planning and implementation ... States tend to express rhetorical support for this right but neglect its basic precepts in development practice'.[14] This may be attributed to the non-binding nature of the Declaration coupled with the resistance of some countries to the kind of global efforts and sacrifice that would be necessary to implement the right.

One area where this neglect is most apparent is in the area of intellectual property, where the freedom to legislate in the way and manner most compatible with attainment of the developmental goals and aspirations of individual countries has, in the face of the current wave of globalisation, given way, to an international system of protection under the Agreement on Trade-Related Aspects of Intellectual Property (TRIPS).[15] It sets minimum, uniformly applicable IP standards regardless of their levels of development, and socio-economic circumstances. Furthermore, it is a reflection of the trends in economic globalisation, which promotes a private, profit oriented approach within an economic and proprietary framework. This is characterised by the extension of IP rights, broadening of subject matter with dire consequences for many countries of the South.[16]

---

13 General Assembly Resolution A/RES/48/14. More recently, at the fifty-ninth General Assembly of the UN, in November 2004, the need to pay special attention to the right to development was again reiterated (see GA/SHC/3796).

14 S. Marks, 'The Human Right to Development: Between Rhetoric and Reality' (2004) 17 *Harvard Human Rights Journal* 137.

15 Annex IC to the World Trade Organization (WTO) Agreement, 1993, GATT Document MTN/FA II-AIC.

16 The impact is felt more keenly in the pharmaceutical sector, where the difference between countries with product patents on drugs, and those without, may be as high as 300 to 1200 per cent. See D. Nayyar, 'Intellectual Property, the New Millennium and the Least Developed Countries: Some Reflections in the Wider Context of Development' in *New Millennium, Intellectual Property and the Least Developed Countries* (WIPO Publication No 766(E)), 25.

Some of the fallouts of the current globalization of the world economy such as the wave of privatisation and commercialisation of government assets have, not surprisingly, affected general outlooks and expectations particularly with regard to the function of the State. Thus, the role of the State has now evolved from sponsor and provider to regulator, while it sheds and privatises many of its functions in terms of provision of basic needs to the public. Given this change in the role of the state, and the corresponding empowerment of private, profit-oriented institutions, the effectiveness of the state to assume direct responsibility for the welfare of the populace, as defined by human rights norms, become increasingly compromised. This is because the values of protection of human dignity and common good are at the core of human rights approach, but these are often at variance with private interests and profit maximisation which characterises economic globalisation. Thus, the role of the state has gradually evolved to the creation of a conducive legal and institutional framework for private sector players to operate.[17]

As mentioned above, the trends, developments, and attitudes underlying economic globalisation are also reflected in the international framework for the protection of IPRs. Not surprisingly therefore, given the divergences in outlook between the human rights school and the promoters of economic globalisation and IPRs, critical human rights implications of certain key IPRs were not adequately factored into TRIPs Agreement.[18]

Concerned about the consequences of such developments if unchecked and with a view to the safeguarding of human rights, a number of United Nations human rights mechanisms have called attention to the human rights implications of globalisation. These include the Economic and Social Council, the Commission on Human Rights, and the Sub-Commission on the Promotion and Protection of Human Rights, which have reiterated the need for a human-rights-compliant international trade regime.[19] According to a Preliminary Report by the UN Special Rapporteurs on globalisation and its impact on human rights:

> the phenomenon of globalization, the processes and institutional frameworks through which it is propagated, and its multifaceted nature have numerous implications for the promotion and protection of all human rights. This implies that there is a need for a critical re-conceptualization of the policies and instruments of international trade, investment and finance. Such re-conceptualization must cease treating human rights issues as peripheral to their formulation and operation. In other words, there is a dire need for human rights … to be brought directly into the debate and the policy considerations of those who

---

17 See A. Chapman 'A Human Rights Approach on Intellectual Property, Scientific Progress and Access to the Benefits of Science' in *Intellectual Property and Human Rights* (WIPO Publication No 762(E)), 129–31.

18 Although Article 7 of the TRIPS Agreement makes reference to the need for the protection and enforcement of IP rights to be implemented in a manner conducive to social and economic welfare, while Article 8 touches on the freedom to adopt measures necessary to safeguard public health and nutrition in the formulation of national laws, however, such measures are required to be consistent with the provisions of the TRIPs.

19 See the Sub-Commission on Human Rights Resolution 2000/7 on Intellectual Property Rights and Human Rights.

formulate the policies and operate the institutions that are at the forefront of the drive for the increased globalization of contemporary society.[20]

The report further reiterates the importance of the right to development when examining the human rights implications of globalisation, particularly in its role as a process that enables the human person to fully enjoy all the economic, social, cultural and political rights embodied in the diverse human rights instruments.[21]

A major set-back, however, is the inadequacy of international efforts to promote the enforcement of these human rights obligations; unlike the WTO TRIPs Agreement, which has been secured within a powerful global framework, with adequate monitoring and enforcement schemes. The scenario is further complicated by what has been described as 'the politics of the right to development', and the polarisation of views along North/South lines.[22]

The overall implication of these factors is the considerable difficulty in reaching a consensus on more specific and enforceable obligations pertaining to the right to development, particularly in the realm of international economic law. The essence of the problem was captured by the Commission on Human Rights Independent Expert, Arjun Sengupta, who attributed the reticence to the fact that the right 'raises issues about which the world has been fundamentally divided – such as issues related to the ideas of justice, equity, *and priorities of international policy*'.[23]

This statement is particularly relevant in connection with the grant of private exclusive proprietary rights in respect of living organisms, vis-à-vis public interest in access to these organisms in their natural and reformed states, given their critical importance in the context of the realisation of the right to food, health, culture, and livelihood. Beyond rhetoric therefore, the critical issue at stake now, as far as Africa and many other developing countries are concerned, is the practical implementation of the right to development, in the face of an increasingly uniform and equal treatment of very unequal parties in the global marketplace. The question is, how is the right to the 'constant improvement of the well-being of the entire population, and of all individuals, on the basis of their active, free and meaningful participation in development and in the fair distribution of benefits resulting there from'[24] to be assured? How does Africa access a process that 'expands the capabilities or freedom of individuals to improve their well-being' and quite importantly to 'realize what they value' within the meaning and intendment of the DRD? Before examining these issues, this chapter will highlight IPR provisions within the human rights framework.

---

20 See J. Oloka-Onyango and D. Udagama, 'The Realization Of Economic, Social And Cultural Rights: Globalization And Its Impact On The Full Enjoyment Of Human Rights' , Sub-Commission on the Promotion and Protection of Human Rights, Fifty-second session, E/CN.4/Sub.2/2000/13 15th June 2000. Online at: http://www.unhchr.ch/Huridocda/Huridoca.nsf/2848af408d01ec0ac1256609004e770b/21a92d3d0425a0cec125693500484d2f?OpenDocument (accessed 1 August 2007).

21 *Ibid*, par 48.

22 Marks, n. 14.

23 Sengupta, n. 6.

24 See Preamble to the DRD.

3. Beyond the DRD: Intellectual Property Rights Within the Context of the UDHR, ICESCR and the ACHPR Framework

Intellectual property systems attempt to strike a balance between two seemingly competing interests – the private ownership rights of authors, creators or inventors on the one hand, and public interest in the general progress and development of mankind, through the free dissemination of knowledge, on the other.[25] Thus, exclusive rights of exploitation, importation and use granted to right owners are often balanced by the provision of limited durations, exclusion of specific subject matter from protection, permission to utilise inventions or other subject matter of protection for research purposes and, in appropriate circumstances, compulsory licensing rights and government user schemes. However, the freedom to balance private/ public interests in a manner consistent with the peculiar needs and circumstances of each country was better assured in the past when IP laws were based mainly on national legislation. With the advent of internationalisation and globalisation of IP, driven mainly by the industrialised countries of the world, the balance appears to tilt decisively in favour of technology owners rather than technology users. TRIPS, for example, not only stipulates minimum standards of protection for IP rights, but also expands the scope of protectible subject matter in a hitherto unprecedented manner, particularly in its requirement for the protection of living matter, as stipulated under Article 27(3) (b) of that Agreement.

The need to balance private rights vis-à-vis public rights is also reflected under the Human Rights provisions of the UDHR, ICESCR and the ACHPR. Article 27(1) of the UDHR provides that everyone has the right to freely participate in the cultural life of the community, to enjoy the arts and to share in the scientific advancement and benefits, Article 27(2) on the other hand, provides that everyone has the right to the protection of the moral and material interests resulting from any scientific, literary or artistic production of which he or she is the author. Article 17 further reinforces the right to private ownership by providing that 'everyone has the right to own property alone, as well as in association with others'; while Article 17(2) adds that 'no one shall be arbitrarily deprived of his property'.

On the other hand, however, the public is also entitled to share in results of artistic and scientific advancements, and benefit from them. The implementation of the right to access may therefore require the imposition of some limitations on the private right to property. Indeed this point is buttressed by Article 17(2) which implies a right to regulate property rights so long as this is done according to law.

On its part, the ICESCR also reflects this delicate balancing act, and further contains several provisions that are germane to the theme of this conference. These include Article 1(2) which provides for the freedom of all peoples to, for their own ends, 'freely dispose of their natural wealth and resources, without prejudice to any obligations arising out of international economic cooperation, *based upon the principle of mutual benefit* …',[26] and Article 11, which recognises the right to, inter

---

25 Perhaps the oldest and most succinct evidence of this is Article 1, Paragraph 8 of the US Constitution.

26 Emphasis added.

alia, adequate food. This is reinforced under Article 11(2) which, while recognising the fundamental right of everyone to be free from hunger, requires the taking of steps by State Parties (either individually or through international co-operation) including specific programmes and measures needed to:

> improve methods of production, conservation and distribution of food *by making full use of technical and scientific knowledge ... and by developing or reforming agrarian systems in such a way as to achieve the most efficient development and utilization of natural resources.*[27]

Article 12 recognises the right to the highest attainable standard of physical and mental health, while Article 15 recognises the right to participate in cultural life, enjoy the benefits of scientific progress and its applications and to benefit from the protection of the moral and material interests resulting from any scientific, literary or artistic production of which a person is author.

States are required to take steps to achieve the full realisation of the above rights, including those necessary for the conservation, development and diffusion of science and culture and to respect the freedom indispensable for scientific research and creative activity.[28] Article 2 further requires each State Party to the Covenant to take steps individually *and through international assistance and co-operation,*[29] especially economic and technical, to progressively realise the rights recognised in the Covenant by all appropriate means, including legislative measures. Special concessions are also given to developing country member states to determine the extent to which the economic rights recognised under the Covenant would be guaranteed to non-nationals.[30]

As mentioned above, the responsibility for the implementation of these programmatic, directive policies lies with individual states as well as regional and international institutions and there is a need to ensure that basic human rights tenets are factored into economic, social and political policies, for the collective benefit of the human race. In particular, individual states must have the freedom and flexibility needed to fulfil their obligations under the ICESCR, in terms of ensuring equal and adequate access to essential resources at the three basic levels that have been articulated under international norms. The first is an obligation to respect the rights of the citizens, and not infringe or otherwise interfere with their enjoyment of economic, social and cultural rights. The second obligation is to protect the interests of the people, and this requires the putting in place of regulations, which protect against the infringement of these rights by private actors as well as governments.[31] The third arm of this tripartite duty is the obligation to least design policies that improve the access of the people, especially its most vulnerable to food producing resources, health care etc.

---

27 Emphasis added.
28 Article 15(3).
29 Emphasis added.
30 Article 2(3).
31 Thus the duty to protect will guard against unfair market practices, such as the creation of monopolies.

The African Charter on Human and People's Rights reaffirms its commitment to eradicate all forms of colonialism (including neo-colonialism) from Africa, and intensify co-operation and efforts to achieve a better life for the peoples of Africa.[32] It further reiterates the need to pay particular attention to the right to development, while emphasising that the safeguarding of economic, social and cultural rights as a guarantee for the meaningful enjoyment of civil and political rights.[33]

Specific articles of the Charter deal with the right to property,[34] right to health,[35] right to take part in the cultural life of the community,[36] right to development,[37] and the right to a generally satisfactory environment favourable to development.[38]

Part II of the Charter further puts in place safeguards to ensure the actualisation of the provisions of the Charter through the establishment of the African Commission of Human and People's Rights, with the mandate to promote human and peoples' right and ensure their protection in Africa.[39]

The emphasis of international and regional human rights standards goes beyond the promotion of the interests of private, proprietary and economic rights and interests of property owners. Rather it is more public oriented and exacting, in terms of the need to ensure that the nature and extent of protection afforded to right owners is such as directly promotes and facilitates the promotion and diffusion of science, and is otherwise beneficial to the public.

Consistent with this approach, the UN Sub-Commission on Human Rights Resolution 2000/7 on Intellectual Property Rights and Human Rights has in unequivocal terms asserted the primacy of human rights obligations over economic policies. It further requests all governments and national, regional and international economic policy forums to take international human rights obligations and principles fully into account in international economic policy formulation.[40]

Beyond policy formulation, there is also a need to ensure that the provisions are implemented in a manner beneficial to the most disadvantaged and vulnerable. In the context of patenting of living organisms, for example, a human-rights-compliant regime will require that patent laws consistent with the right to food, health and also the dignity of the human person and that people are treated fairly and equitably, in terms of the protection of their knowledge systems and the sharing of the benefits of the exploitation of products resulting from the utilisation of their biological resources and traditional knowledge.

Thus, introducing the human rights approach will take international economic policies beyond economic and proprietary interests of a few individuals, firms or the powerful countries. It will rather be applied in a way that will help to improve the lot

---

32 See Preamble to the Charter.

33 *Ibid.*

34 Which shall be guaranteed, and may only be encroached upon in public interest, and in accordance with the provisions of appropriate laws: Article 4.

35 Both physical and mental: Article 16.

36 Article 17(2).

37 Development broadly encompassing economic, social and cultural aspects: Article 22.

38 Article 24.

39 Article 30.

40 The Resolution was adopted on the 17 August, 2000.

of humanity at individual and collective levels. It will thus allow sufficient flexibility to cater for the disempowered, vulnerable and weak: descriptions which eminently fit the continent that has the unenviable status of being the region with the highest incidence, as well as the greatest depth, of extreme poverty.[41]

4. The African Context

The grim realities of unemployment, hunger, disease and conflict on the African continent reveal beyond a shadow of doubt that the continent faces a development crisis. Poverty rates are at an all-time high level, diseases like polio and tuberculosis, which have long been eradicated elsewhere, have resurfaced to plague the young and old alike, while the HIV/AIDS pandemic ravages the populations mercilessly.

Admittedly, many of these challenges also confront other countries classified as developing countries, but there are wide disparities in terms of social and economic conditions and technological competence of each country. For example, while some of the newly industrialising economies like Malaysia, India and Taiwan have significant scientific and technological capabilities and decent infrastructure, the same is not so for many African countries, who labour under relatively weak technical capacity and are plagued by poor infrastructure. In fact, it takes a great deal of optimism to continue to describe many of the countries as developing countries, given the socio-economic set-backs resulting from their severe circumstances. Moreover, most of the economies are agrarian and the appropriate IP policies to address the needs of these African countries merit separate consideration.

Efforts to adopt a collective approach to dealing with some of the challenges of the continent under the auspices of the African Union (AU),[42] as well as its precursor, the Organization of African Unity (OAU),[43] have emphasised the need to promote research and development in all fields;[44] the making of concerted efforts to halt the marginalisation of Africa in the globalisation process; and the enhancement of its full and beneficial integration into the global economy as critical. In particular, the development-focused initiative of the continent, the New Partnership for Africa's Development (NEPAD),[45] has as its key priority the implementation of the food security and agricultural development programme in all sub-regions.

Access to the benefits of scientific research in the biotechnology sector, as well as the safeguarding of Africa's biological resources and traditional knowledge (TK) from biopiracy are critical to the attainment of these goals.

---

41 See Chen and Ravallion, n. 3.

42 The Constitutive Act of the African Union: adopted in 2000 at the Lome Summit (Togo), entered into force in 2001.

43 Established by the OAU Charter of 23 May, 1963, and entered into force the same year. One of the stated objectives of the OAU was, inter alia, the promotion of unity and solidarity among African States, as well as the coordination and intensification of cooperation among these states for development.

44 Article 3 of the Constitutive Act of the AU.

45 Adopted as a Programme of the AU at the Lusaka Summit (2001).

5. The Agricultural Sector, Biotechnology and the Right to Development: The Interface

Beyond being a source of food, agriculture is also a source of livelihood for the vast majority of Africa's people. The World Bank estimates that it accounts for well over 60 per cent of employment in many African countries. The agricultural sector also has a profound impact on the meaningful realisation of the right to health both in the preventive and curative aspects. This makes access to safe and nutritious food, as well as medicinal herbs, an absolute necessity. Thus, there is a strong interconnection between Africa's agricultural performance and its socio-economic well-being, both at the individual and collective levels. And anything that affects the sector strikes at the very existence and well-being of the people.

However, a recent Food and Agriculture (FAO) release has disclosed that twenty-four sub-Saharan African countries face food emergencies, with over thirty million people on the continent needing food assistance.[46] This development constitutes a reversal of the efforts of the continent to eradicate poverty, increase life expectancy and otherwise improve the living conditions of Africa's teeming populace. The food crisis becomes more critical in the face of estimates that the continent is likely to more than double in population size by 2050. This necessitates the need to deploy strategies to revolutionalise food production to sustain the growing population.[47]

It is in this context that the vast advances in biotechnological research become relevant as a means of enhancing food production and safeguarding the livelihood of the millions of farmers and agricultural workers.[48]

Biotechnology refers to any technique that uses living organisms (or parts of organisms) to make or modify products, to improve plants or animals, or to develop micro-organisms for specific uses. Research and development activities in the field of biotechnology have resulted in increased nutritional value of staple foods, increased yield and reduced production costs, tolerance of poor environmental conditions including pest resistance and drought tolerance.[49] The informed application and utilisation of these developments can be of tremendous assistance in the enhancement of food production and poverty alleviation.

However, the commercialisation of science and the consequent restriction of access to these technologies under patent regimes for living organisms and biotechnological products constitute a serious threat to the utilisation of biotechnology to secure the realisation of the right to food and other associated rights. This is because the large

---

46 See the FAO '24 sub-Saharan African countries face food emergencies', 28 September 2005 (http://www.fao.org/newsroom/en/news/2005/107852/index.html) (accessed 1 August 2007).

47 See T. Goliber, 'Population and Reproductive Health in Sub-Saharan Africa' (1997) 52(4) *Population Bulletin.*

48 FAO 'World Food Summit: Five Years Later Reaffirms Pledge to Reduce Hunger', 27 August 2002. Online at: http://www.fao.org/worldfoodsummit/english/newsroom/news/8580-en.html (accessed 1 August 2007).

49 See J. Omiti *et al* 'Biotechnology Can Improve Food Security In Africa' (2002) 3(1) African Journal of Food, Agriculture, Nutirtion and Development. Online at: http://www.ajfand.net/issueIIIfiles/IssueIII-policies.htm#BIOTECHNOLOGY (accessed 1 August 2007).

multinational businesses, which often dominate the biotechnology sector, will be armed with the tools to set exploitative market prices. This situation is compounded by the possibility of genetically engineered products supplanting traditional varieties, with grave implications for the millions of poor, socially disadvantaged, small-scale farmers who may be unable to afford the product. This could lead to diminished earning capacity or passing on the increased cost of farming inputs as higher prices to consumers.[50] Additionally, the propriety of handing over such a vital sector to private interests has been questioned given the possibility of technology-inherent risks, which may endanger public health and environmental safety.[51]

Beyond biosafety issues, the application of biotechnology in the political and socio-economic circumstances of most African countries also gives rise to certain other concerns. First is the exploitation of African indigenous genetic resources without appropriate compensation by the North, which broadens the gap between the North and the South.[52] Coupled with this is the loss of biodiversity as traditional local varieties give way to the more productive genetically engineered varieties with dire consequences for present and future generations.

These concerns require specific measures aimed at addressing the problems: to protect future generations, to reduce the unhealthy disparity between developed and developing countries, and to address the dwindling competitiveness of many African countries whose economies rely on agricultural exports. This is because the goals of global sustainable development cannot be achieved with growing socio-economic disparities and an endangered environment. Thus, from an African perspective, the framework for protection should deal with these biosafety and equity issues, as well as the issue of access to the technologies, which are critical, not only in terms of physical availability, but also of affordability.

The point must be made that where trying to balance public interests against the private interests of the plant breeders the intricate research in this field involves great skill and ingenuity, higher committal of time and resources and great risks. However, once a successful recombinant product has been created, either in form of a modified seed, bacterium, plant or animal variety, the possibility of free riding is high.[53] The need for a conducive environment which affords the opportunity to make adequate returns is thus critical to the private biotechnological firms at whose initiative and

---

50 In Africa, agricultural research is mostly carried out by publicly funded research institutes, who thus do not charge exploitative prices for the improved seedlings and other inputs. However, these institutes are often hampered by inadequate funds, thus limiting the scope and level of their R&D activities, and necessitating private sector participation.

51 These are risks which occur, when due to the interaction of genetically engineered organisms in the environment into which they are released damage is caused to the environment, and harm to human life or health. The issue of biosafety is thus critical, and calls for the putting in place of appropriate legal and regulatory biosafety framework, supported by the required infrastructural facilities and manpower crucial to effective implementation.

52 Discussed below.

53 See M. Dolmans 'rDNA as a Protectable Database/Copyrighted Work? Lessons From The Software Sector', presented at the 8th Fordham Conference on International Intellectual Property Law and Policy, New York (April 2000), 3–5.

expense much of the research is undertaken, if further time, money and efforts are to be committed into the R&D process, for the benefit of all.[54]

6. Patenting of Living Organisms, Right to Health and the Protection of Traditional Knowledge

The patenting of living organisms has important consequences for the actualisation of the right to health. In an interesting discourse, Silvar Salazar stated 'it is perhaps in the field of health that the most questions have been asked about intellectual property and its role as a promoter of development, as health is a factor that is crucial to the survival and welfare of mankind'.[55]

The connection is most obvious in respect of the mandatory requirement in TRIPS that pharmaceutical products can be patented.[56] Beyond this issue, however, the interrelationship between the right to health and the patent system raises other questions relating to access to biological resources, biopiracy from TK-rich countries of the South, including Africa. This issue is particularly critical given the increasing popularity of nature-based products in many sectors of modern life. As one commentator put it 'the search for alternative ways of doing things and for renewed cultural infusion has led to an interest in the cultures of local communities particularly by people from the industrialized countries … [T]he climate for a new relationship with practitioners of "authentic" or "complementary" medicine is based on the world-wide call for "health for all". A large proportion of the population is going for traditional medicine as a first resort and there is world-wide renaissance for the use of traditional medicine.'[57] Thus, increasingly, biotechnological, pharmaceutical, cosmetic and other sectors are turning to natural products, particularly medicinal plants and herbs, rather than synthetic products to meet the health needs of consumers.

However, the possibility of patent protection for living organisms, including medicinal plants and herbs and their derivatives, has introduced some controversy into the issue. The controversy stems from the fact that the ecological distribution of biological diversity is unequal, with the countries of the South, and especially Africa, being much better endowed in this respect than the North. On the other hand, when compared with the North, the South has limited R&D capacity. This leads to

---

54 Unlike when research is undertaken by publicly funded institutions, altruism and peer recognition are inadequate incentives to private R&D efforts, ibid.

55 S. Salazar, 'Intellectual Property and the Right to Health' in *Intellectual Property Rights and Human Rights* (WIPO Publication No 762(E)), 65.

56 Due to the effects of the patent system on access to drugs and medicines in LDCs, certain concessions were granted to these countries during the WTO Doha Rounds. The resulting Doha Declaration thus extends the deadline for least-developed countries to apply provisions on pharmaceutical patents until 1 January 2016.

57 E.N. Mensah, Director, Institutional Care Division, Ministry of Health, Accra, Ghana, as reported in *Intellectual Property Needs and Expectations of Traditional Knowledge Holders, World Intellectual Property (WIPO) Report on Fact-Finding Missions on Intellectual Property and Traditional Knowledge* (1998–9) (WIPO Publication No. 768(E)), 147.

a dichotomy of interests between the owners of the resources and associated TK and the multinational corporations who through their R&D activities are able to develop and package these natural resources into commercially marketable products. The injustice here lies in the securing of patents and exploitation of TK-based products and processes without obtaining the prior informed consent of the original knowledge holders, acknowledging their contributions, or sharing the benefits of commercial exploitation with them. This inequity further tilts the scales against the already economically disempowered peoples and countries of the continent and runs contrary to the letter and spirit of international human rights norms.

Beyond the narrow confines of traditional medicine, it has also been asserted that:

> biodiversity, and the knowledge associated with using it in a sustainable manner, are a comparative advantage of those Least Developed Countries that are biodiversity-rich, enabling them to participate more effectively in global markets and thus rise above current levels of poverty and deprivation.[58]

However, the full economic potentials of the increased interest in biological resources and the associated TK of African people (and others similarly endowed) have not been effectively realised by these peoples. Thus, while annual global business in natural products in the pharmaceutical, biotechnology and health industries are estimated at billions of dollars, hardly any benefits accrue to the source countries and traditional communities who provide the leads for research into the use of products. In fact, according to a source, total trade in herbal remedies and botanicals in 1995 yielded over US $56 billion, but the only payments to the communities were for the manual labour involved.[59]

As mentioned earlier, there are also moral rights issues involved in the context of foreign multinationals seeking to obtain exclusive rights in respect of products originating from traditional knowledge holders, without any reference to the source of the product.[60]

The patentability of such nature-based products and processes in this context raises complex ethical and moral issues pertaining to the identification and ownership of all those involved in the development of the product and their status and rights. It also has profound implications on the actualisation of the right to development, health, food and culture of Africans. It further creates a dilemma because while on the one hand, there is dire need to promote the right to development of the continent, which in the short term can be facilitated by a 'no patent' regime which facilitates

---

58 *Protection of Traditional Knowledge: A Global IP Issue* (WIPO Document WIPO/RT/LDC/14).

59 D. Posey, 'Intellectual Property Rights For Native Peoples: Challenges to Science, Business, and International Law', (1991) cited in Mugabe, 'Intellectual Property Protection and Traditional Knowledge' in *Intellectual Property Rights and Human Rights* (WIPO Publication No 762(E)), 103.

60 Examples include the Neem Tree Patent, (popularly referred to as 'dogonyaro' among the natives) (see http://news.bbc.co.uk/1/hi/sci/tech/745028.stm) (accessed 1 August 2007); the Turmeric Patent (see http://www.twnside.org.sg/title/tur-cn.htm) (accessed 1 August 2007).

copying and imitation and makes for cheaper products affordable to the people. In the long run this is actually counterproductive because failure to put in place adequate provisions to protect innovation may hinder technological development and discourage private sector involvement in biotechnology.[61]

Ultimately, what is needed is a framework which strikes the right balance between the regulation of access and utilisation of biological resources and the protection of innovations and knowledge systems, including TK, without discrimination, while at the same time, taking care to put in public interest safeguards.[62]

The International Convention for the Protection of New Varieties of Plants (UPOV), whose provisions are more tilted towards the protection of breeders' rights, to the detriment of farmers' and community rights clearly fails to meet this need.[63] However, the Covention on Biodiversity (CBD), as well as the FAO International Treaty on Plant Genetic Resources for Food and Agriculture,[64] have both responded to these issues by providing for access to, as well as the conservation and sustainable use of, plant genetic resources on the one hand and the fair and equitable sharing of benefits derived from their use on the other. The obligations contained in these instruments need to be taken into account in the formulation of an appropriate scheme for the protection of living matter.[65]

On its part, the human rights community has responded to these issues via a Declaration on the Rights of Indigenous Peoples,[66] and Draft Principles and Guidelines for the Protection of the Heritage of Indigenous People,[67] by which national laws are to be enacted to protect indigenous peoples' heritage, by providing the means for these peoples to prevent infractions though injunctions and to provide

---

61 This is particularly important to many African countries that are at present making concerted efforts to attract foreign investment, and to create a conducive framework to strengthen the private sector and encourage their participation in a number of key sectors of the economy.

62 The difficulty of a consensus in this regard is revealed in the sheer number of efforts and initiatives by diverse groups, organisations and institutions to tackle the issues. While some advocate a regime of private contracts, others are promoting codes of practice in access and benefit sharing, while yet some others maintain that nothing short of legislation would work. Among the latter category are the advocates of the modification of patent application procedures to integrate the tripartite requirements of disclosure of origin, evidence of prior informed consent, and satisfactory benefit sharing arrangements.

63 This is particularly the case with the 1991 Act of the UPOV Convention.

64 Adopted by the FAO Conference in November 2001.

65 This point has been succinctly made in the Proposal of the African Group to the WTO on the review of Article 27.3(b). According to the Proposal, the implementation of the article is subject to clarification to allow developing countries to meet other international obligations, for example under the Convention on Biological Diversity, and the FAO International Undertaking for Plant Genetic Resources, and also satisfy their need to protect the knowledge and innovations in farming, agriculture and health and medical care of indigenous people and local communities.

66 This was adopted on 13 September 2007.

67 Sub-Commission on the Promotion and Protection of Human Rights, Decision 2000/107, UN Doc. E/CN.4/Sub.2/DEC/107/2000/107 (2000). 30 Revised Draft Principles and Guidelines, Guidelines 24(b).

redress through damages, 'the acquisition, documentation or use of their heritage without proper authorization', while also requiring states to deny patents, copyrights, and other exclusive rights over 'any element of indigenous peoples' heritage' that does not provide for 'sharing of ownership, control, use and benefits' with those peoples.[68]

7. Patenting of Living Organisms in Africa? The Issues at Stake

With regard to the framework for the recognition and protection of patents, most countries of the continent have, in the post-independence era, either continued with their national systems of protection or opted for one of the two regional IP systems – the African Regional Industrial Property Organisation (ARIPO)[69] or the African Intellectual Property Organisation (OAPI).[70]

Under these systems the patenting of life forms, (with the exception of microbiological inventions) have been excluded from the scope of protection.[71] In other countries, however, particularly the developed countries, the situation is different. In the United States, for example, in the landmark case of *Diamond v. Chakrabarty*,[72] the United States Supreme Court extended the scope of utility patents to living organisms when it held that a living, man-made, genetically modified

---

68 Guidelines 24(b) and (c) respectively. WIPO and UNESCO have also been active in this regard. See, for example, the WIPO *Technical Study on Patent Disclosure Requirements Related to Genetic Resources and Traditional Knowledge*, Study No 3, (WIPO Publication No 786(E)), as well as the WIPO-UNEP Study, *Role of IPRs in the Sharing of Benefits Arising From the Use of Biological resources and Associated Traditional Knowledge*, Study No 4, (WIPO Publication No 769(E)).

69 Established by the Lusaka Agreement on the Creation of an Industrial Property Organization for English-Speaking Africa December 9, 1976, as amended (1982), (1986), (1996), and (2004) Lusaka Agreement on the Creation of the African Regional Intellectual Property Organization (ARIPO) (1976). ARIPO's members are primarily English-speaking African countries.

70 Formerly known as The African and Malagasy Patent Rights Authority, created under the defunct 'Libreville Agreement' (1962) for the Establishment of the African and Malagasy Patent Rights Authority. The transformation to the African Intellectual Property Organization (OAPI) was effected through the adoption of the Bangui Agreement for the Establishment of the African Intellectual Property Organization (1977) as revised (1999). In the ARIPO countries, a single application can provide patent protection across all member countries that belong to ARIPO, although national offices still need to register patents in accordance with national law. By contrast OAPI operates a truly regional patent, which without more, is effective in all the designated states.

71 Article 6 of Annex 1 to the OAPI Agreement; section 1(4)(a) of the Patents and Designs Act of Nigeria (Chapter 344 of the Laws of the Federation of Nigeria, 1990) provides that 'patents cannot be validly obtained in respect of plant or animal varieties, or essentially biological processes for the production of plants or animals (other than microbiological processes and their products)'. However, the lack of a clear line between biological and microbiological processes may create some difficulty about the exact scope of excluded inventions.

72 447 U.S. 303 (1980).

bacterium was protectible under the US Patent Act. This development was followed in 1985 by the grant of patent protection to a new variety of maize with higher protein content, and in 1988, the 'inventor' of a genetically modified mouse was successfully granted a patent in the European Patent Office.[73]

The desirability or otherwise of these developments in the law of patents raises complex issues of bioethics, human rights, and morality, among others.

The question now is whether Africa should follow suit in granting patents on life? In proffering an answer, as discussed above, there is a need to consider the implications of such to the availability and access to food, medicine, technology transfer, and the preservation and sustainability of the environment. There is also a need to protect all the stakeholders involved in the evolution of the biological variety or product by safeguarding the rights of these stakeholders to reward and equitable sharing of benefits derived from the exploitation of the variety, product or process.[74] Thirdly, there needs to be appropriate limitations on the rights granted to owners, with a view to safeguarding relevant public interests.[75] Finally, administrative challenges in terms of infrastructure, manpower etc must be duly taken into account.[76]

A further issue, which arises with regard to the patenting of living organisms, has to do with the suitability of patents for the protection of genes, DNA sequences, cells, and other parts of plant or animal forms. The identification and selection of these are undoubtedly time consuming, expensive, and useful in understanding nature and tackling diseases, but there is a fundamental issue about whether they are inventions, and thus protectible under the patent laws, or discoveries, which are not. Where they pertain to humans, further issues pertaining to the right to the dignity of the human person are raised.

Taking into account the above issues, the patent system, in its present form, does not satisfactorily address all the underlying issues affected, at least from the African perspective. This makes substantial modifications to the framework for patents, within the TRIPs Agreement, desirable to enable it respond to some of these issues, particularly to protect traditional knowledge holders who are seriously shortchanged present scheme. These modifications may include the introduction of certain additional requirements prior to the grant of patents. Examples include the disclosure of origin requirement,[77] proof of prior informed consent of the owner of

---

73 See *Onco-mouse/HARVARD* (2003) OJ EPO 10.

74 TK holders are presently left out of the scheme of things, because the tripartite requirements of newness, inventive activity and industrial application are couched and interpreted in ways inconsistent with the recognition and protection of TK which often has evolved over time, through generations.

75 See below.

76 This has to do with the administrative and technical procedures involved in the grant of patents. Due to manpower and infrastructural challenges, Nigeria, in particular operates the formal, as opposed to the substantive examination system.

77 By which patentees will be required to disclose the source of information and/or genetic material, basis of the patented invention. See the Directive 98/44/EC (recital 27). A major limitation of this however is that non-disclosure or inadequate disclosure does not prejudice the validity of patents, thus rendering the provision merely cosmetic. For a critical appraisal of

the knowledge,[78] and satisfactory benefit sharing arrangements.[79] Such provisions will go a long way in ensuring the realisation of economic, social and cultural well-being of the owners and source states of traditional knowledge. However, so far, no headway has been made at the WTO towards the introduction of these provisions into the TRIPS. It is, however, gratifying that Africa has taken some steps towards the fashioning of a Model Law, which seems to address a number of the issues which lie at the heart of the protection of its biological resources.

8. The AU Model Law on the Protection of the Rights of Local Communities, Farmers and Breeders and For the Regulation of Access to Biological Resources

The inadequacies of the existing framework for the protection of plant breeders' rights under the UPOV 1991 Agreement, in particular the primacy accorded to breeders' rights over and above farmers and community rights, as well as the lack of recognition accorded to traditional knowledge led to the development of the AU Model Law.[80]

According to Ekpere,[81] the Model Law represents an important initiative on the part of the African continent to strike the right balance between the protection of the investment of plant breeders on the one hand and Africa's biological diversity and the livelihoods dependent on it on the other. It thus provides a framework for the recognition of the innovative and creative efforts of African societies, providing a tool for the protection of their knowledge.[82] The specific objectives of the Model

---

the disclosure of origin requirement: see M. Blakeney, *Proposals for the Disclosure of Origin of Genetic Resources in Patent Applications* (WIPO/IP/GR/05/01).

78 In line with the provisions of the CBD Article 2.

79 This is also in line with the CBD. Benefit sharing in this context includes both financial aspects and technology sharing/transfer. See M. Beglund, 'The Protection of Traditional Knowledge Related to Genetic Resources: The Case for an Amended Patent Procedure, Paper Presented at the Nordic Environmental Law Workshop on the New Instruments for the Protection of Biodiversity and Biosafety' (2005) 2(2) *SCRIPT-ed*.

80 Endorsed in Ouagadougou, Burkina Faso, in 1998

81 See J.A. Ekpere, 'The OAU (AU) Model Law and Africa's Common Position on the TRIPs Review Process' discussion paper presented at 'Eastern and Southern Africa Multi-Stakeholders Dialogue on Trade, Intellectual Property Rights and Genetic Resources' Nairobi, Kenya, July, 30–31, 2001. Online at: http://www.ictsd.org/dlogue/2001-07-30/Ekpere.pdf#se arch='oau%20model%20law%20implementation%20africa (accessed 1 August 2007).

82 The revised Bangui Agreement (1999). However, the OAPI member countries have acceded to the UPOV Agreement although there are claims that they acceded under intense pressure from the international community: see GRAIN 'OAPI Undermines Farmers' Rights in Africa' (http://www.grain.org/nfg/index.cfm?id=7) (accessed 1 August 2007), as well as GENET, 'Legal 'Terminator' Threatens Francophone Africa's Farmers' (http://www.gene.ch/info4action/1999/Mar/msg00017.html) (accessed 1 August 2007). The ARIPO states and most other African countries have however opted to pursue a sui generis system of intellectual property rights, in recognition of the fact that neither the patent system, as outlined under the TRIPs Agreement nor the UPOV system of plant breeders' rights suitably satisfy local conditions and circumstances in Africa.

Law include: the recognition, protection and support of the inalienable rights of local communities including farming communities over their biological resources, knowledge and technologies; the recognition and protection of the rights of breeders; the provision of an appropriate system of access to biological resources as well as community knowledge, subject to the prior informed consent of the state and concerned communities, and based on the principles of benefit sharing; the development of appropriate and effective mechanisms for the enforcement of community, farmers', and breeders' rights; the promotion of the supply of good quality seed and planting material to farmers; the ensuring of the effective involvement and participation of concerned communities in decisions about the sharing of benefits, with a special focus on the role of women in the conservation and sustainable utilisation of biological resources; and to ensure the effective and equitable utilisation of biological resources, in order to strengthen food security.[83]

The law, while preserving traditional systems of access, use and exchange of knowledge by local communities[84] precludes collectors of biological resources from applying for patents over life forms and biological processes as these are not recognised under the Model Law.[85]

The Model Law also regulates access to biological resources based on the principles of benefit sharing and prior informed consent outlined in the CBD. It further assures community participation and involvement by specifying that decisions made by the national government regarding the sharing of biological resources or community knowledge must be made in cooperation and consultation with the local community in question.[86]

Part VI protects plant breeders' rights in respect of new varieties, conferring the exclusive right to sell and produce the plant variety and propagating material in respect of the variety, subject to the farmer's right and the right of the community to propagate or use the variety for purposes other than commerce.[87] Thus, unlike UPOV, it balances the rights of breeders with provisions for farmers' and community rights.

With regard to farmers, the law grants broad rights to farmers both as a reward for past contributions to the development of biodiversity,[88] and as a way of ensuring the preservation of food security. The farmers' rights include the right to save, use, sell and exchange seed/propagating material and to use a breeder's variety to protect under the law in the development of new farmer varieties, provided that the farmer is precluded from selling farm-saved seed of a breeder's protected variety on a commercial scale, in the seed industry.[89]

---

83 Part 1 of the Law.

84 Section 2(2).

85 Section 9. It should be noted however, that the patent exclusion does not extend to products derived from such biological resources, subject to the collector obtaining the consent and approval of the community in question, and making arrangements for equitable benefit sharing.

86 Part III.

87 See Section 32 and 33.

88 Part V; see also the FAO's International Undertaking on Plant Genetic Resources.

89 See Section 26.

The Model Law awaits incorporation into the domestic legislation of different African states, either individually, under national legislation, or collectively, through the regional system.

9. Conclusion

The patent system both benefits and challenges the realisation of the right to development, particularly in the context of the right to food and right to health. However, for the system to be truly beneficial it has to be fair. In its present form, the stringently high level of protection afforded by the existing international patent regime decisively tilts the delicate private/public interest in favour of the private interests of corporations. It is therefore ill adapted to safeguard the wide range of interests directly affected, including the right to food, health and overall development. A system which appears to permit the plunder of biological resources, gaining of market domination and the subjugation of the rights and interests of local communities and poor peoples, is clearly inconsistent with human rights requirements. These require the introduction of safeguards to protect public interests, especially in sectors which affect the weak and vulnerable. Such a system further supports the widening of the inequities between the haves and the have-nots.

There is a need for both the human rights community and the intellectual property group to work together to achieve a fairer and more balanced system. After all, their *ultimate* goals are not so fundamentally different from each other. The one is for the development, empowerment and protection of individual as well as group rights. The other protects and encourages those who contribute to human welfare, through their efforts and investments. In both cases, the ultimate goal is societal advancement and well being. Thus, there must be some give and take and a middle ground to give a human, development-centred face to the legal protection of property rights in the biotechnology sector.

PART 3
Medicine and Public Health

Chapter 4

The Genetic Sequence Right: A *Sui Generis* Alternative to the Patenting of Biological Materials

Luigi Palombi

There's always a tension between those who would like to garner wealth, and they contribute a lot to society. There's also those who say, 'I believe in the common good. I want that to be enlarged.' They contribute a lot to society. The tension, the debate, between these two views is extremely important to our progress.[1]

Part I

The patent system has at its core an exclusionary right. It is designed to exclude third parties from *making, using, vending or exercising*[2] the 'invention' of the patent within its jurisdiction. A patent is an asset just like any other. It can be traded. It has a value. It is property.[3] Therefore, although a patent right is 'exclusionary', the 'invention' which comes within the scope of its twenty-year statutory monopoly is the property of the patent owner.[4] It belongs to the patent owner just like a piece of land belongs to

---

1 Prof. Sir John Sulston, Interview with ABC TV Reporter, Jonathan Holmes, on July 9, 2003 at the International Genetics Conference in Melbourne, Australia. Prof. Sir John Sulston is Head of the British contribution to the Human Genome Project and was awarded the Nobel Prize for Physiology or Medicine in 2002.

2 In Australia, the exclusionary right is described as the right to 'exploit' the patent: Patents Act 1990 s.13(1) (Au). The word 'exploit' is defined to mean in respect of a product 'to make, hire, sell or otherwise dispose of the product, offer to make, sell, hire or otherwise dispose of it, use or import it, or keep it for the purpose of doing any of those things.'

3 See, for example, Patents Act 1990 s. 13(2) (Au) provides that 'The exclusive rights are personal property and are capable of assignment and of devolution by law.'

4 Stephen Crespi, a well-known proponent of patents over biological materials, argues that the term 'property' means nothing more than a farmer that owns the animals or plants that he or she has produced. It does not extend to ownership of a 'species' of animals, plants or organisms. He explains that 'objectors draw a distinction between owning specific plants and animals and the ownership of "whole species" which they claim is achieved by patenting. This is a clever debating point but it has no substance.' See S. Crespi, 'Biotechnology Patenting: The Wicked Animal Must Defend Itself' (1995) 17 *European Intellectual Property Review* 431. There is of course no substance in this argument. One only has to look at AU Patent 624,105 over hepatitis C virus polypeptides and nucleotides to realise that its claims do practically appropriate all HCV genotypes.

the landowner.[5] It may be an intangible asset, not real property, but trespassing upon it provides the patent owner with the right to unleash an arsenal of legal weaponry that includes injunctions, damages and accounts of profits. Each of these weapons are designed first, to punish the trespasser so as to deter further trespass and other potential trespassers and, second, to expropriate any financial benefit received as a result of the trespass. In patent law, a trespass is called an infringement. Therefore, if any third party *makes, uses, vends or exercises* an 'invention' without the authority of the patent owner, that party will infringe the patent, just as a person who enters upon land without the authority of the landowner will trespass upon the land.

Just as landowners are not obliged to work their land, patent owners are not obliged to work their inventions. They may simply use it to exclude all others from using the invention for twenty years. Although compulsory licences[6] supposedly provide a check against this eventuality, whether these licences are effective is another issue. For example, in Australia there has only ever been one application for a compulsory licence in the entire 102-year history of its patent law; and that application failed.[7]

Therefore, patented inventions are the exclusive property of the patent owner. With respect to patented biological materials this means that an isolated genetic sequence of a natural gene[8] or protein[9] becomes the *absolute* property of the patent owner if the claim is directed to the isolated genetic sequence *per se* as a product, or the *conditional* property of the patent owner if it is directed to the isolated genetic sequence as a component in a process or method. The distinction between the absolute property and the conditional property is important because ownership of the absolute means that no matter how the isolated genetic sequence is used or made, patent owners can exercise their patent rights; however, the conditional means that patent owners can only exercise their rights over isolated genetic sequences in the patented processes or methods.

---

5 This analogy is imperfect. Although it must be understood that while a landowner owns a single piece of land and a patent owner owns a single invention, the way that the 'invention' is described in the patent can give him or her ownership which is much broader in scope than a single physical entity. This is because the exclusionary right applies to an intangible thing which may have application in a myriad of physical applications.

6 A ground for the grant of a compulsory license is the non-working of the invention: Article 5(A)(4) of the Paris Convention for the Protection of Industrial Property.

7 *Fastening Supplies v Olin Mathieson Chemical Corporation* (1969) 119 CLR 572 (HC), per Menzies J.

8 Usually described by its nucleotide sequence. There are four DNA nucleotides (bases), adenine (A), guanine (G), cytosine (C), and thymine (T). A codon is made of three nucleotides e.g., ATG, GGC, and there can only be sixty-four different codons. Each codon codes for an amino acid or peptide.

9 Usually described by its amino acid sequence. The are only twenty amino acids, but depending on the nucleotides sequence, the polypeptides that result can be simple or complex. These twenty amino acids are common to all organisms. Polypeptides (many amino acids) are proteins.

1. The Absolute Genetic Patent Claim and its Consequences

An example of the *absolute* type is claim 1 of Australian Patent 624,105 entitled 'NANBV Diagnostics and Vaccines' granted to Chiron Corporation in 1991.[10]

> A polypeptide in substantially isolated form comprising a contiguous sequence of at least 10 amino acids encoded by the genome of hepatitis C virus (HCV) and comprising an antigenic determinant, wherein HCV is characterized by (i) a positive stranded RNA genome; (ii) said genome comprising an open reading frame (ORF) encoding a polyprotein; and (iii) said polyprotein comprising an amino acid sequence having at least 40% homology to the 859 amino acid sequence in Figure 14.

This is an example of a *genetic product claim*. It gives Chiron ownership in Australia of any protein (which is what a polypeptide is) that is 'isolated' from its natural environment (that is, not inside a human or animal) and which is comprised of (a) at least ten amino acids (amino acids are natural chemicals that are the building blocks of all proteins) and (b) an antigenic determinant (an antibody-binding site) derived from any positive stranded RNA virus[11] that has 'at least 40% homology to the 859 amino acids' of the NS4 region (a hyper-variable non-structural region of the HCV virus genome).

While this claim does not give Chiron ownership of natural HCV *per se*, it gives Chiron ownership over specific isolated proteins that correspond to those contained in any natural HCV. Therefore, ownership of natural HCV is unnecessary because ownership over specific isolated proteins that correspond to those contained in natural HCV is good enough.

In short, the genetic products of claim 1 are nothing more than bits and pieces of naturally occurring HCV cut and spliced together in an artificial environment. While these identical bits and pieces (natural genetic components) can be brought together to form fused polypeptides which themselves do not exist in naturally occurring HCV (i.e., are artificial genetic products), the natural genetic components are nevertheless individually identical to the corresponding sections of the HCV genome from which they have been derived. It is important to appreciate that in *many* instances the artificial genetic product is identical to, and corresponds precisely with, a natural genetic component and the only point of distinction is that the artificial product is *isolated*[12] whereas the natural is not.[13]

---

10 This claim, incidentally, is identical to claim 1 as granted by the European Patent Office in European Patent 318, 216.

11 HCV is an RNA virus. Its genome is made up of a single positive stranded ribonucleic acid molecule. The molecule is made up of nucleotides containing one of four bases represented by the letters, A, G, C and U (uracil).

12 This means that it has been removed from its natural cellular environment.

13 This distinction is crucial to the argument that a product of nature can be transformed into a product of man. See the First Art. 16(c) Report of the European Commission to the European Parliament on the operation of the EC Biotechnology Directive [October 7, 2002] where it states at section 4: 'an element isolated from the human body, including a sequence or partial sequence of a gene, by techniques of identification, purification, characterisation and multiplication, may constitute a patentable invention, even if the structure of that element

With this type of absolute claim the application of the genetic product in any kind of technology, such as a component in an immunoassay, vaccine or anti-viral, is irrelevant to the issue of infringement. The mere use of a genetic product that comes within the claim, even by a university conducting research, can amount to an infringement.[14] For example, when a vaccine to HCV infection is eventually developed, if that vaccine makes use of a genetic product of claim 1, then even if it is the subject of a separate patent owned by a third party, that third party will need the authority of Chiron before it can exercise its patent rights because its patent will be subordinate to Chiron's. In fact, it is arguable that even the vaccine research conducted by that third party will itself infringe Chiron's patent if there is use of a genetic product of claim 1.[15]

The impact which this HCV genetic product claim had over medical and scientific research in the 1990's was explained by Prof. Baruch Blumberg[16] in his testimony to the Federal Court of Australia:[17]

> I have reviewed Chiron's Australian Patent No. 624105 [and] [i]n my opinion, the claims in this patent … represent a view in scientific thought, i.e., that '[a]*nything that is done with the HCV virus is covered by this patent and all research and development on the virus is subservient to it.*' This patent essentially does not distinguish between genotype and phenotype, whereas geneticists are very aware that such a distinction should be made. It is the reductionism argument taken to the extreme and it is not supported by the great weight of the history of scientific discovery in biology and medicine. To the extent that

---

is identical to that of a natural element. The same reasoning can obviously be applied to any element produced otherwise synthetically by a technical process.' This distinction, however, is spurious because the mere isolation of a natural gene or protein does not produce something that is substantially different to the natural. The US Supreme Court in *Diamond v Chakrabarty*, 447 U.S. 303 (1980) only permitted the patenting of a genetically modified bacterium because it displayed 'markedly different characteristics from any found in nature' (at 309). The Danish Council of Bioethics in its 2004 report entitled *Patenting Human Genes and Stem Cells* noted that 'it cannot be said with any reasonableness that a sequence or partial sequence of a gene ceases to be part of the human body merely because an identical copy of the sequence is isolated from or produced outside of the human body' (at 98). See also L. Palombi, *The Patenting of Biological Materials in the Context of TRIPS* (PhD University NSW, September 2004) and L. Palombi 'The Impact Of TRIPS On The Validity Of The European Biotechnology Directive' (2005) 2 *Journal of International Biotechnology Law*, 15.

14 See for example *Madey v. Duke University*, 307 F.3d 1351 (Fed. Cir. 2002).

15 Ibid. Cf: According to the US Supreme Court in *Merck KGaA v. Integra Lifesciences I, Ltd.*, 545 US 193 (2005), even pre-clinical commercial research will come within the US statutory exemption (s.271(e)(1) Patents Act, (1952)) provided that there is an intention to conduct those experiments with a view to ultimately seeking FDA approval.

16 Prof. Blumberg identified the causative agent of hepatitis B (HBV) in 1967. In 1976 he was awarded the Nobel Prize for Physiology or Medicine in recognition of his studies concerning mechanisms involved in the origin and spread of infectious diseases and, specifically, for the discovery of the hepatitis B virus and for the development of methods for detection of HBV and the vaccine for HBV. He never sought to patent HBV.

17 *Murex Diagnostics Australia Pty Ltd v Chiron Corporation* NG 106/1994 (Federal Court of Australia). There is no judgment as the case settled in week nine of the trial in August 1996 as part of a global settlement.

this extreme view is backed-up by broad claims, which it is in this patent, the effect will likely be inhibition of research on HCV. Based on the unusually broad nature of the patent, if I were a research director for anti-virals and had the option of working on several viruses, the existence of this patent would weigh against my deciding to undertake HCV research. A company, or even an academic laboratory, might well be deterred from conducting research on HCV because the patent is, in effect, intimidating. With the patent as it stands, any investigator, particularly in commercial laboratories (where much of the work on hepatitis has been done) would have to seriously consider that Chiron would bring an action against them if they attempted any commercialization of anything related to HCV.[18]

Some commentators argue that these types of statements are not supported by empirical evidence and are irrelevant because the cross-licensing of the patented technologies will overcome any obstacles.[19] But these counterarguments are beside the point. Firstly, the paucity of empirical evidence is probably due to the fact that research and medical research institutions are unlikely to publish information about where their research priorities are not heading. It is more likely that they will simply divert their research towards areas where they are not hampered by patents. Secondly, with regard to the actual behaviour of patent holders, it is noteworthy that Chiron refused all of Murex's requests for a patent licence despite that fact that Murex had patent rights to the only HCV serotyping assay in the world that enabled laboratories to detect a particular type of HCV infection. This was an important diagnostic tool because the only form of HCV treatment that then existed used interferon alpha alone or in combination with ribavirin and this treatment was effective only in some HCV patients.[20]

The substantive point is that even where patent owners license their patent rights on reasonable commercial terms, the fact that they can, in their absolute discretion, choose not to do so means that legally there is little, if anything, that can be done to redress the cooling effect on the medical and scientific research that is covered by the patent's monopoly.

In 1999, Dr Michael Houghton, one of the 'inventors' of the HCV genetic products, admitted that after ten years of research there was no HCV vaccine.[21] Many may see

---

18 Ibid. See the first affidavit of Prof. Baruch Blumberg filed by Murex at pars 5.1 and 5.2.

19 See Crespi, n. 4.

20 See affidavit of Dr Peter Simmonds filed by Murex in *Murex v Chiron* NG 106/1994 (Federal Court of Australia); Dr Simmonds testified at par 7.5 'There is evidence that it helps determine the outcome of interferon therapy although it is unclear whether genotypes vary in their properties to cause severe liver damage …'.

21 'There is no vaccine for HCV and the only available treatment, IFNalpha alone or in combination with ribavirin, has proven efficacious in less than 50% of patients. Given that approximately 200 million chronic HCV infections have been estimated worldwide, there is a pressing need to develop vaccination strategies aimed at preventing and possibly eradicating HCV infection. However, several major practical and scientific problems arise in designing an HCV vaccine. First, HCV is only readily detected as RNA by PCR. Second, the only species that can be infected by HCV are humans and chimpanzees. Third, the virus does not replicate efficiently in vitro. Fourth, some viral proteins have very high mutability. Last, there is little information on correlates of immunity. Although an ideal vaccine should protect from

this as an unexceptional admission given that vaccines generally take many decades to develop. Nonetheless, Chiron made specific claims to HCV vaccines in its HCV patent application which was first filed with the US Patent and Trademark Office (USPTO) in November 1987.[22] It may be that Chiron's claims to HCV vaccines did not impede vaccine research, but given Chiron's behaviour in vigorously prosecuting its HCV patent rights around the world, its refusal to license even on reasonable commercial terms and the concerns expressed by eminent scientists such as Prof. Blumberg, it is stretching credibility to suggest that Chiron's claims to HCV vaccines had no, and continue to have, no negative impact on scientific and medical research into HCV vaccines and treatments.

2. The Conditional Genetic Patent Claim and its Consequences

An example of the *conditional* property right is claim 1 of European Patent 148,305 entitled 'Production of Erythropoietin'[23] and granted to Kirin-Amgen. This patent expired in Europe in December 2004 (other than in the UK where some claims of the patent were held to be invalid in October 2004).[24] Claim 1 read:

> A DNA sequence for use in securing expression in a procaryotic or eucaryotic host cell of a polypeptide product having at least part of the primary structural confirmation [*sic*] of that of erythropoietin to allow possession of the biological property of causing bone marrow cells to increase production of reticulocytes and red blood cells and to increase hemoglobin [*sic*] synthesis or iron uptake, said DNA sequence selected from the group consisting of:
> (a) the DNA sequences set out in Tables V and VI or their complementary strands;
> (b) DNA sequences which hybridize under stringent conditions to the protein coding regions of the DNA sequences defined in (a) or fragments thereof; and
> (c) DNA sequences which, but for the degeneracy of the genetic code, would hybridize to the DNA sequences defined in (a) and (b).

This is an example of a *genetic process claim*. It gave Kirin-Amgen ownership of the use of the human erythropoietin gene (Epo gene) in a specific process, namely the use of host cells (for example, *E.coli* and *chinese hamster*) into which the Epo

---

infection, in that it should elicit sterilizing immunity, this is quite an ambitious goal in the PCR era.' See S. Abrignani *et al.*, 'Perspectives for a Vaccine against Hepatitis C Virus' (1999) 31 *Journal of Hepatology*, Supplement 1, 259.

22 Claim 64: 'A vaccine for treatment of NANBV infection comprising an immunogenic polypeptide encoded within NANBV, wherein the NANBV contains a genome which encodes a polypeptide which is immunologically reactive with an antibody to a polypeptide encoded by a cDNA selected from the cDNAs in clones 5-1-1, 1-2, 81, and 91, and wherein the immunogenic polypeptide is present in a pharmacologically effective dose in a pharmaceutically effective excipient.'

23 Epo is a hormone that is produced naturally in humans and regulates the level of red blood cells. Its principal source of production is the kidneys and people that suffer from kidney failure benefit from therapeutic treatment with Epo.

24 *Kirin-Amgen v Hoechst Marion Roussel* [2005] RPC 9 (HL).

gene DNA[25] was cut and spliced so as to have the host cells express or produce Epo, a human protein.

Therefore, although Kirin-Amgen did not own the human erythropoietin gene *per se*, it owned a process[26] for the recombinant production of a recombinant Epo (rEpo), a substance that was identical to the natural human Epo (uEpo).[27] However, in Kirin-Amgen's opinion, ownership of the process was as good as ownership of the natural Epo gene because the product of the process, rEpo, was identical to the product of the natural Epo gene, uEpo.

Before the English courts, Kirin-Amgen maintained, all the way to the House of Lords, that its patent covered all processes and methods of rEpo production because the disclosure of the genetic sequence of the Epo gene was the underlying piece of information that was central to the production of rEpo howsoever made. It argued that its claim, even though it was to a process, was an absolute claim to rEpo *per se* because the *end product* of the process was rEpo.

Kirin-Amgen's argument was so persuasive that Neuberger J. agreed. In his opinion, even though the DNA sequence of the Epo gene was a 'discovery' it was an 'essential feature' of the 'invention' because it 'made a technical contribution'.[28] In other words, the DNA sequence of the human Epo gene was an 'invention' because it made the production of rEpo possible. The fact that rEpo and uEpo were indistinguishable products physically, genetically and biologically was irrelevant to both Kirin-Amgen and the trial judge. He explained that he was 'comforted' in his ruling by the fact that 'over the past 20 years or so, it has been the regular practice of the European Patent Office (and, I think, of the US Patent Office) to grant claims substantially in the form of Claim 1.'[29]

The House of Lords, however, was not so comforted or persuaded. Lord Hoffmann, who delivered the unanimous decision of their Lordships, disagreed that the invention was to rEpo howsoever produced. In their Lordships' opinion,

---

25 Genes are located on chromosomes in the nucleus of a cell and are made of deoxyribonucleic acid ('DNA'). DNA is composed of two strands of nucleotides in double helix formation. The nucleotides contain one of four bases, adenine (A), guanine (G), cytosine (C), and thymine (T), that are linked by hydrogen bonds to form complementary base pairs (i.e., A-T and G-C).

26 See *Kirin-Amgen v Hoechst Marion Roussel* [2002] RPC 31 (CA). In its decision (this part was upheld by the House of Lords) the Court of Appeal held that the Kirin-Amgen invention did not capture the production of erythropoietin howsoever made and that therefore the erythropoietin manufactured by Transkaryotic Therapies Inc did not infringe the patent. The Court of Appeal rejected Kirin-Amgen's submission that the claim covered all processes for the recombinant production of erythropoietin.

27 *Kirin-Amgen v Hoechst Marion Roussel* [2005] RPC 9 (HL), par 96; also see *Amgen, Inc v Chugai Pharmaceutical Co and Genetics Institute, Inc*, 13 USPQ 2d 1737 (U.S. DC Mass, 1989).

28 *Kirin-Amgen v Hoechst Marion Roussel* [2002] RPC 1, par. 540, 'Claim 1 is to a DNA sequence which is "suitable for" the claimed purposes, and I accept Mr Waugh's submission [Kirin-Amgen's counsel] that it is "plainly the application of the discovery which is capable of industrial application (whatever the origin of the DNA sequence)".'

29 *Ibid*, par. 541.

this was not possible because such a claim would be a claim to a 'discovery' per se.[30] Lord Hoffmann explained that 'an invention is a practical product or process, not information about the natural world ... [and] it cannot be right to give him a monopoly of the use of the information as such.'[31] It was therefore wrong to permit Kirin-Amgen to monopolise the production of rEpo because that would have been tantamount to transforming the DNA sequence of the Epo gene, being a product of nature, into an *invention*, being a product of man. In their Lordships' opinion, the process of claim 1 was restricted to that which the claim described, namely a process that used a 'host cell'. The *invention* was the specific process, not the isolated Epo gene.

Even so, the House of Lords held claims 19–26, 29 and 31 of the patent to be invalid because the *end product* of that process, rEpo, was indistinguishable from uEpo, a natural product that was known to exist before the date of the patent application. In other words, despite the fact that the specific process was the *invention*, it was not a *patentable invention*, because even though the process was artificial, the product of the process was a substance that was identical to a product of nature.

The ruling, however, made little, if any, impact upon Kirin-Amgen because it came at the very end of the twenty-year monopoly. Arguably, the position which Kirin-Amgen adopted and which found favour with the trial judge (and the EPO) probably encouraged many European biotechnology companies to keep clear of the production of rEpo and the development of alternative processes for its production. Whether this was a good thing for European biotechnology is unquantifiable, but what is quantifiable is the extra cost that this illegal monopoly (at least in the opinion of the House of Lords)[32] placed upon the health care budgets of European countries to which this patent applied. Even without having done the calculations it is reasonable to infer that the price of rEpo would have been higher with this patent than without it.

What is particularly concerning is that in granting this European patent to Kirin-Amgen, the EPO effectively gave ownership of *information about the natural world* (using the rationale that 'isolated' biological materials are 'inventions') to a corporation that was then able to dictate, by law, how that information could be used in Europe for a period of twenty years. Clearly, the House of Lords found this idea repugnant, but its rejection merely echoed the objections that were first raised by the English Court of Appeal in *Genentech*.[33]

---

30 *Kirin-Amgen v Hoechst Marion Roussel* [2005] RPC 9, par. 76.

31 *Ibid*, par. 77.

32 Although claim 1 was not held to be invalid this was because its validity was not challenged in this litigation and therefore was not in issue either at trial or in the appeal before their Lordships. Nevertheless, it is arguable, based on the reasons given by their Lordships, that had claim 1 been in issue that it would have been held to have been invalid. Apart from the fact that the subject claims were all dependent on claim 1, this claim was to a process that used a DNA sequence (human Epo gene) to produce a protein (rEpo) that was indistinguishable to a known natural protein (uEpo). In other words because the product of the process of claim 1 was not *new* (see par 132) and therefore not patentable, the process itself was not patentable: see *Kirin-Amgen v Hoechst Marion Roussel* [2005] RPC 9 (HL), pars 88–101, particularly pars 90–2.

33 *Genentech Inc's Patent* [1989] RPC 147.

Interestingly, the EPO upheld the validity of this patent[34] all the way through the opposition process, from grant to the appellate hearing before the Technical Board of Appeal (TBA). The TBA, so it seemed, was unable to grasp the point which the House of Lords saw as obvious. With diplomacy Lord Hoffmann explained away the discrepancy in results by pointing out that the TBA had found that there was a physical difference[35] between rEpo and uEpo and this distinguished rEpo from uEpo so as to not be identical to the natural product.[36] Even so, he expressed 'being a little puzzled by these findings'.[37]

Lord Hoffmann was perfectly justified in being 'puzzled' because the evidence of the similarity of the two products, one artificial and the other natural, had been clearly recorded in a 1989 decision of the US District Court for the District of Massachusetts in *Amgen, Inc v Chugai Pharmaceutical Co and Genetics Institute, Inc.*[38] There the District Court held:

> the *overwhelming* evidence, including Amgen's own admissions, establishes that uEPO and rEPO are the same product. The EPO gene used to produce rEPO is the same EPO gene as the human body uses to produce uEPO. The amino acid sequences of human uEPO and rEPO are identical. There are no known differences between the secondary structure of rEPO produced in a CHO cell and EPO produced in a human kidney … Amgen's own scientists have concluded that by all criteria examined, rEPO is the 'equivalent to the natural hormone.' In particular, they noted that the uEPO preparation had an equivalent biological activity in the RIA and bioassays. Amgen's Product License Application to the FDA states that all 'physical tests performed on both r-HuEPO and u-HuEPO … show these proteins to be indistinguishable'; that r-HuEPO and u-HuEPO are 'indistinguishable in their biological and immunological properties'; and that testing 'confirms the similarity of the secondary and tertiary protein structures of r-HuEPO and u-HuEPO as predicted by the equivalence of their immunological and biological activities.

Given this decision it is difficult to see how the decision of the TBA can be as easily explained away as Lord Hoffmann diplomatically did. The lack of a full and proper explanation for the divergence of result suggests that the lack of independence of the TBA from the EPO may have influenced the TBA, especially in view of the fact that, as discussed below, (a) the EPO had been a party to the 1988 joint communiqué and (b) the EPO was a proactive supporter of the EC Biotechnology Directive.

It needs to be understood that the TBA is not a truly independent tribunal and therefore there resides within the EPO opposition process, as established by the European Patent Convention, a conflict of interest. Apart from the fact that the TBA is not a judicial body, its close association with the EPO must mean that the policy of the EPO is influential, to some degree, and from that it is fair to infer that the TBA was affected by EPO policy in reaching the decision that it did in the Kirin-Amgen

---

34 T636/97 *Production of erythropoietin/Kirin-Amgen*. 26 March 1998.

35 'The Board is on the evidence prepared to presume that the limitation to the polypeptide being a product makeable using the DNA of Claim 1 is a technical feature which ensures that it has a glycosylation pattern different from the known uEPO', ibid, 9.

36 *Kirin-Amgen v Hoechst Marion Roussel* [2005] RPC 9 (HL), pars. 93–5.

37 *Ibid*, par. 95.

38 13 USPQ.2d 1737 (DC Mass, 1989).

opposition. Clearly, the TBA was prepared to come to a finding of fact that was at odds with the evidence in order to come to a decision that was sympathetic with EPO policy.

3. The EC Biotechnology Directive

The EC Biotechnology Directive[39] (the Directive) was passed in 1998 by the European Parliament. The Directive became law principally at the behest of the European biotechnology industry. The question which must be asked is: why was the Directive necessary if pre-Directive European patent law permitted the grant of the types of patents discussed earlier?

The answer is simple. The patent cognoscenti had known for some time there was a problem and so as early as 1988 the EPO, the USPTO and the Japanese Patent Office (JPO) had issued a joint communiqué which stated:

> Purified natural products are not regarded under any of the three laws [US, EU and Japan] as products of nature or discoveries because they do not in fact exist in nature in an isolated form. Rather, they are regarded for patent purposes as biologically active substances or chemical compounds and eligible for patenting on the same basis as other chemical compounds.[40]

It is not clear what event triggered this action, but it is noteworthy that a number of biotech patent cases were brewing in the mid- to late 1980s and that *Genentech* was one of them. That case concerned a patent granted to Genentech, which was at the time a relatively new biotech company. The invention was isolated human tissue plasminogen activator (t-PA), a protein which occurs naturally in humans in very small quantities, and the recombinant production of t-PA. T-PA activates the conversion of existing precursor plasminogen into plasmin, an enzyme capable of dissolving fibrin in blood clots.[41] The Court of Appeal's decision in October 1988 was unfavourable to Genentech. The entire patent was held to be invalid for a number of reasons, one of them being that isolated t-PA was not an 'invention'. The impact of the decision was felt throughout Europe because the applicable UK law was based on the EPC.[42]

Whether it was a mere coincidence that in 1988 the EPO, USPTO and JPO issued their joint communiqué, or whether it was in response to this decision, or even in anticipation of it, is immaterial. What is material is that first, the English Court of Appeal disagreed with their central rationale and, secondly, under the EPC it is the

39 Directive 98/44/EC on the Legal Protection of Biotechnological Inventions. OJ. L 213, July 30, 1998, 13–21.
40 1988 Joint Statement of USPTO, EPO and JPO; see footnote 9, Nuffield Council of Bioethics Discussion Paper, *The Ethics of Patenting DNA* (2002) 26, 3.14.
41 *Genentech Inc's Patent* [1989] RPC 147.
42 Patents Act 1977 s. 130(7) (UK).

exclusive role of the national courts to decide patent validity in a revocation action, not the role of the European Patent Office to pre-empt them.[43]

Undoubtedly, the Court of Appeal's decision in *Genentech* sent a chill down the collective spines of European patent agents, the CEOs of European biotechnology companies and the officials at the European Commission in Brussels (EC), for soon thereafter the EC initiated the process which led to the Directive. Indeed one of the principle architects of the Directive, Dominique Vandergheynst,[44] explained that the Directive was a 'true revolution ... between the ethical dimension and a technological sector of which certain aspects cannot but arouse control by public powers.'[45]

The Directive took ten years and two attempts by the EC to become law. The first attempt in the mid-1990s failed. However, the EC persisted and eventually a compromise was reached between the various factions within the European Parliament.

The Directive is a revealing document because its two principle articles, Article 3 and Article 5, expose the very weakness which the EPO tried to address with the 1988 joint communiqué. Ironically, in trying to strengthen the European patent system to cater for biotechnology, the European Parliament through the actions of the EPO and European Commission (EC) highlighted the very problem.[46]

The Directive provides that 'biological materials'[47] derived from *any natural source*, including 'elements' from the human body that are either 'isolated'[48] or 'produced by means of a technical process',[49] even those identical to the 'natural' elements are presumed to be 'inventions'. The term 'biological materials', as defined by the Directive, include, but are not limited to, such things as viral, plant, animal and human proteins and genetic materials that code for them.

The Directive therefore reverses the impact of the Court of Appeal decision in the *Genentech* decision insofar as the 'invention' requirement of patentability is concerned. Patents granted by the EPO after July 2000, with respect to the Directive,

---

43 There is, of course, the possibility of centrally opposing a patent under the European Patent Convention.

44 Former Responsible Official at the European Commission from 1990 to 1999 for the European Biotechnology Directive – see Foreword, in G. Kamstra *et al.*, *Patents on Biotechnological Inventions: The E.C. Directive* (London: Sweet & Maxwell 2002).

45 Ibid.

46 'The European Parliament and Council directive 98/44/EC ... was crucial in order to foster the innovation and provide European companies *with adequate protection of their domestic market*' (emphasis added) per Philippe Busquin and Frits Bolkestein of the European Commission in their foreword to the EC report entitled *Patenting DNA Sequences (Polynucleotides) and Scope of Protection in the European Union: an Evaluation,* 2004, EUR 21122.

47 Article 2(1) of the Directive defines 'biological material' to mean 'any material containing genetic information and capable of reproducing itself or being reproduced in a biological system.'

48 The word 'isolated' in this context means that the biological material or human element has been separated or removed from its natural environment and has been purified to some degree.

49 A technical process includes the process for the recombinant production of a protein.

can only be revoked if they fail to meet the thresholds of the remaining patentability conditions which include novelty, inventive step and industrial applicability.[50]

In other words, according to the reasoning of the Court of Appeal in *Genentech*, pre-July 2000 European patents that claim inventions over isolated or purified genetic sequences and the process or methods of production of the corresponding natural proteins, are invalid. This was reinforced by the House of Lords in *Kirin-Amgen* which held that even though the primary claim was to 'a perfectly good and ground-breaking process for making [Epo] and its analogues, [Amgen] were determined to try to patent the protein itself, notwithstanding that, *even when isolated*, it was not *new*'.[51]

Clearly, the House of Lords was not prepared to accept that the isolation of the Epo gene nor the elucidation of the genetic sequences of the Epo gene and Epo made any difference to what it was and its ruling therefore contradicted the 1988 joint communiqué. In other words, the isolation of the Epo gene and the elucidation of its nucleotide sequence did not *turn a pig's ear into a silk purse*.[52]

But the law changed with the Directive, so that from July 2000 'isolated' biological materials and those produced by technical means are presumed to be 'inventions'. Even the Court of Appeal in *Kirin-Amgen,* which was considering a pre-Directive patent, was influenced by the Directive.[53] However, as the House of Lords overruled it, whatever reliance the Court of Appeal placed on the Directive may have been misplaced. But for post-Directive biotechnology patents, the Court of Appeal's comments suggest that the European biotechnology industry may have finally fixed the problem which the 1988 joint communiqué sought to address.

Unfortunately, the EC's solution may not be legitimate.[54] The uncertainty surrounding its legitimacy stems from its inconsistency with Article 27.1 of the Agreement on Trade Related Aspects of Intellectual Property (TRIPS). TRIPS is one of the key agreements binding all 151 member countries and the European Community

---

50 European Patent Convention, Pt 2, Chp 1.

51 *Kirin-Amgen Inc v Hoechst Marion Roussel Ltd and others* [2005] RPC 9, par 132. (emphasis added).

52 The scepticism expressed by the House of Lords to the distinction between a natural human protein and an isolated human protein was also expressed by the Danish Council of Ethics in their 2004 report entitled *Patenting Human Genes and Stem Cells.* On page 98 they state, 'In the members' view, it cannot be said with any reasonableness that a sequence or partial sequence of a gene ceases to be part of the human body merely because an identical copy of the sequence is isolated from or produced outside of the human body.'

53 'We *draw comfort* from the Directive which allows claims to biological elements "isolated ... or otherwise produced by means of a technical process even if the structure of that element is identical to that of a natural element"': *Kirin-Amgen v Hoechst Marion Roussel* [2003] RPC 31, par. 57 (CA) (emphasis added).

54 See *Netherlands v European Parliament (supported by the European Commission)* [2001] 3 CMLR 49. In this case the Court of Justice held that the Directive did not violate TRIPS Art. 27(3)(b), but it left open the issue of whether it violated other aspects of TRIPS. It held, 'the legality of a Community instrument can be called in to question on grounds of breach of international agreements to which the Community is a party ... if the provisions of those agreements have *direct effect*' .

(as a separate member) to the Agreements of the World Trade Organisation (WTO). It is a requirement of the World Trade Agreement that all WTO members 'ensure the conformity of [their] laws, regulations and administrative procedures with [their] obligations as provided in the annexed Agreements.' TRIPS is one of the 'annexed Agreements'.

Article 27(1) TRIPS provides as follows:

> patents shall be available for *any inventions*, whether products or processes, in all fields of technology, *provided* that they are *new, involve an inventive step and are capable of industrial application* [and] … *patents shall be available* and patent rights enjoyable *without discrimination as to* the place of invention, *the field of technology* and whether products are imported or locally produced.

Article 27(1) stipulates that there are four conditions of patentability. The first is the *invention*. This is a prerequisite condition of patentability because unless something is an 'invention' the subsidiary conditions of patentability are irrelevant. The second is the *novelty* of the 'invention'. The third is the *inventive step* of the 'invention'. The fourth is the *industrial applicability* of the 'invention'. This means that each of these parameters must be satisfied before any WTO member may grant a patent, or enable one to 'be available' under its national patent laws. It also requires the administrative and regulatory patent regimes of WTO members to be applied and interpreted consistently with these parameters. A granted patent that does not satisfy these parameters violates TRIPS and, as a consequence, the patent law from which it derives its legal status also violates the World Trade Agreement. Furthermore, it stipulates that these conditions shall apply to all patents 'without discrimination as to … the field of technology'.

It is important at this juncture to appreciate that the word 'invention' in TRIPS cannot mean whatever a WTO member deems it to mean. It follows that if the Directive was not a 'mere clarification' of European patent law as it stood before July 2000, then arguably it represented a significant variation from that law. The extent of that variation is the contrast between the UK court decisions in *Genentech* and *Kirin-Amgen* and the 1988 joint communiqué.

While TRIPS does not provide a definition of the word 'invention', the lack of a definition does not mean that anything made by man is an 'invention'. There are limits and one of the most significant limitations was restated by the US Supreme Court in 1980 in *Diamond v Chakrabarty* where the Court held:

> The laws of nature, physical phenomena, and abstract ideas have been held not patentable … Thus, a new mineral discovered in the earth or a new plant found in the wild is not patentable subject matter. Likewise, Einstein could not patent his celebrated law that $E=mc^2$; nor could Newton have patented the law of gravity. Such discoveries are 'manifestations of … nature, free to all men and reserved exclusively to none.' *Funk, supra*, at 130.[55]

---

[55] *Diamond v Chakrabarty*, 447 U.S. 303, 309 (1980) (citations omitted). For a complete explanation see L. Palombi, *The Patenting of Biological Materials* and 'The Impact of TRIPS'.

Accordingly, it is suggested that because (a) the Directive circumvents the necessity for biological materials to be 'inventions' *within the meaning of that word in TRIPS* when TRIPS mandates that all patents must only concern 'inventions' and (b) the circumvention itself positively discriminates *in favour* of biotechnology, that there is a plausible argument that the Directive violates TRIPS.[56]

Interestingly, the EC has recently turned its attention to the potential conflict between the Directive and TRIPS. In a report it released in 2004 entitled, *Patenting DNA Sequences (Polynucleotides) and Scope of Protection in the European Union: an Evaluation,*[57] Philippe Busquin, Research Commissioner, and Frits Bolkestein, Internal Market Commissioner of the EC, noted in their foreword:

> The European Parliament and Council directive 98/44/EC of 6th July 1998 on the legal protection of biotechnological inventions came into place almost a decade after its first draft had been proposed by the Commission. *This piece of legislation was crucial in order to foster the innovation and provide European companies with adequate protection in their domestic market.*[58]

At this time, some seven years since it was passed, four countries[59] of the European Communities have refused to implement the Directive into their domestic patent law. Given that both Commissioners accepted that the Directive was 'crucial' to providing the European biotechnology industry 'with adequate protection in their domestic market', the obvious question is: why has it not been fully embraced in Europe?

This EC report[60] documented the discussions of an expert group[61] that met in March 2003 to discuss the impact of the Directive as required by Article 16(c). This article of the Directive requires the EC 'to monitor "the impact of patent law on biotechnology and genetic engineering" and provide annual reports ("Article 16(c)

---

56 See also L. Palombi, 'The Impact of TRIPS'.

57 European Commission Report n. 46.

58 Ibid. (Emphasis added.)

59 The last country to implement was Luxemburg who implemented on 23 April 2006. A list of implementation dates was: http://ec.europa.eu/internal_market/indprop/docs/invent/state-of-play_en.pdf (accessed 1 August 2007).

60 European Commission Report n. 46. was written by Prof. Sven Bostyn who is not only a member of the Faculty of Law, University of Amsterdam, but also is Legal Counsel to a Belgian patent agent firm, De Clercq Brants & Partners.

61 The expert group was made up of Ms Anne McLaren (Wellcome CRC Institute, University of Cambridge); Ms Stobhan Yeats (Director, Biotechnology Directorate, European Patent Office); Mr Jacques Warcoin (Patent Agent, Cabinet Regimbeau); Mr Daniel Alexander (Barrister, London); Mr Bo Hammer Jensen (Director, Senior Patent Counsel, Novozymes A/S); Mr Francisco Bernardo Noriega (Deputy Director, Intellectual Property, PharmaMar S.A.); Prof. Joseph Straus (Managing Director, Max Planck Institute for Intellectual Property); Mr Francis Queitier (Genoscope); Mr Ingwar Koch (Director, Patent Law Directorate, European Patent Office); and Mr Kjeldaard (Senior Counsellor, Biotechnology and Genetic Resources, WIPO). It is noteworthy that the majority of the members of the expert group came from the biotechnology industry, the European Patent Office, European patent agents or WIPO, all of whom have a vested interest in maintaining the patent system.

reports")'.[62] So although this particular report is not an Article 16(c) Report, it is a document that was created as part of the process leading to the second Article 16(c) Report which was released on 14 July 2005.[63] Accordingly, the statements contained in the report are relevant to this discussion because the expert group was established specifically to 'advise the Commission on the preparation of future 16(c) Reports through the examination of important issues relating to biotechnological inventions'.[64]

In this report Professor Bostyn explained that a major issue under European patent law is the 'distinction between patentable inventions and non-patentable discoveries'[65] and that the requirement that the 'invention' be technical in nature has made the threshold of patentability 'problematic' in biotechnology 'especially in view of the fact that it is *very difficult* to define what technical means'.[66] Not content to leave the discussion to European patent law, he proceeded to discuss the issue of 'invention' under US patent law[67] explaining that even there the legal position was uncertain, although he suggested that the absence of a 'technical' requirement provided 'the advantage of clarity'.[68]

Despite the stated uncertainty of the law regarding the invention condition of patentability he confidently asserted that DNA coding for industrially useful expression products; genes as diagnostic tools and genes which control biological pathways are 'inventions'.[69] He confirmed that the Directive made it clear that the only exception is the human body which cannot be patented under any circumstances[70] and specified that a 'specific [human] DNA sequence without more' is not an 'invention'.[71]

Then he made the usual intellectual leap, consistent with the 1988 joint communiqué, that the isolation of a genetic sequence from its natural environment is an 'invention' because it has been so removed 'via a reproducible technical process' which involves the making of a 'selection in the sequence' and the production of cDNA[72] 'which does not occur as such in nature'.[73] He concluded therefore that the Directive was a 'mere clarification' of European patent law.[74] But in doing so, he

---

62 European Commission Report n. 46, foreword.

63 EC Commission, *Development and Implications of Patent Law in the Field of Biotechnology and Genetic Engineering*, COM (2005) 312 final, July 14, 2005.

64 The second Article.16(c) EC Report specifically refers to the expert group and their deliberations at heading 1.2, p. 2.

65 European Commission Report EUR 21122, December 2004, *Patenting DNA Sequences*, at heading 3.3 (p. 12).

66 Ibid (Emphasis added.)

67 Ibid, 13–14.

68 Ibid, 14.

69 Ibid, 38–9.

70 Ibid, 40.

71 Ibid. He also refers to recital 16 of the Directive which states that 'the simple discovery of one of [the human body's] elements or one of its products, including the sequence or partial of a human gene, cannot be patented.'

72 cDNA means copy DNA.

73 Ibid, 41.

74 Ibid, Heading 4.6.2 (p.53).

focused only on the practice of the EPO and completely ignored the English Court of Appeal decision in *Genentech*.

Finally he arrived at the crucial issue – Article 27(1) of TRIPS. Although he limited his discussion to the discrimination prohibition in Article 27(1) and acknowledged that 'it could be argued that TRIPS does not allow discrimination as to the field of technology for which patent protection must be available' he suggested that in the absence of any 'uniform interpretation' of Article. 27(1) that 'member states can determine the type of protection they provide'.[75]

His argument that there can be disparity in the patentability thresholds between WTO members provided that the four conditions of patentability are incorporated into domestic patent law, however, failed to take the fundamental objectives of TRIPS which is to 'reduce distortions and impediments to international trade' and to 'promote effective and adequate protection of intellectual property rights'.[76]

Enabling WTO members to individually determine the type of protection they provide detracts from, rather than enhances, *the effective and adequate protection of intellectual property rights* because once the individually set thresholds to the patentability conditions are met, those set by Article 27(1) become meaningless. It suggests that something that can be an 'invention' according to the patent laws of one WTO member may not be according to the patent laws of another. Seriously, if that were the case, Article 27(1) TRIPS would be redundant.

Part II

The nub of the problem for biotechnology is the simple fact that much of the commercial value of its intellectual property resides in the production of recombinant proteins that merely replicate the function or performance of natural proteins. It is the *in vivo* identity that is valuable but it is this which cuts across the prohibition against the patenting of 'laws of nature, physical phenomena, and abstract ideas' as restated in *Chakrabarty*.[77]

It is important to appreciate that not only are the recombinant proteins produced by the patented processes not substantially different to natural proteins, but neither are the isolated genetic materials used in those processes. The genetic components and the end products of these processes are therefore indistinguishable from the natural and, as has been long recognised by *Chakrabarty* and *Genentech* and most recently by *Kirin-Amgen*, they are not inventions. This must mean that the patent system cannot provide the level of intellectual property protection that the biotechnology industry seems to demand. Critically, it means that the creativity, ingenuity and invention which an efficient patent system should nurture and encourage is being

---

75 Ibid, 66.

76 'Desiring to reduce distortions and impediments to international trade, and taking into account the need to promote effective and adequate protection of intellectual property rights, and to ensure that measures and procedures to enforce intellectual property rights do not themselves become barriers to legitimate trade.' 1st recital in the TRIPS Agreement.

77 Also see, EPC Article 52(2).

undermined by the grant of patents that are creating patent thickets so dense[78] that they are adding costs to medical and scientific research and, in some instances, hindering it altogether.

Stephen Crespi has said that 'the word "invented" sounds strained when applied to something already existing.'[79] Of course he is right, because it is impossible to invent something that already exists, even if its existence is unknown. But to suggest, as he does, that 'the word "discovered" ... glosses over the painstaking work that has to be done by the scientist before he can see the pure substance in the test tube,'[80] and that therefore 'isolation' is a legitimate device to transform a product of nature (i.e., a 'discovery') into a product of man (i.e., something capable of being an 'invention'), is an attempt to distort the patent system. It is true that the word 'discovery' glosses over 'the painstaking work that has to be done by the scientist,' but the threshold of invention is not 'painstaking work'. If that were the case, then literally anything 'made by man' could be considered to be an 'invention'.

Unfortunately, rebutting this argument does not address the fact that the ability to mass produce recombinant proteins is commercially, medically and scientifically advantageous and there can be no doubt that the isolation of genes and proteins has greatly contributed to the betterment of human health throughout the world. In these circumstances it is not only fair, but appropriate, that the work that has facilitated the isolation of these proteins be rewarded, if for no other reason than the work leading to their isolation is not only 'painstaking' but necessarily involves high-risk investments. This is the point which Stephen Crespi and the biotechnology industry[81] have made time and time again. Their error, however, has been to stubbornly rely upon the 'international' patent system, rather than to argue for a sui generis intellectual property right. What they have failed to accept is that the patent system has its limits and consequently biotechnology cannot be wholly served by it.[82] Then, neither should it be.

---

78 Researchers K. Jensen and F. Murray conducted a survey of US patents granted with respect to nucleotide sequences to the human genome (i.e. genes or gene sequences). Their survey, however, did not include claims to human proteins (amino acids). Even so, their results show that 'nearly 20% of human genes are explicitly claimed as U.S. I.P.' which 'represents 4382 of the 23,688 genes in the database of the U.S. National Center for Biotechnology Information.' These genes alone represent '4270 patents within 3050 patent families' and these patents are owned by 1156 different organizations: see K. Jensen and F. Murray 'Intellectual Property Landscape of the Human Genome' (2005) 310 *Science* 239.

79 Crespi, n. 4, 432.

80 Ibid.

81 The British BioIndustry Association has argued, 'the patentability of genes *per se* strikes the most appropriate balance between rewarding the inventor for their contribution to the technical field and the monopoly conferred by the patent. We admit that this is an imperfect balance, but we believe that this balance is more equitable than that achieved by denying *per se* patent protection for genes or other molecules.' See BioIndustry Association (UK): statement published 21 December 2001 in response to British Medical Association's discussion paper on gene patenting.

82 See A. McInerney, 'Biotechnology: Biogen v Medeva In The House Of Lords' (1998) 20 *European Intellectual Property Review* 14.

This chapter therefore proposes the creation of the Genetic Sequence Right (GSR) as a sui generis system of intellectual property.

Under this proposal the GSR would be administered using the existing administrative system utilised by the present patent system so as to minimise establishment costs and to facilitate its adoption. A GSR would be granted to the first person to file and disclose a genetic sequence defining genetic material of any origin and explaining its function and utility. A GSR would be the subject of a written application filed in a patent office. The GSR would become part of an international electronic database which would be freely accessible by any person.

Upon registration the GSR holder would have the right to a *GSR use fee* (GSR fee). The GSR fee would vary depending on the nature of the use. For publicly funded institutions such as universities, experimental use would not attract a GSR fee, but for commercial entities, the fee would apply commensurately with the nature of the use. For example, there could be a scale for commercial entities starting at experimental use and moving through to full commercialisation. It is envisaged that there would be a multitude of variations in between. The fee would be set by a published scale which is determined by a centralised world body responsible for the global administration of the GSR (for example, WIPO). This body would collect and distribute the GSR fee revenue and could earn revenue by the collection of application and annual administrations fees, as well as by retaining a small percentage of the GSR fee revenue collected. Specific allowance could also be made for GSR holders to seek GSR fees above the published scale if the GSR holder could establish that due to factors relating to the nature of the GSR or unforeseeable events (e.g. war), the total amount of GSR fees would be insufficient to recoup a fair return on the investment in the research and development leading to the GSR.

GSR users would be required to register their use with the local administrative authority and that use would be registered on the GSR electronic database. This would provide a public record of use.

The life of the GSR would be ten years from the date of registration. Infringement of GSRs could be dealt with through the relevant national courts. The holder would accordingly have the right to seek injunctions, declarations, or damages. Criminal provisions could also make it an offence for breaches the holder's GSR rights.

Moreover, if the GSR were to be identified through the provision of traditional, tribal or indigenous knowledge or information a portion of the GSR fee due to the GSR holder would be paid to the persons who are the owners of that knowledge or information. Their entitlement would be commensurate with the contribution made in the identification of the GSR and would be determined by the central administrative authority, which would also oversee the distribution of the GSR fee revenue to the relevant peoples.

The GSR would thereby provide a system by which investors in genetic research could be remunerated without the GSR holders having the power to control the uses to which that GSR may be put. The GSR would thereby facilitate the publication of genetic sequence information and encourage its use and the production of corresponding biological materials. Thus, by removing the element of absolute control, the GSR would prevent GSR holders from controlling further downstream research or other uses.

The GSR holder would not need to satisfy any 'invention' or 'inventive step' criteria. Novelty of the genetic sequence could be established by a search of the GSR database or other genetic sequence databases. Novelty of the GSR could also be established by function and utility, so that even if the genetic sequence is already known or the subject of an existing GSR, establishing a novel function and utility not previously known could give rise to a new GSR. However, broad GSR description regarding function and utility would not be permitted unless substantiated throughout the breadth of the description. The GSR would therefore incorporate a description of the function and utility of the GSR.

The GSR would also address the many concerns that surrounding experimental use. One issue that is problematic with experimental use exemptions for patent infringement in the context of biotechnology is that many patents have been granted over 'research tools' that are useful in the search for new drugs. In the context of each of these applications, the patented biological materials have been used by research institutions, such as universities, and the issue that has arisen is whether such use is or should be exempted from patent infringement.

Under the GSR, use by a teaching or research institution would be zero rated for fee purposes. However, a commercial entity's use of a GSR, either directly or indirectly through a university, would attract a GSR fee commensurate with such use. The obligation to pay the GSR fee would remain with the commercial entity. Therefore, if any commercial entity entered an agreement with a university to conduct research on its behalf or as part of a joint enterprise or collaboration, the obligation to pay the GSR fee would continue. This would remove the debate about when, and if, universities that are conducting commercially funded research should be the subject of an experimental use exemption.

The dilemma which today confronts the patent system in this regard has been illustrated most aptly in the case of *Madey v Duke University*.[83] In this case the US Court of Appeals for the Federal Circuit (CAFC) considered whether the common law research exemption under US patent law applied to Duke University in respect of its use of certain equipment that was the subject of two US patents granted to Dr Madey. The equipment had been used in a physics laboratory while Dr Madey was associated with the university. After Dr Madey resigned, the university continued to use this equipment without Dr Madey's authority and he sued the university for patent infringement. On appeal to the CAFC, Dr Madey prevailed. Crucially, the CAFC held that the university was not able to rely on the common law research exemption to patent infringement because 'use in keeping with the legitimate business of the alleged infringer does not qualify for the experimental use defence'.[84] The CAFC explained,

> Our precedent clearly does not immunise use that is in any way commercial in nature. Similarly, our precedent does not immunise any conduct that is in keeping with the alleged infringer's legitimate business, regardless of commercial implications. For example, major research universities, such as Duke, often sanction and fund research projects with arguably no commercial application whatsoever. However, these projects

---

83 *Madey v Duke University*, 307 F.3d 1351 (Fed. Cir. 2002).
84 Ibid.

unmistakably further the institution's legitimate business objectives, including educating and enlightening students and faculty participating in these projects. These projects also serve, for example, to increase the status of the institution and lure lucrative research grants, students and faculty.[85]

The CAFC's reasoning essentially means that *any* use of a patented biological material or process which is related to the business of education, in the case of a university, or the business of research, in the case of a research institute, will not come within the US common law exemption to patent infringement.

Conclusion

The GSR proposal recognises that the use of genetic sequences or biological materials (that are identical to naturally occurring sequences and materials) for whatever purpose should not be controlled nor come under the ownership and control of any one organisation or person. Its purpose is to encourage third-party use, rather than attempting to control or restrict it. It recognises that irrespective of whether a genetic sequence is an 'invention' or not, the elucidation of a genetic sequence and the identification of its function is important work that should be encouraged. It therefore enables universities to fund their research projects by becoming GSR holders without incurring any obligation to pay GSR fees. It provides a system to record GSRs and assess the uses to which they are put. The fact that universities are in the business of education or, that today, see themselves as part of a broader commercial world becomes irrelevant.

The patent system which creates property in the patented invention and gives the patent owner the exclusive right to deal with that property as he or she sees fit; the GSR does not. Rather the GSR holder is recognised as being the first to enable the publication of new biological materials and their function and accordingly the *quid pro quo* for its disclosure is the entitlement to receive a GSR fee revenue. Thus, the more use of that GSR the greater the potential GSR fee revenue. Moreover, with the patent system, the price of the patented invention can be subject to manipulation through the patentee's ability to control third party use. It is this ability to control and restrict use that provides the rationale for the experimental use exemption, in an attempt to balance the needs of the patentee with the needs of society. However, with the GSR there is no further balancing or fine tuning required because the whole system is designed to encourage both commercial and non-commercial use equally.

This proposal is merely in its infancy. Therefore this is not the time to accept nor to reject it. Rather it is time for careful reflection, suggestion and constructive criticism. After all, as Prof. Sir John Sulston said, the tension, the debate, between those garnishing wealth and the enlargement of the common good is extremely important to our progress and this proposal is put forward in the context of this debate.

---

85 Ibid.

Chapter 5

Forfeited Consent:
Body Parts in Eminent Domain

Angela A. Stanton

1. Introduction

In the United States, the laws regulating ownership in the body are ambiguous. On the one hand, anyone can go to a blood bank and offer his or her own blood for sale or donate it to victims of natural catastrophes, such as the earthquake in Indonesia or the hurricane in New Orleans; yet in recent history the courts have held that bodily fluids are not considered to be the property of the person who provided them. How can someone donate (or sell) something that one does not legally own? And how can doctors or researchers take this same property and use it for monetary gain as though they have ownership in it, knowing that they do not own it any more than the patient does? This chapter introduces the reader to a case in which this conflict is clearly demonstrated. Further, there is inconsistency among the laws of the several states as well, so that in one state the sale of one's blood may provide for a comfortable living and is considered to be a 'full-fledged commodity,' while in the state next door the rights to earnings from one's bodily fluids is not an acceptable practice.

A couple of examples for the rights of bodily-fluid sales are *Green v. Commissioner*,[1] and in *United States of America v. Dorothy R. Graber*[2] respectively, where Margaret Cramer Green and Dorothy R. Graber earned their living by repeatedly selling their rare blood. According to the Tax Court, blood was a tangible product for sale, similar to

> hen's eggs, bee's honey, cow's milk, or sheep's wool for processing and distribution... [and the Court could] find no reason to legally distinguish the sale of these raw products of nature from the sale of petitioner's blood plasma... any salable part of the human body, is tangible property.[3]

This Court, in fact, decided that earnings from the sale of blood were taxable income, 'subject to ordinary business expenses.' Both of these cases were decided by the Courts a few years before *Moore v Regents of University of California.*[4]

---

1 74 TC 1229 (1980).
2 607 F.2d 92, 44 A.F.T.R.2d 79-6095 (1979).
3 *Green v Commissioner*, 74 TC 1229, 1233 (1980).
4 51 Cal.3d 120 (1990).

Yet, in *Moore*, the patient's blood and other body fluids were taken for research without his consent and without compensation. They were used for research that earned the doctor-researcher, the university, and a couple of pharmaceutical companies billions of dollars in profits. After major battles through several Courts for several years with twists and turns on who has the rights and for what, the Supreme Court of California ruled against the rights of Moore in 11 of the 13 causes, leaving the breach of fiduciary duty and patient's lack of informed consent for re-hearing by the lower Court. However, that hearing never took place. According to the Court records all the defendants were dismissed without charge and Moore had to drop the case because no attorney would take it under consignment and he was a poor man.

How could the Courts come to such drastically different conclusions on such similar issues? The Moore story started in 1976 and arrived in the Courts in 1988. The difference between the several states convey mixed messages about human rights and values to the whole country, particularly when the issue is this important. As it happens, this case became the legal guide for the biotechnology era. It also showcased the unusual relationships between patients, universities, doctors, and corporations in partnerships. It is this case that now serves as a guideline for other cases involving cell donations and sales, such as sperm, eggs, surrogate mothering and so forth.

The purpose of this chapter is to evaluate *Moore* through the legal definition of the human body, ownership in the body, patenting rights and industry views, as well as to show the logic of how the decision was made by the judges and what they thought of future implications. Ruling over the applicability of new technology forces judges to face the dilemma of whether to follow indirect precedents as close to the letter as possible or apply translation and implication that often come from confused reasoning. The limitations of the courts in dealing with scientific and technical issues are generally well acknowledged, but in most cases, no matter how scientific, eventually the end judgment hinges on ethical and moral issues. The *Moore* case was an exception to this rule. In *Moore*, it is easy to find major logical errors and counter-productive statements forming the commentary of the same Justice within a few paragraphs of each other.

This chapter is a critique of the Court's handling of this case and its failure to 'discover' new laws, as it is supposed to do in cases of 'first impression.' The definition of the rights is documented in the Fifth Amendment to the Constitution of the United States, which reads: 'nor shall private property be taken for public use, without just compensation.' However, as this chapter shows, while certain parts of the body are considered to be private property, others are not. This property 'in part' causes considerable confusion and provides for inconsistencies in the law that allows for differing judgments over identical issues. In *Moore*, the unintended consequence was that body parts ended up as subjects of eminent domain.

2. The Moore Story in Brief

In 1976, John Moore was in Alaska working as an engineer on the Alaska Pipeline when he was diagnosed with a rare and deadly form of cancer known as hairy-cell leukaemia, a disease which affects the spleen. Normally, the spleen acts as a filter to remove old and dead cells. However, when the spleen is struck by hairy cell leukaemia, it overproduces a type of white blood cell known as a T-Lymphocyte. Upon the discovery that he had a rare cancer, John Moore sought treatment from Dr David W. Golde, a famous UCLA physician.

In the initial tests, Golde found that Moore's cells had a rare quality that was of high interest in biomedical research. A week later, Moore authorized the surgical removal of his spleen, which, according to Golde, was necessary to save Moore's life. However, unbeknown to Moore, and well before the surgery, Golde arranged to deliver parts of Moore's spleen to a research lab, rather than to the usual pathological examination lab, as required by law. Blind to all the research behind his back, Moore continued his visits to Golde (from Seattle, Washington to Los Angeles, California), because Golde told him that further treatment at *his office* was necessary and required for his health and well-being.

During each visit from Seattle to Los Angeles, during the eight years of aftercare, Golde withdrew additional samples of blood, blood serum, skin, bone marrow aspirate and sperm. All this time Golde never asked for consent and, without Moore's knowledge, used the bodily fluids and tissues for his own research. Moore became suspicious when, tiring of the long and expensive commute between Seattle and Los Angeles, he asked Golde if he could have his fluids and other bodily tissues tested in Seattle with only the results sent to Golde. Golde vehemently disagreed. Moore was firmly told that doing this was not in his best interest and that, if money was a problem, he could be compensated from Dr. Golde's research grant for his travel costs.

At one point, Golde even offered to pay for Moore to stay at the Beverly Wilshire Hotel. This seemed very strange to Moore; why were his follow-up tests of such importance to Golde that he was willing to pay for Moore's trips? It is highly unusual for a doctor to pay the expenses for a patient to come for treatment. But just as Moore begun to ask questions, about eight years after his initial visit, and before he was able to voice his surprise and suspicion, he was served a consent form for the use of his bodily substances for research by Golde. He circled *no* indicating that he did not wish to participate in any research. However, unbeknown to Moore, Golde's patent on the Mo cell line, the one he created from Moore's cells, was just a couple of weeks from gaining approval. As a result, Moore was hounded by letters, phone calls, and special deliveries of consent forms over and over again because he did not sign it 'correctly'. At this point, Moore retained a law firm to find out what had actually occurred behind his back.

On September 11, 1984, Moore filed claims against Golde, his assistant Quan, the Regents of the University of California, and two pharmaceutical companies that paid for Golde's research. The original 13 causes of action fell, by broad definition, into three categories: the first cause dealt with conversion and the rest could be encapsulated under fiduciary duty and lack of informed consent. Figure 5.1 sums up the Court events in brief.

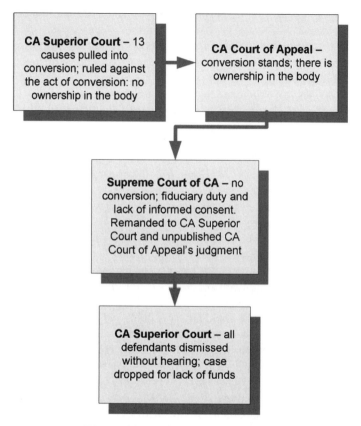

Figure 5.1 Court actions in brief

The Superior Court of Los Angeles County decided that all 13 causes were contained in the first cause, conversion, but as it did not find that conversion took place, it dismissed the case.[5] The decision was based, broadly, on the fact that for the act of conversion to have taken place, Moore must have had property rights in his body and bodily fluids. However, the Court considered those body parts to be abandoned and not something that could be owned. As a result, conversion could not have taken place.

Moore appealed to the California Court of Appeal, which, still retaining all causes under conversion, reversed for the plaintiff, ruling that Golde *did* commit conversion.[6] However, Moore had little time to celebrate since in 1990, the defendants petitioned to the California Supreme Court, which separated the 13 causes into two kinds: conversion as one and grouped breach of fiduciary duty, lack of informed consent, and the remaining ten causes, into the second acceptable cause for discussion.[7] The

5 *Moore v Regents of University of California*, 249 Cal.Rptr. 494 (Cal.App. 2 Dist. 1988).
6 51 Cal.3d 120 (Cal., 1990).
7 Ibid.

case, as decided upon by the Court of Appeal with conversion standing as cause of action, was *ordered unpublished* and is not citable. The Supreme Court of California remanded the case of breach of fiduciary duty and lack of informed consent to the Superior Court of California.[8]

However, upon visiting the Los Angeles Superior Court, one encounters a number of obstacles attempting to find information about this case. The final Court decision was made on 23 October 1992, 'Order of Dismissal with Prejudice'. The Court dismissed all defendants one by one. Moore was forced to drop his case of breach of fiduciary duty and lack of informed consent because of lack of funds and lack of an attorney willing to take the case on consignment. With this, the last part of the case was closed and the details of the final records destroyed. Thus 'Golde was free to return without punishment to his millions of dollars received from his patent'.[9]

Actions Filed by Moore

Originally Moore filed 13 causes of actions: Conversion, lack of informed consent, breach of fiduciary duty, fraud and deceit, unjust enrichment, quasi-contract, bad faith breach of the implied covenant of good faith and fair dealing, intentional infliction of emotional distress, negligent misrepresentation, intentional interference with prospective advantageous economic relationships, slander of title, accounting, and declaratory relief. The first cause of action, conversion, is the most important one in this case. Conversion is strict liability. If a person takes that which is the rightful property of another, the victim is eligible to collect for the full value of the product at the time of the theft. However, the item must fit within the definition of property in order to gain this protection.

Troubled Consent

When Moore grew suspicious about Golde's actions, he retained attorney Gage. Gage discovered that by 1979 Golde had developed a cell line from Moore's T-cells and had applied for a patent in 1983. The patent, covering the cell line and various methods for using it to produce lymphokines was issued in 1984, naming Golde and Quan as the inventors and the Regents as the owner. Golde also negotiated agreements with a couple of pharmaceutical companies to commercially develop the cell line along with derivative products.

> Under an agreement with Genetics Institute, Golde became a paid consultant and acquired the rights to 75,000 shares of common stock. Genetics Institute also agreed to pay Golde and the Regents 'at least $330,000 over three years, including a pro-rata share of [Golde's] salary and fringe benefits, in exchange for ... exclusive access to the materials and research performed' on the cell line and its derivatives. In 1982, Sandoz joined the agreement, and compensation payable to Golde and the Regents was increased by $110,000.[10]

---

8 499 US 936 (1991).

9 M. Burke and V. Schmidt, 'Old Remedies in the Biotechnology Age: Moore v. Regents' available at: http://www.piercelaw.edu/Risk/Vol3/summer/Moore.htm (accessed 1 August 2007).

10 Ibid.

Let's pause for a moment and recount the events: a UCLA doctor, acting on behalf of his patient, while under medical oath, without patient consent and with full knowledge and intent of deceit, took organs and bodily fluids from a patient under his care, patented and profited from the stolen goods without disclosing any of this to his patient. There is more to this than meets to eye. Golde was not only Moore's doctor and confidant; he was also a service-provider for fees. Joshua Kalkstein[11] voiced his disappointment that no one was talking about the 'patient's ethical duty to the doctor and to the others who came before' Moore. In his view, Moore was the 'inheritor of Dr. Golde's knowledge and skill derived from the treatment of those who preceded him'.[12]

What would encourage, from economic and ethical points of view, a generally non-altruistic society to have its members offer their own bodies for experimentation *and* pay for the privilege of being used? Clearly, if, as Kalkstein suggests, the patient has an ethical duty to the *others* (other patients) *who came before him*, there must be a long history of taking cells from patients without their consent. Thus all patients before Moore are some sort of martyrs in Kalkstein's eyes. And martyrs they were, as they were 'harvested,' just as Moore was. But in an altruistic and utopian society the members are willing and informed participants. This case is about *not* being informed! Justice Mosk, in his dissent, called this 'commercial exploitation'.[13] Thus the ideals of an utopian society do not apply.

One might ask why there is an expectation in the research community for receiving payments at both ends of a deal – getting payment from the patients for services provided and sell the 'parts and rights' of patients to someone else for a fee. According to the Court papers, the cell line derived from Moore was worth about $3 billion for the pharmaceutical industry. By the time Moore was asked by Golde to give his consent, the Mo cell line, unbeknown to Moore, had already 'been sold to a biotechnology company for $1.7 million'.[14] At the same time, the 'U.S. biotechnology industry has more than doubled in size since 1993, with revenues increasing from $8 billion in 1993, to $22.3 billion in 2000. In the biotechnology industry patents are widely licensed and are considered to bring some of the highest profits.'[15]

The patient–doctor relationship is based on trust, which, so far has not included concerns over the privacy and ownership of our body tissues. In the mind of the public, research by the universities implies 'research for the sake of research' and not for economic or commercial interest. Of course, in reality, such idealistic views are not applicable to the modern, competitive biotechnological research arena. Whether a researcher working at a university should have the right to 'sell' the creation of

11 J. Kalkstein, 'Moore v. Regents of the University of California Revisited' (2000) 3 *Yale Journal of Law and Technology* 4.

12 Ibid, 1147.

13 *Moore v Regents of University of California*, 51 Cal. 3d 120, 163 (1990).

14 Kalkstein, n. 11, 1146.

15 http://www.bioethics.gov is the general site; see also http://www.bioethics.gov/topics/patenting_index.html which is the transcript of the meeting specifically on Property in the Body. For in-depth study of biotechnology and public policy, see http://www.bioethics.gov/topics/biotech_index.html which contains links to all transcripts available.

his or her mind rather than having to offer it free to the society, as discussed by dissenting Justice Mosk briefly, is too large an issue to be considered here.

The Court sided with the research community because, as Judge Mosk stated, Moore wanted to characterise

> the invasion of his rights as a conversion ... [under which he would continue] to own his cells following their removal from his body ... [he could claim] a proprietary interest in each of the products that any of the defendants might ever create from his cells or the patented cell line ... it raises a flag of caution ... impose[s] a tort duty on scientists to investigate the consensual pedigree of each human cell sample used in research ... would affect medical research of importance to all of society, implicates policy concerns ... Moore claims ownership of the results of socially important medical research, including the genetic code for chemicals that regulate the functions of every human being's immune system.[16]

Judge Mosk's opinion reverberated in the President's Council on Bioethics meeting in 2002, in which the discussion started by exclaiming that there is no need to 'unduly burden the biotech industry' because that would hamper research.[17] Importantly, Judge Mosk stated that Moore had wanted to enforce 'a tort duty on scientists to investigate the consensual pedigree of each human cell sample used in research'. This completely ignores blood banks, sperm banks and other formal depository and storage institutions that were specifically created to avoid such investigational nightmare. Because donation to a specifically designated institution by a donor implies 'blind consent' to all future activities, if the contract is so signed, there is no need to seek out each individual donor for additional permit. If Moore had wanted to donate his bodily tissues to an institution like this and if Golde had taken them from there to his research, there would not have been a lawsuit.

The United States Patent and Trademark Office argued, in the same Council on Bioethics meeting, that their policy does not grant patents on human organisms but this is contrary to the fact that patents already have been issued, as Golde's *Mo* cell line that was derived from Moore, suggests. Research conducted at the cost of the individual's privacy and freedom of choice has never been the custom of American society. For a doctor to steal cells and deny informed consent for the purpose of profiting is, it is suggested, undeniably unethical no matter how it serves the research industry or the public. What the Court said, in effect, places the bodily tissues of every single patient in every single hospital and medical office into 'eminent domain' status with the twist that the doctors and researchers have the right to profit from these cells. This is not a 'business as usual' approach to medical treatment.

---

16 *Moore v Regents of University of California*, 51 Cal. 3d 120, 134 (1990).
17 Ibid.

The Case in Court

In brief, Figure 5.2 sums up the events in Court with the specific outcome.

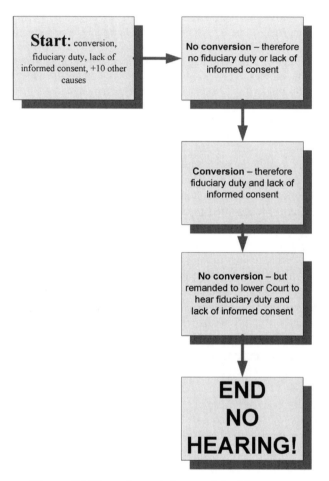

Figure 5.2 Flow of events in court decisions

Before the trial began in the Superior Court of Los Angeles, the trial judge sustained the demurrers of the Regents to the question of conversion. The attorneys for the Regents argued that there was no basis in law for a conversion claim and that the claims to breach of fiduciary duty and others were subsumed within the claim of conversion. In consultation with Moore's attorneys, the judge indicated that he would be willing to entertain the cause of conversion if the plaintiff's attorneys could show Golde's intent to wilfully keep the information about the use of the spleen from Moore. Although this would have been rather easy to do, since there was written proof of Golde arranging for the receiving of the spleen from surgery in his research lab well before the surgery took place, Moore's attorney felt that the case of intent was irrelevant to conversion. This was later shown to be true by the Court following *Poggi v. Scott.*[18] In a letter to Judge Deering dated 7 March 1986 (obtained from Court records), Moore's attorney, Gage, discussed his desire to appeal the case so that it could be tested without the question of intent:

> we do not believe that it is necessary that we establish that the defendant had an improper motive at the precise moment they took the cell line from the plaintiff. We believe that a breach of the fiduciary duty and lack of informed consent constitute a conversion at any time the physician or other defendant acted financially to the detriment of the patient (experimental subject). Since we can prove these facts unequivocally, we prefer to stand on the Complaint and present the matter on appeal. All parties are interested in obtaining appellate review which would greatly facilitate the further handling of this landmark case ...[19]

The demurrers moved to appeal in late 1987 and the decision of the Court of Appeals, was announced on 21 July 1988. The Court's ruling might seem to be basic to the point of being obvious to some, but its meaning was, in another sense, quite incredible. The Court found that a person *has* a property right interest in his or her own body, using *Poggi v. Scott* as precedent:

> The foundation for the action of conversion rests neither in the knowledge nor the intent of the defendant. It rests upon the unwarranted interference of the defendant with the dominion over the property of the plaintiff from which injury to the latter results. Therefore, neither good nor bad faith, neither care nor negligence, neither knowledge nor ignorance, are of the gist of the action. 'The plaintiff's right of redress no longer depends upon his showing, in any way, that the defendant did the act in question from wrongful motives, or generally speaking, even intentionally; and hence the want of such motives, or of intention, is no defense. Nor, indeed, is negligence any necessary part of the case. Here, then, is a class of cases in which the tort consists in the breach of what may be called an absolute duty' ...[20]

However, this judgment was subsequently was overturned on appeal and later dismissed altogether.

3. Analysis

Logical Mishaps, White Lies, and Mere Ignorance

To prove that Moore had no property rights in his own cells, the majority used the conclusion of the argument as the means of the argument itself. They stated: 'Moore's

---

18 167 Cal 372 (1914).

19 www.biology.buffalo.edu/courses/bio129/medler_lectures/visuals/John_Moore.html for details of conversations between the author of 'The Strange Case of John Moore and the Splendid Stolen Spleen' and John Moore, found at this website. This site also refers to many Court documents that were not available for the time period of the research for this chapter. It is my intention to get copies of all original documents in this case.

20 *Poggi v Scott*, 167 Cal. 372, 375 (1914).

allegations that he owns the cell line and the products derived from it are inconsistent with the patent, which constitutes an authoritative determination that the cell line is the product of invention.'[21] This is a circular argument that can easily be inverted to state the exact opposite: Golde's ownership of the patent and his allegation that the cell line henceforth patented is a product of his invention is inconsistent with the fact that the cells were taken from Moore's body. Further, the modified cells had to be different from the cells of Moore, because the patent was received for the cell line and not the process that created the new cells. According to US patent laws to patent a cell line it is not enough to take merely cells to multiply in a petri-dish; the cells themselves must be different from those taken from something, in this case the cells that were taken from Moore. The Court continued by stating that:

> Lymphokines … have the same molecular structure in every human being …[the cells taken from Moore are] *no more unique to Moore than the number of vertebrae in the spine or the chemical formula of hemoglobin.*[22]

The dissent noted a discrepancy in this argument and questioned Golde why he used Moore's cells for his invention if there was no unique value inherent in those cells.

Hence we may ask: if the cells taken from Moore were not unique, since everyone has exactly the same kind of cells, why didn't Golde use his own cells? Secondly we may also ask: since Golde had to make the cells unique to receive the patent but, as the Court stated, every human being has the same molecular structure and thus uniqueness is actually a disadvantage, then these cells cannot be useful since they are different from all other cells in humans – thus are unpatentable. We must conclude the following two points: (1) if the cells taken from Moore were *unique* then Golde either merely kept them unique and just multiplied them in a petri-dish, in which case the cells are not patentable only the *process* is, or (2) the cells are unique but then could not possibly be useful if everyone else otherwise has the same molecularly structured cells that are different from Moore's and thus, again, the cells are not patentable. In sum, Figure 5.3 provides a visual representation of what was wrong in the patent support of the Court.

Since something cannot simultaneously be both distinct and undifferentiated, the Court's argument was seriously flawed. The majority's reasoning, with respect to the patent, is based on two false premises: (1) because the end result is undistinguishable, the beginning must also have been undistinguishable and thus insignificant. We clearly know that the beginning was distinguishable and significant or else there would have been no meaning in the exercise of taking bodily fluids from Moore; (2) the created cells are both distinct and indistinguishably identical to cells in every human – an impossible hypothesis.

Critically, upon visiting the US Patent Office's website, one may search and find the specific patent granted to Golde. The patent abstract states the following:

---

21 *Moore v Regents of University of California*, 51 Cal. 3d 120, 142 (1990).

22 Ibid, 139 (emphasis added).

A human T-lymphoblast cell line (Mo) maintained as a continuous culture constitutively produces proteins, including immune interferon, neutrophil migration inhibition factor, granulocyte-macrophage colony-stimulating activity and erythroid-potentiating activity, as well as other proteins produced by T-cells.[23]

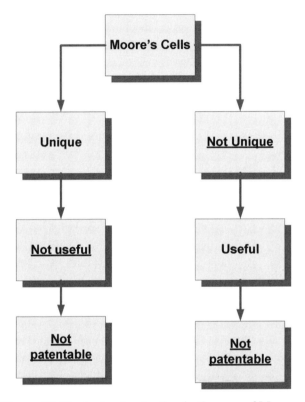

Figure 5.3 The logic of patenting in the case of Moore

From the patent we can precisely tell that the Mo cell line was patenting the actual cells taken from Moore and what Golde added was a medium that provided 'continuous culture' to sustain the cells life. The cells themselves produced the 'proteins, including immune interferon, neutrophil migration inhibition factor, granulocyte-macrophage colony-stimulating activity and erythroid-potentiating activity, as well as other proteins produced by T-cells.' Hence, Golde really should have had the right to patent the *process* and not the cells; the patenting of the medium itself was not patentable because it was in general knowledge already at that time. It is thus arguable from the abstract alone that this patent should not have been grantable. One might wonder why the court never looked at the patent to help them with reaching their judgment.

---

23 US 4,438,032.

Further, since genetic research shares similar patenting concerns to cell research, it is appropriate here to include the cynical but extremely important remark made of intellectual property during the Council on Bioethics meeting in 2002:

> Gene patents are treated as absolute property rights, and we can see already that the way that private companies are dealing with their property rights in human genes is creating problems for medical research, and even in the diagnostic area. Problems are arising in medical research from the fact that expensive licensing fees are being charged by some companies for people just to do research on these genes. And it seems sort of paradoxical and bizarre to a number of observers that if you wanted to take a gene from your own body and do research on it that you can't do it without paying a license fee possibly to whoever owns the patent.[24]

The most critical part of the Court's statement was based on their decision to disallow the conversion claim. Moore could not have owned his own cells because he had no property rights in them. There were several references brought to support this. One such reference stated that '[w]hile it ordinarily suffices to allege ownership generally, it is well established that a complaint's contentions or conclusions of law do not bind us'.[25] Thus in this instance the Court did not surrender its judgment to the law. Yet, as the next several paragraphs show, other times it surrendered to the decision of the lower Court, used precedents that did not fit, sometimes extended the law to embrace and other times reduced the law to bind seemingly with no discernable reasoning.

Fiduciary duty is related to property rights. Informed consent had only been discussed in cases of malpractice before this case. Thus, the Court justly felt it important to establish whether Moore had property rights over his tissues, to see if fiduciary duty and informed consent could have been established in this case as property-right issues. If he did have property rights, conversion should be used in future cases that debate body parts. Fiduciary duty and informed consent can be looked at from property-rights as well as privacy-rights perspectives. It is important to note that the Court concluded that the 'concept of informed consent ... [was] broad enough,' as discussed in malpractice cases, to encompass the Moore case.[26] Thus the Court extended informed consent to encompass this application.

As part of this analysis, the Court evoked the Health and Safety Code (H&SC)[27] to show that had the lower Court reached the issue of breach of fiduciary duty and lack of informed consent, this Court would also have included it in its decision. This means that this Court decided to follow the decisions of the lower Court. We must remember that this Court, the highest Court of California, was hearing the case because the lowest Court did not provide a satisfactory decision. However, following an unaccepted decision is not meaningful. Under the Medical Experimentation Act of H&SC, Golde could have been charged with different levels of violations.

---

24 See the transcripts of the Council on Bioethics meeting in 2002 at http://www. bioethics.gov/topics/biotech_index.html.

25 *Moore v Regents of University of California*, 51 Cal. 3d 120, footnote 19 (1990).

26 Ibid, 129.

27 Health and Safety Code (H&SC) sections 24173 and 24176.

However, because the lower Court did not reach the issue of breach, the Supreme Court decided that it also did not need to 'determine whether the alleged research on Moore's cells would amount to a violation'.[28] Thus, here the Court reduced the laws it could have considered applicable instead of extending them.

The Supreme Court actually stated that had the lower Court *considered* Golde as having committed illegal activities, this Court *would have found him guilty* and the listed penalties would be applied according to the H&SC's specific penalties ordered for this sort of crimes. The Court listed these penalties in the following way:

> Health and Safety Code ... provides *maximum* damages of $1,000 for negligent violations, $5,000 for willful violations, and $10,000 for willful violations which 'expose[ ] a subject to a known substantial risk of serious injury ...'[29]

In reality, these penalties were incorrectly stated. These fines are required as the *minimum* for the violation rather than the maximum. The maximum for offence (a) is $10,000, for (b) $25,000, and (c) is a different bird altogether; it is a *misdemeanour* 'punishable by imprisonment in the county jail for a period not to exceed one year or a fine of fifty thousand dollars ($50,000), or both.'

The laws created by the Legislature provide mandatory sentencing guidelines and not options for recommended action by the Courts. To further its case, the Court heavily depended on the H&SC:

> [n]otwithstanding any other provision of law, recognizable anatomical parts, human tissues, anatomical human remains, or infectious waste following conclusion of scientific use shall be disposed of by interment, incineration, or any other method determined by the state department [of health services] to protect the public health and safety.[30]

The Court further purported that this law limited a patient's right over the excised cells. However, the term 'scientific use' is extremely broad and ambiguous. Justice Mosk, in his dissent, stated that the phrase likely:

> includes routine postoperative examination of excised tissue conducted by a pathologist for diagnostic or prognostic reasons ... [or] purely scientific study of the tissue by a disinterested researcher for the purpose of advancing medical knowledge ... It would stretch the English language beyond recognition, however, to say that commercial exploitation of the kind and degree alleged here is also a usual and ordinary meaning of the phrase ...[31]

'Scientific' means 'relating to or based on science, systematic, methodical' and the word 'use' has multiple meanings to the extent that it includes 'deploy as a means of achieving something' and 'consume' all the way to 'exploit unfairly'.[32] Thus, 'scientific use' could very well have meant what the Court purported it meant.

28 *Moore v Regents of University of California*, 51 Cal. 3d 120, footnote 7 (1990).
29 H&SC section 24176 (emphasis added).
30 *Moore v Regents of University of California*, 51 Cal. 3d 120, 140 (1990).
31 Ibid, 164.
32 *The Compact Oxford English Dictionary*.

Scientific use seems to include *any* type of use, even for one's personal gain and advantage. As a result, rather than limiting the patient's rights, the definition of scientific use actually increases the rights of the physician to do whatever he or she wishes to do with the excised cells, over and above the decision of the patient from whom the cells were taken. This definition aligns with the dissent in noting that:

> [a]bove all, at the time of its excision [Moore] at least had the right to do with his own tissue whatever the defendants did with it ... Defendants certainly believe[d] that their right to do the foregoing [was] not barred by section 7054.4 and [was] a significant property right, as they have demonstrated by their deliberate concealment from Moore of the true value of his tissue, their efforts to obtain a patent on the Mo cell line, their contractual agreements to exploit this material, their exclusion of Moore from any participation in the profits, and their vigorous defense of this lawsuit.[33]

The Court suggested that the decision whether any part of the body should become private property with all the rights and duties associated with such a bundle of proprietary rights is in the faculty of the Legislature to be decided and not in the Court system.

Next the Court brought up the rules of Uniform Anatomical Gift Act (UAGA). According to the UAGA, a donor may donate any body part he or she wishes. However, a person does not actually have ownership rights over his or her body parts. How does the UAGA imagine allowing a person to give away something that the person does not own? This is a disturbing proposition. Furthermore, a statement from the UAGA was brought up in Court in discussion over how the 'act does not, however, permit the donor to receive "valuable consideration" for the transfer'.[34] Alarmingly this quote was taken out of context by the majority. The full quote actually includes an important part that was conveniently left out: 'A person may not knowingly, for valuable consideration, purchase or sell a part for transplantation, therapy, or reconditioning, if removal of the part is intended to occur *after the death of the decedent*'.[35] Moore was not dead; this rule did not apply to him.

Lastly, *Venner v. State*,[36] was used as a reference to show that it 'is not unknown for a person to assert a continuing right of ownership, dominion, or control... over such things as ... blood, and organs or other parts of the body'.[37] But because this case involved a criminal action of illegal drug use, the Court did not find it appropriate to use even those sections where the ownership of property rights in bodily substances were independent from the criminal activity itself but would have been of outmost importance to the Moore case.

---

33 *Moore v Regents of University of California*, 51 Cal. 3d 120, 166 (1990).
34 Ibid, footnote 22.
35 H&SC 7155 (italics added for emphasis).
36 30 Md.App. 599 (1976).
37 *Moore v Regents of University of California*, 51 Cal. 3d 120, footnote 28 (1990).

Precedents and Laws the Californian Supreme Court Ignored

There were precedents which might have been applied in *Moore*. However, the Supreme Court selectively chose some and discarded others with no clearly understandable pattern. In some cases the Court extended (stretched) precedents, other times limited them, and often ignored them altogether.

What Other Courts Said in the Past

At the time the Moore case was filed, ownership over body parts had already been established in other cases. For example, in *York v. Jones*,[38] the Court evaluated frozen sperm (not unlike excised bodily substance), which was held by the defendant in cryopreservation (a special frozen state), was the personal property of the plaintiff. The couple moved to another state and wanted the cryopreserved sperm to follow them but the storing company refused. The Court noted that the 'Agreement created a bailor-bailee relationship between the plaintiffs and defendants' and that the defendants had the 'duty to account for the thing as the property of another ... [because] the essential nature of a bailment relationship imposes on the bailee... an absolute obligation ... to return the property [which] is implied from the fact of lawful possession of the *personal property* of another'.[39]

Many Courts had come to view at least some body parts, such as blood, as a 'full-fledged commodity' before the Moore case. In *Green v Commissioner*[40] and in *United States of America v Dorothy R. Graber*,[41] Margaret Cramer Green and Dorothy R. Graber earned their living by repeatedly selling their rare blood. According to the Tax Court, blood was a tangible product for sale, similar to 'hen's eggs, bee's honey, cow's milk, or sheep's wool for processing and distribution ... [and the Court could] find no reason to legally distinguish the sale of these raw products of nature from the sale of petitioner's blood plasma ... any salable part of the human body, is tangible property'.[42] The Court, in fact, decided that payments received for the blood were taxable income, 'subject to ordinary business expenses.'

Golde took Moore's blood on several occasions, specifically for the purpose of taking advantage of its rare quality. Moore's blood had significant rarity and there is little distinction between Moore and Margaret Green or Dorothy Graber. Thus ownership rights in some bodily substances have been established prior to Moore's final hearing. In particular, the right to selling one's own blood was considered to be a right. One of the substances taken from Moore for the use of research without his consent was his blood. So on the one hand, people living in some states in the United States earn taxable income from selling their *own* blood with clear ownership granted to them in their blood, while in California Golde had the right to sell Moore's blood, which apparently Golde owned and not Moore. Therefore in some states,

---

38 717 F. Supp 421 (1989).
39 Ibid, 425 (emphasis added).
40 74 T.C. 1229 (1980).
41 607 F. 2d 92 (1979).
42 *Green v Commissioner*, 74 T.C. 1229, 1233 (1980).

such as California, a patient does not own his or her blood; the doctor in charge of treatment does.

The Council on Bioethics meeting in 2002 also discussed the meaning of commodity in the human body. David Kevles submitted, 'The basic argument advanced is that to patent life is to hold that it has no vital or sacred character but it is commodifiable in ways that are no different from, say, tennis balls.' Commodification takes place by the means of the research activities of the medical research industry. Referring to the hearings by Congressman Robert Kastenmeier, Kevles stated, 'U.S. patent law is literally amoral. All it does is to grant an exclusive right to make, use, or sell an invention, or to exclude others from making, using, or selling it.'

While rulings by Courts of one state do not bind Courts of another state, in instances of *universal concern*, such as our right over our body, all states should have a pattern of validation and ruling system that is recognisably uniform in its values.

Extension Example

A similar case to Moore took place in 1969, *Berkey v. Anderson*,[43] a suitable precedent, in which the Court of Appeal of California decided on a complaint of malpractice that resulted in unconsented medical treatment of myelogram, and which concluded in injury to the patient. The patient sued for lack of informed consent and breach of fiduciary duty. The California Court of Appeal stated that although a *technical battery* was *neither part of the charges nor discussed in the pretrial statement*, the Court still felt that it was *appropriate to extend* the case *to meet the type of crime* committed. It appears that the California Court of Appeal applies some flexibility in its approach to cases of first impression. This is also visible in that they ruled in favour of conversion.

Similarly to the California Court of Appeal, both the Supreme and the Superior Courts of California had the opportunity to extend and investigate options suggested by the Court of Appeal. It would have been possible and appropriate to extend the case against Golde by introducing charges appropriately fit for his actions for not providing informed consent option to Moore and for breaching fiduciary duty. By the California Supreme Court choosing not to do so, it actually reduced the case to *exclude* charges.

Limitation Example

The Superior Court also ignored *Berkey v. Anderson*,[44] where the Court of Appeal of California noted that a motion for *nonsuit* (meaning failing to make a case stand for cause of action) may only be granted when after 'giving to plaintiff's evidence all the value to which it is legally entitled, indulging in every legitimate inference which may be drawn from that evidence, the result is a determination that there is no

---

43 1 Cal.App.3d 790 (1969).
44 Ibid.

evidence of sufficient substantiality to support a verdict in favor of the plaintiff'.[45] Thus, the option for dismissal is questionable in *Moore* because much of the evidence the plaintiff brought to Court was given no value.

Paradox

The Health & Safety Code establishes the minimum requirement to be met under the 'experimental subject's bill of rights'. These include the list of actions required for informed consent to be adequately met, such that the patient is

> informed of the nature and purpose of the experiment … given an explanation of any benefits … given an opportunity to ask any questions concerning the experiment … instructed that consent to participate in the medical experiment may be withdrawn at any time … without prejudice … given a copy of the signed and dated written consent form … given the opportunity to decide to consent or not to consent to a medical experiment without the intervention of any element of force, fraud, deceit, duress, coercion, or undue influence on the subject's decision[46]

Clearly none of these requirements was met in *Moore*. One might wonder if Golde could make the argument that he had thought that Moore would want to donate his cancerous spleen; after all what good was it for him after it had been removed? But the H&SC, the UAGA, governs what and under what conditions one might donate or accept a donated body part. Although the UAGA discusses the donation of body parts, it does not actually state whether the donor owns the body part prior donation.

It is not at all clear how one might donate a body part that one clearly does not own. The UAGA only sets specific rules for the requirements for a donation to become officially acceptable. The requirements are that a 'document of gift' is either signed by the donor or an 'oral statement [is] made in the presence of two individuals or by means of a tape recording in the donor's own voice'.[47] If none of these took place (and none had in *Moore*), Golde could neither have made the assumption that Moore's cells were donated to him nor could he have accepted them as such even if Moore had given them to him as gifts.

It is very clear that had the Court acted on Moore's claim of Golde's breach, as detailed by the H&SC, Golde might have ended up a lot poorer and possibly in jail. But the Court decided not to act and felt it important to protect the researchers and the pharmaceutical industry. The meaning of this is not easy to decipher and, from a social responsibility standpoint, impossible to fathom. The Court spent a considerable time detailing the conflict of interest of the physician acting as a doctor and a researcher with financial interests. The Court argued that this subject too fell under informed consent, which they did not want to discuss further in this Court room but sent it back to the lower Court. The Supreme Court of California used a circular argument to demonstrate the existence of a desired 'end' (have the subject

---

45 Ibid, 794.
46 H&SC section 24172.
47 H&SC section 7150.

fall under lack of informed consent in order to discuss it) by the lack of existence of the 'means', without the intent of a discussion (no intent to actually discuss the issue if indeed it fell under lack of informed consent cause); this creates a paradox.

Another paradox stems from the ownership of Moore's bodily substances, such as his spleen, for example. Unlike blood cells, for some reason, spleen cells are not yet considered to be property of the beholder. This is not to say that spleens can never become property, as Justice Mosk pointed out, because while taking them from Moore's body by Golde did not constitute a crime, the theft of Moore's spleen cells from Golde's laboratory by Moore would have been considered to be a crime. Instead, it simply states that Moore's spleen was not Moore's property; '[a]s a result, the case paradoxically reinforces the image of the body as property in its partial'.[48] It also clearly demonstrates that ownership rights of Moore's spleen are granted to Golde but not to Moore. Again, this paradox can be formulated as follows: in some states, such as California, a patient does not own his or her spleen; the doctor in charge of treatment does!

Precedents the CA Supreme Court Did Not Ignore

The Court used a variety of precedents, many of which were tangential to the case at hand. *Daar v Yellow Cab Company*,[49] was a case dealing with a class-action lawsuit for charging unfair prices to taxi customers. This case received several negative treatments by the time *Moore* came along; a fact that must have been known by the Court. Further, the arguments in this case were very distant from that of *Moore* and to compare one with the other requires a great deal of imagination.

The majority also referred to several journal articles in support of their argument. Interestingly, some of these articles undermine the points they wanted to make more than helped. For example, Mary Taylor Danforth's article[50] was quoted by the majority, but it showed no familiarity with *Moore*. Her writing was based on false premises. In the introduction she wrote: 'the doctors *received [Moore's] consent* to use his blood and bodily substances in research ... Moore's *consent to the research* was *adequate* to permit the development of the cell line.' This is contrary to anything that actually transpired in this case. It is underclear how she ever could conclude that there was consent but the bigger puzzle is why the Court would ever refer to an article completely based on erroneous information.

The majority used *People v. Guerra*[51] for 'salient solution', *People v. Shirley*[52] to argue that 'hypnotic recall "form[ed] a scientifically inadequate basis for drawing conclusions about the memory processes of the large majority of the population"' but there was neither hypnotic recall of any kind nor any discussion of memory

---

48 R. Rao 'Property, Privacy, and the Human Body' (2000) 80 *Boston University Law Review* 374.

49 67 Cal.2d 695 (1967).

50 M. Danforth 'Cells, Sales, and Royalties: The Patient's Right to a Portion of the Profits' (1988) 6 *Yale Law and Policy Review* 179.

51 37 Cal. 3d 385, 412 (1984).

52 31 Cal. 3d 18, 59 (1982).

processes in *Moore*, and *People v. McDonald*[53] to demonstrate 'that eyewitness testimony can be unreliable'.[54] There were no eyewitnesses in this case as neither did *Moore* contain violent crime or hypnosis. The use of so unrelated cases with historical quotes of the other justices had the appearance of throwing flying objects with sharp pins, like that of a porcupine, toward justices in the opposite camp.

As discussed in an earlier section, the Court also used *Poggi v Scott*,[55] for the applicability of a tort conversion to show that it was immaterial whether the conversion took place knowingly or without intent.[56] *Poggi* established conversion as a breach of *absolute duty* and that intent was irrelevant since the Court decided that the cause of conversion did not stand. Thus rather than showing support for the majority's argument that conversion did not take place, *Poggi* actually strengthened the case of Moore by showing that it did not matter if Golde deliberately or without intent breached fiduciary duty and informed consent in the process of taking Moore's cells secretly.

Diamond v. Chakrabarty,[57] was used as precedent.[58] This was a landmark case about a scientifically designed oil-eating bacterium; the first engineered live being to have become patentable. But the genetic engineering of bacterium-research does not use human cells; the patentability of this new line of live organism is not really useful as a precedent, except to show that new and unique creations engineered in the biology lab are patentable. Because, there is a contradiction in the Court's reasoning about whether the Mo cell line really represented something new, different, and useful like the oil-eating bacterium so that it could also have become patentable with reason, the oil-eating bacterium merely amplifies the differences between a patentable cell design and one that is not patentable, demonstrating that the Mo cell line should not have been granted patent.

The Conclusion of the Moore Case

In March of 1991, Moore was denied Certiorari by the Supreme Court of the United States. Moore's attorney Gage thought that, with the caps on medical liability in place in California, further pursuing of the case was not economically viable. John Moore passed away in 2001. He has lived over 20 years after his original doctors gave him six months to a year to live. Although Golde clearly extended Moore's life, the patent that Golde received for the Mo cell line did not provide benefits to Moore, neither financial nor in extending his life. The MO cell line has not proved to be as profitable as was originally expected as a result of competing products developed by Genentech and others, though it has remained commercially viable. Dr Golde's stock in Genetics Inc., at of the close of the Market on 5 April 1996, was worth over

---

53 37 Cal. 3d 351, 365-367 (1984).

54 *Moore v Regents of University of California*, 51 Cal. 3d 120, footnote 35 (1990).

55 167 Cal. 372, 375 (1914).

56 *Moore v Regents of University of California*, 51 Cal. 3d 120, footnote 38 (1990).

57 447 U.S. 303, 309–310 (1980).

58 *Moore v Regents of University of California*, 51 Cal. 3d 120, 142 (1990).

five million dollars. Golde left UCLA shortly after the Moore case and passed away a few years later.

4. After Moore

Moore is the landmark case that addresses the issue of ownership in one's cells. As there has been an international market in human body parts for some time with the poor selling off organs to people with money, as feared, the concern might seem reasonable on the part of the Court for limiting Moore's property rights over his body. But many body parts have already been commonly treated as commodities in the United States, with legal support from several Courts in many states. 'Blood, semen, hair, teeth, sweat, and urine' were the most common but 'pieces of skin and muscle from living persons have been sold without raising any controversy'.[59] Pignatella suggests that recognition of property rights in the human body may actually reduce, rather than increase, the market in body parts because people will realise that they are in control of those rights. Ambiguous laws, such as what was established by *Moore*, lead to confusion and continual inappropriate access to bodily tissues without patient knowledge or consent. Further, as discussed in the Council on Bioethics meeting in 2002, the biggest threat to commodification of body parts comes from the researchers and scientists using body parts without consent and selling their findings for profit.

Should the scientific industry have an incentive to take body parts secretly and sell their modifications of them to the industry? If there is an incentive to be had to the trade of body parts, surely the incentive be given to those who 'live' in these body parts? (It might have been desirable to have said that 'the people who own their body parts' but that is clearly not defined according to the law currently; hence the awkward statement.)

Justice Mosk pointed out in his dissent the irony in what the majority was proposing: Golde could own Moore's tissue, but Moore could not. Further he pointed out the inequity in bargaining positions between Moore and Golde. Justice Mosk believed that ownership rights in the body would give patients a 'right of participation'. He further asserted that the doctrine of informed consent would not be sufficient for dealing with the advancing biotechnology that uses the patient's biological materials.

According to Judith Fischer[60] the strong criticism of the Moore decision 'rests on its failure' to signify personal considerations. Justice Broussard, concurring and dissenting, criticised the Court's inconsistency in allowing an exception to conversion liability by permitting Golde and the drug companies to retain their 'ill-gotten gains free of their ordinary common law liability, thus foreclosing an important avenue of

---

59 C. Pignatella and S. Amy, 'Property Rights in Human Biological Materials: Studies in Species Reproduction and Biomedical Technology' (2000) 17 *Arizona Journal of International and Comparative Law* 477.

60 J. Fischer, 'Misappropriation of Human Eggs and Embryos and the Tort of Conversion: A Relational View' (1999) 32 *Loyola of Los Angeles Law Review* 381.

recovery to the plaintiff'.[61] Indeed, some commentators have faulted the Court as engaging in 'unsound legal analysis' in order to protect the research industry.[62]

The Court also discussed the doctor's conflict of interest in having to tell his patient his involvement in research that provided financial incentives. Patients have the right to not participate in any research if they so desire, reducing the doctor's opportunity to reach the extra economic gain. Thus, the physician is affected by the tradeoff between the financial gain and consideration for the patient's health when proposing a specific treatment:

> The Court's decision in Moore endorsed the Kaldor-Hicks theory of economic efficiency. The Kaldor-Hicks theory is not concerned with whether or not a reallocation of resources will make certain individuals worse off, but it is concerned with whether or not society's aggregate utility will be maximized. According to this theory, reallocation of resources is efficient if those who gain from the transaction obtain enough to fully compensate those who lose from the transaction, even though there is no requirement that actual compensation occur.[63]

The Court noted that Californian law prohibits the doctor from making the final decision for the patient; it is the 'prerogative of the patient to determine for himself the direction in which he believes his interests lie'.[64] However, there is a sliding scale in the evaluation of when to disclose and to what degree. The Court stated that:

> a physician's research interest might play such an insignificant role in the decision to recommend a medically indicated procedure that disclosure should not be required because the interest is not material. By analogy, we have not required disclosure of 'remote' risks that 'are not central to the decision to administer or reject [a] procedure'.[65]

Because of this sliding scale, it is plausible the Court believed that removing cells from the spleen that was already surgically separated from the patient constituted no harm – as long as the spleen was removed exclusively to benefit the patient and not for the purpose of furthering the doctor's research effort. In ruling against Moore, the Court referenced the economic and social benefits that cell research provided. The Court concluded that economically it was not rational to grant Moore rights in his cells. By deciding in favour of the Regents, the Court implied that the transaction costs and externalities that research institutions and hospitals would incur if individuals were granted property rights in their cells was too high to justify the imposition of those rights. While socially it may have been more preferable for individuals to have rights in their cells, economically the costs associated with the maintenance and enforcement of those rights was not justified in light of the social

---

61 *Moore v Regents of University of California*, 51 Cal. 3d 120, 160 (1990).

62 Fischer, n. 60, 405.

63 J. Muchmore, 'Proprietary Rights and the Human Genome Project: A Legal and Economic Perspective' 8 *The Digest* 45.

64 *Moore v Regents of University of California*, 51 Cal. 3d 120, 132 (1990).

65 Ibid, footnote 9.

benefit that cell research created. The Court was more concerned with economic policy considerations and the formulation of biotechnology law than ethical justice.

The UC Irvine Fertility issue, *Clay v Asch*[66] came on the scene a few years after *Moore* ended. The UC Irvine case shares with Moore a fundamental property: human cells (eggs at UC Irvine: spleen and blood cells in *Moore*) were misappropriated without consent. 'The question then is whether Moore is applicable to all genetic material, including embryos, of patients' or is the UC Irvine case more applicable even for cases that involve spleen cells?[67] Embryos are cells that have a significant difference from just plain cells; embryos may become people, while Moore's cells just remained that, cells. However, the *act* of misappropriation of human cells is the same regardless what cells we are talking about.

Doctors Asch, Stone and Balmaceda worked in the UC Irvine fertility clinic, where they stored and were supposed to implant the patients' own eggs preserved in a frozen state using in-vitro fertilisation technology. The problem arose when, with the help of several whistleblowers, it became known that embryos were taken from certain women and, without their knowledge and consent, were implanted into other women. According to the reports, there are as many as fifteen children who were born in this way, not to their biological parents, without knowledge and consent. Some of the Clay eggs apparently also ended up in the research laboratory of Cornell University. The *Los Angeles Times* alleged inappropriate action, in response to which a 'top federal official who reviewed the documents … told the newspaper that Cornell did not use the embryos for the benefit of the patient'.[68] Later Cornell was also sued by two couples and charged with 'fraud and professional negligence for using the embryos in research without learning whether patients had given consent'.[69] In both cases responding parties stated that there does not seem to be specific laws regulating the industry and the definition of 'research' is ambiguous.

All three doctors were charged. Dr Asch and Dr Balmaceda left the country and could not be brought to justice but Dr Stone served a jail sentence. The university settled with all patients out of Court, some receiving as much as $500,000.

The California Supreme Court made it very clear that the lack of *property* status, implying lack of convertibility, of Moore's cells was the main issue and that it was based on the lack of *uniqueness* of those cells. But based on the United States patent information on Golde's 'invention,' we know that Golde converted Moore's unique cells. The uniqueness of his cells lay in their rare ability to mass produce for an infinite length of time, which made them unique, valuable, and definitely different from the cells of other people.

---

66 *Clay v Asch* (No. 752294) (Orange County Super. Ct.); related cases include *Challender v Regents* (No. 748303) (Orange County Super. Ct.).

67 S. Paine *et al.*, 'Ethical Dilemmas in Reproductive Medicine' (1996) 18 *Whittier Law Review* 51, 54.

68 Associated Press 'Records Spur Calls for Fertility-Industry Controls Court Papers Show Human Embryos From UC Irvine Were Used for Research at Cornell University Without the Consent of Donors.' The Press-Enterprise (Riverside, CA), 13 July 1999.

69 Ibid.

In *Clay*, the genetic material involved was also unique. Since the California Supreme Court originally considered Moore's cells not to be unique, they did not have to render the same decision in *Clay* as *Moore* – the consideration of the uniqueness of genetic material seems to be of the highest importance. Thus, given our new knowledge of the patent issue that proves the uniqueness of Moore's cells, and since in the fertility clinic's case the Court came to the conclusion that the doctors were guilty of conversion because of the uniqueness of the cells, so Golde must also have been guilty of conversion in the Moore case.

In another case, shortly after *Moore*, *Hecht v. Kane*,[70] the debate was over sperm that the deceased deposited, specifically for the purpose of the impregnation right of his girlfriend of five years, before he committed suicide. Although he expressly stated in his will that Deborah Hecht was the owner of the sperm that was preserved under cryopreservation, the children from his first marriage sued and the California trial Court judge ordered the sperm to be destroyed. Luckily, that did not happen. In the California Court of Appeal, the decision placed the sperm vials in the category of 'estate property' and under probate Hecht received the designated portion of all other property between the children and her, yielding 20 per cent of the sperm to her. In the Supreme Court of California, the decision included the definition of sperm as *property* relying upon statutory authority, stating that sperm met the definition of property under the California Probate Code and stated that 'decedent's sperm is a unique material, not subject to the terms of a property settlement between claimants under the will'.[71] Thus, here is an additional example of the definition of genetic material, other than ova, as property.

It is clear from the few cases set out above that came after *Moore* that the view of the body and whether it constitutes property is changing. It is unclear if the entire body will eventually be considered to be property of the person who uses it for life. For now, we have to settle for the few parts that can legitimately be owned by us and do with as we wish, including selling them for money. Currently parts that can be sold are hair, blood, sperm, and human eggs. We may even sell the 'service' of our bodies for surrogate maternity, in which a woman lends her entire body for a fee.

Again, it is important to mention that it is difficult to fathom how one can lend her body for a fee as a surrogate mother, yet it is a body she does not legally own. This conflict, it is certain, will eventually be resolved to the advantage of ownership.

5. Concluding Thoughts

From the discussion the following issues clearly stand out for future decisions:

(1) We must decide what we own and what we don't own, in terms of our bodies, with great precision – partial ownership is meaningless and ambiguity leads to inconsistent and confusing decisions that increase costs on all sides.

(2) The California Supreme Court has few rules that it cannot blatantly break or ignore and that there are no checkpoints along the way to ensure that appropriate steps are taken

---

70 59 Cal.Rptr.2d 222 (1996) (ordered unpublished).

71 Ibid, 226.

to reach ethical decisions. We must design a better functioning legal system that deals more expertly and with consistency with the issues of handling and manufacturing human organisms.

(3) Although most institutions have implemented strict rules whose adherence is overseen by their Institutional Review Boards, the general laws have not grown to reflect the same rigor. This is inadequate and embarrassing.

(4) It might be helpful for Courts to consider applying mathematical rigour, economic analysis, and ethical evaluations to their judgments before they settle with their final draft.

The issues this chapter discussed point to inefficiencies of the California legal system and the legislated laws. An exciting area for future work could be to create a permanent legal and ethical committee that specialises in evaluating potential new laws and regulations with respect to research on human cells, tissues, and organisms. A great challenging area of research also exists in developing a model to help recognise inconsistencies in the laws so corrections may be attempted by the court system during each argued case rather than only retroactively.

6. Implications and Recommendations

Golde was not a lone researcher interested only in benefiting humanity, but had tremendous financial incentives to create a commercially viable product. But Golde worked within an institution that also had a variety of economic and social motives and the rights to make the product were given to for-profit corporations who were interested in a variety of social and economic goals as well as profits for themselves. It is clear that regulating only one chain in the link of many will not do a good enough job. Regulating the entire chain requires the co-operation of the legislature and the Courts. It also requires some form of unity between, and within, the states so that the consistency of regulations reflects the uniformity of the human body and its associated value system throughout our nation. Courts today, in the course of resolving cases and controversies, create a variety of scientific and technological policies with broad costs and benefits without being appropriately equipped to do so successfully. *Moore*, shows that we do not own our bodies, placed the human body into a weird eminent domain in which the power lies in the ~~state~~ [researcher] to appropriate private property for its own use without the owner's consent.

PART 4
Traditional Knowledge

Chapter 6

Beyond 'Protection': Promoting Traditional Knowledge Systems in Thailand

Daniel Robinson

With the extinction of each indigenous group, the world loses millennia of accumulated knowledge about life in and adaptation to tropical ecosystems.[1]

In the development of traditional knowledge (TK) regulatory systems there has been a tendency to focus on developing mechanisms to control the scientific and commercial use of TK (facilitated access), with the apparent aim of enabling indigenous and local communities to capture the anticipated benefits of the commercialisation of TK (usually profit sharing).[2] Whilst benefit sharing is important for reasons of compensation and justice, there is no guarantee that it will assist with the continuation of TK-associated local customs. Databases, registers and gene banks provide only a *static* record of knowledge and associated genetic resources. The *promotion* of traditional knowledge and associated local innovation more generally has often been forgotten. TK is highly situated within complex local cultural and environmental conditions and is perpetuated by local practice, which is threatened by a range of often ill-considered factors outside of biopiracy threats. This chapter describes these issues with reference to legal developments and current events between stakeholders in Thailand. Specifically, this intends to illustrate the need for greater 'community rights' and TK promotion amidst a backdrop of exclusion from lands, political marginalisation, and cultural assimilation that are eroding the local customs and associated traditional knowledge of the ethnic minorities of northern Thailand.

1. What is Traditional Knowledge?

There is no one universally accepted definition of 'traditional knowledge' and it is a term that takes on many meanings for different people. There are, however, some generally accepted concepts associated with discussions on TK. The following provides some general criteria based on the collective understandings of the term

---

1 D. Posey, 'Indigenous Knowledge and Development and Ideological Bridge to the Future' in K. Plenderleith (ed.), *Kayapó Ethnoecology and Culture* (New York: Routledge 2002), 59.

2 See for example B. Tobin, *Customary Law as the Basis for Prior Informed Consent of Local and Indigenous Communities* (Tokyo: UNU-IAS undated).

made in international fora, based on comments by the leading experts and academics and direct research experience. This is by no means a finite definition.

Traditional knowledge is widely understood as:

- knowledge developed over time;
- transmitted generation to generation;
- typically, transmitted orally;
- typically, collectively held and owned;
- typically of a practical nature, and relating to natural resources (as has been defined in intellectual property circles, otherwise it falls under folklore or cultural expression);
- is dynamic and evolving with environmental and external influences;
- often involves elements of innovation and experimentation;
- typically is imbedded in specific environmental settings;
- is imbedded in customs, language, local practices and cultural heritage;
- when removed from its local cultural or environmental setting may still exist in memory, but becomes less 'traditional';
- often taking the form of stories, songs, folklore, proverbs, cultural values, beliefs, rituals, community laws, local language, and agricultural practices; and
- having an holistic aspect.[3]

Furthermore, traditional knowledge[4] has been broadly recognised for playing the following important roles:

1. for sustaining or improving the livelihoods of a vast array of local communities,
2. as part of the sustainable use and conservation of the environment,
3. for experimentation and provision of innovations that can be used to benefit society more broadly,
4. for its benefits to national economies.

---

3 This definition draws upon the discourses of the CBD Secretariat (8(j) Working Group), the WIPO Secretariat (Traditional Knowledge Division), and discussions of traditional knowledge by G. Dutfield, *Intellectual Property, Biogenetic Resources and Traditional Knowledge* (London: Earthscan 2004); D. Posey and G. Dutfield, *Beyond Intellectual Property: Toward Traditional Resource Rights for Indigenous Peoples and Local Communities* (Ottawa: IDRC 1996) and J. Gibson, 'Traditional Knowledge and the International Context for Protection' (2004) 1 *SCRIPT-ed* 48 and local experiences and observations made by the author from several field trips in three of the regions of Thailand.

4 Reference to 'traditional knowledge' throughout this chapter generally refers to the traditional biodiversity-related knowledge of indigenous and local communities, including traditional agricultural, medicinal and ecological knowledge. Cultural expressions and folklore are beyond the scope of the paper unless specifically mentioned.

2. How is TK Protection Discursively Framed?

If new to the debate on the legal treatment of traditional knowledge, then one might assume that 'TK protection' would entail a broad range of means for which traditional knowledge holders may continue to pursue these roles. This is not necessarily the case. The primary reason that countries have sought to protect traditional knowledge to date has been to stop 'biopiracy'. This term is applied broadly to refer to the use of biological resources and/or associated traditional knowledge (typically from developing countries or from indigenous communities) without adequate authorisation, and/or to patents which utilise such knowledge or resources without adequate compensation or recognition. As Dutfield notes, it is not always clear who the victims are, or indeed if there are any, particularly in cases where a resource is widely distributed and traditional knowledge applications are widely applied.[5] This is not to play down the concerns of indigenous and local communities and indeed there have been numerous cases where extensive public outcry has occurred at the potential moral and economic implications of biopiracy.

A curious result arising from the broad attention that biopiracy cases received was that TK and biological resources came to be recognised as having enormous value. The developing world, where the world's biological wealth is predominantly located, has since taken up the biopiracy discourse as these countries realise the potential to capitalise on such resources and knowledge and thus the importance of protecting it from potential misappropriation. However this drive for protection essentially focuses on the last two roles of TK. In essence, TK and GRs (genetic resources) 'protection' has taken on the meaning of 'protection from biopiracy'. A disclosure requirement has emerged as the primary potential mechanism for TK and GRs protection. Prior informed consent (PIC) has been developed as a principle for the *respect* of TK holders. Means for *promotion* of TK for the maintenance of livelihoods and for conservation/sustainable use of the environment has had a harder time finding adequate policy space. In the case of Thailand, these are perhaps best tackled at the national and local level, but are likely to need various forms of international pressure and support.

Predominantly, the framing of TK protection has taken place in the discourse of Western trade-related intellectual property (IP) rights, gaining a high profile in trade and IP fora. As Tobin notes, there has also been a tendency to focus on developing mechanisms to control the scientific and commercial use of TK (facilitated access), with the apparent aim of enabling indigenous and local communities to capture the anticipated benefits of the commercialisation of TK (usually profit sharing).[6] This chapter argues that this is largely driven by national governments, in many cases without broader recognition for the need to promote TK's other roles and benefits. It is not the intention of this paper to extensively review the technical merits of a potential disclosure requirement, ABS (access and benefit sharing) or PIC mechanisms as

---

5 Dutfield n. 3.
6 See Tobin, n. 2.

there are a plethora of documents which already address these issues.[7] Rather it is to highlight their limited scope given the array of threats that are posed to TK. While the current focus is important for the exchange of technology and for the reduction of biopiracy, it does not necessarily engage the issues that directly and immediately threaten host communities and the continuity of their culture. As Gibson has suggested, there is likely a fundamental difference between the object of protection that is understood in conventional legal discourse, and that sought by traditional and indigenous groups.[8] Conserving the method of knowledge creation must be more directly addressed in order to support the first two roles of TK aforementioned, not just the tangible object or a documented version of the knowledge.

This chapter is based on an analysis of the policy space surrounding the biodiversity/traditional knowledge/intellectual property nexus that has emerged in Thailand. The Thai government has been pursuing mechanisms for the protection of TK and biological resources from biopiracy, but it has also been pursuing some mechanisms for the promotion of community rights and continued local practices linked to TK. Whilst it is considered pertinent that protection from biopiracy should be enforced internationally, addressing the continuation of the local culture of custodian communities in Thailand is occurring through some national and local initiatives.

3. International Fora

Traditional knowledge is not dealt with by any one forum in isolation. Rather, aspects of TK protection are dealt with in numerous fora, meaning there are various perspectives and potential modalities for different forms of legal treatment of TK.

In the World Trade Organisation (WTO) Trade Related Aspects of Intellectual Property Rights Agreement (TRIPS) Council, Thailand has co-sponsored submissions by Peru, India, Brazil and others for a patent requirement for disclosure of the source and country of origin (when GRs or TK have been used in the invention process), and mechanisms for prior informed consent, access to and the sharing of sharing arising from the utilisation and commercialisation of GRs and TK.[9] Thai negotiators also made a proposal to the US for similar requirements in the fifth round of Free Trade Agreement (FTA) negotiations in Hawaii in October, being one of the only countries besides those in the Andean Community to have made such a proposal in the recent flurry of FTAs with the US.

The World Intellectual Property Organisation (WIPO) and its Inter-governmental Committee on Intellectual Property and Genetic Resources, Traditional Knowledge and Folklore has also had a significant effect on the discourse of TK protection.

---

7 For a number of these see www.iprsonline.org/resources/tk.htm or www.iprsonline.org/resources/biodiversity.htm.

8 Gibson, n. 3.

9 See the following WTO webpage for relevant submissions made under the 2001 mandate of the Doha Development Agenda on the review of TRIPS Article 27(3)(b), traditional knowledge and biodiversity: http://www.wto.org/english/tratop_e/trips_e/art27_3b_e.htm (accessed 1 August 2007).

It has provided a useful coordination point for dialogue, fact-finding missions, national case studies, the dissemination of such information and the articulation of the TK issue in a predominantly IP context. It tends to also be the target of a range of criticisms because of its limited mandate, lack of progress on substantive mechanisms for protection from misappropriation in the IP regime and for providing a distraction point for countries, such as the US to deflect progress on the disclosure issue in the TRIPS Council.

The Convention on Biological Diversity (CBD), which essentially initiated debate on the protection, promotion and respect of TK, has through discussions in the Conference of the Parties (COP) established two working groups. One is focused on the development of an international regime on access and benefit sharing to genetic resources and traditional knowledge, and the other is on the implementation of Article 8(j) for local practices and associated TK. The ABS forum has been the more prominent CBD discussion and has the goal of ensuring that fair and equitable benefit sharing arising out of the utilisation and commercialisation of genetic resources and TK can be feasibly implemented internationally.

The Article 8(j) Working Group (and a related advisory committee) on the other hand is a smaller forum which has received less media and academic attention. The forum has a broad mandate for the promotion of TK and associated local practices. One outcome of the working groups has been a series of composite reports from different regions on the status and trends regarding the knowledge, innovation and practices of indigenous and local communities. The reports documented the loss of traditional knowledge and emphasise the relative scarcity of examples of measures and initiatives specifically designed to protect, promote and facilitate the use of traditional knowledge. As a result the working group is now discussing options for sui generis (unique) systems of protection and promotion of local practice and traditional knowledge, with specific emphasis on the respect of customary laws of local and indigenous peoples. Such negotiations have however been hamstrung by the need to have a framework that is broad enough so as not to limit or exclude the applicability of the wide range of customary laws.

There is also a number of other international fora and organisations dealing with TK.[10] It is worth noting at this point that there has been some reluctance by Parties in such fora to link TK to a broader rights-based approach such as human rights, including the 8(j) Working Group.[11] This discussion will return to this point in section 7 of this chapter.

---

10 For example, the World Health Organisation deals with traditional medicines; the United Nations Conference to Combat of Desertification; the Food and Agriculture Organisation Sustainable Development Department as well as the Commission on Genetic Resources for Food and Agriculture; the UN Conference on Trade and Development and various UNEP and UNDP projects either directly or indirectly.

11 Staff at the CBD Secretariat have noted that there is a one-sided interaction between them and the Working Group on Indigenous Populations and the Office of the UN High Commissioner on Human Rights.

4. The Biopiracy Threat

Countries with TK interests have been considering whether or not to implement national sui generis systems of protection from biopiracy. The development of national systems may be useful for the building blocks of an international framework and, by virtue of being closer to the issue, may more specifically address the needs of traditional knowledge holders. They are, however, limited such that they have no extra-territorial effect. For disclosure, ABS and PIC requirements, it makes clear sense to seek an *international* framework for TK protection in order to prevent biopiracy, facilitate benefit sharing and respect TK.

Table 6.1 Documented 'biopiracy' episodes in Thailand

'Jasmati' trade mark case	Famous case of the RiceTec, Inc. trade mark of 'Jasmati' on an unrelated rice product. The product name utilised a combination of the words 'jasmine' and 'basmati'. This is arguably deceptive to consumers about the quality or substance of the rice.
Stepwise Programme: jasmine rice	The Dale Bumpers National Rice Research Center, US Department of Agriculture/ Agricultural Research Service and University of Florida Everglades Research and Education Center have established the 'Stepwise Programme for the Improvement of Jasmine Rice for the US', which includes a breeding programme and induced mutation to improve jasmine rice for the US market. There was controversy over the withdrawal of the materials from the International Rice Research Institute (IRRI) under material transfer agreement (MTA). The University of Florida has since stated it will not patent any resultant products from the programme. Thai officials are concerned that the programme may reduce the need to import Thai jasmine rice.
Kwao krua (*Pueraria mifica*)	This is a well-documented Thai medicinal herb that has been used in Thai households and communities for more than 100 years. The herb has had its extracts patented by Thai, Japanese, Chinese and Korean companies. The use of technical language in the patent description of the Japanese, Korean and Chinese patent applications obscures the origins of the product and associated knowledge.
Marine fungi: University of Portsmouth	More than 200 strains of marine fungi were collected by researchers from coastal areas of Southern Thailand and brought to the national biotechnology authority – Biotec. The marine fungi were transferred to the University of Portsmouth in 1993 as part of a research project sponsored by a pharmaceutical company. A limited 'gentleman's agreement' was made between the parties. In 1998, fearing potential patenting and loss of rights over the commercialisation of the strains, the Thai government asked for the specimens back. The University of Portsmouth gave conflicting responses for several months about the whereabouts of the samples before returning some of them to Thailand.
Plao Noi	Patents by a Japanese company on a chemical extract used for the treatment of ulcers, but based on Thai traditional knowledge. Consent was provided by an official of the Thai Royal Forestry Department without adequate benefit flows.

A number of 'biopiracy' episodes, as well as the heightened perceived value of GRs and associated TK, have triggered national regulatory developments in Thailand. Table 6.1 lists a number of the most well-documented misappropriations that have occurred.

The jasmine rice cases struck the strongest chord with the Thai public, due to the cultural importance of rice in this still primarily rural-based country and its place as the largest rice exporter in the world. Section 6 explains the political and legal response that resulted from this case.

Perhaps less known, until recently, is white kwao krua (*Pueraria mifica*), a plant which is now recognised for its ability to firm or enlarge breasts and revitalise sexuality. Interest groups and non-governmental organisations (NGOs) identified that white kwao krua has become part of the essential subject matter in US patent number 6,352,685 owned by Japanese and Chinese corporations. There is strong evidence that at least one of the four inventors of the patented product had worked extensively with local scientists in Thailand.[12]

Discussions about protection from biopiracy have led commentators and decision makers to question whether these are just a few bad patents (and trade marks), or whether there are genuinely systemic problems with the patent system. As the number of documented 'biopiracy' cases rises, and due to the absurdly broad nature of some patents[13] it seems clear that the system is not adequately coping. So what can be done? There are a number of emerging questions. Is it just a matter of improving the patent examination process or is the examination process inherently limited such that it deserves a disclosure requirement? Given the frequent claims that the patent system is already 'overburdened' as patent application numbers continue to rise, does this mean that patent examination quality will continue to decline? Although NGOs and concerned researchers have done well to uncover and document a growing number of biopiracy cases, why should the burden be on them? Can bad patents be simply remedied through the courts or is the burden of legal and transaction costs too high for those who feel they have been exploited? These are questions for which the WIPO Secretariat and the Parties to the IGC, and the TRIPS Council, have been searching for answers.

Due to the global reach of corporations and large industry interested in accessing the resources and knowledge of local communities the international dimension of a protection mechanism has been emphasised. It is worth noting, however, that in a number of cases Thai companies have also utilised and patented the traditional knowledge and genetic resources held communally by tribal and local communities or broadly across various communities and groups.[14] To what extent adequate prior informed consent and benefit sharing arrangements were obtained is unclear and problematic. Do these cases fit within the definition of biopiracy? The distribution of traditional knowledge and biological resources is often ambiguous. They may be

---

12 *Bangkok Post*, 22 November 2004.

13 See, for example, the *Yellow Enola Bean Case* in Dutfield n. 3.

14 Some of these are indicated or implied in P. Subcharoen *et al.*, 'Indigenous Knowledge and Intellectual Property – a Thai study' (2001) (unpublished document from the Department of Public Health).

freely and openly shared (as is frequently the custom amongst various communities throughout Thailand) or they may be kept more secret, particularly in relation to rituals, traditional medicine practised by tribal shaman, the customary laws of certain groups or even family traditions.[15] Whether or not these cases involving patenting of TK and GRs by Thai companies in Thailand can really be considered biopiracy is linked to a much more complicated question of the state treatment of some unempowered and marginalised local Thai and ethnic groups.

There are, in this sense, both internal and external 'threats' to consider in relation to GRs and TK; however, the international elements of biopiracy draw the most attention and are perceived as the most threatening by far. However, an analysis of these aforementioned and a range of other reported misappropriations emphasises the persistent lack of a clear definition of what exactly constitutes biopiracy having clear effects on protection of the subject matter thereof. Amongst socially responsible academics, NGOs and policy-makers it seems there is a tendency to want to fight injustice for which international corporations are the ultimate target; but there may be some inequities or injustices of equal importance closer to home. History has proved that in a vast number of cases the state is not necessarily paternal of the culture, resources and rights of minority groups. State treatment of minority groups is often controversial and complex and remains so in modern-day Thailand for a variety of reasons.

5. Threats to Local Community Customs, Practice and Traditional Knowledge

Anthropologists and social scientists have noted a range of other threats to the local customs, practices, lifestyles, language, environments, culture and consequently the evolving and dynamic component of traditional knowledge.[16] The following table illustrates some of the threats noted to local practices and traditional knowledge of the ethnic minority tribal groups or 'hill tribes'[17] in northern Thailand. It would be colonial to suggest that their heritage must be preserved in some static form in time and space, for its own sake. Conversely, the continuation of practices, customs and traditional knowledge will likely be lost if nothing is done, and therefore uncritically

---

15 Y. Santasombat, *Biodiversity Local Knowledge and Sustainable Development* (Regional Centre for Social Science and Sustainable Development 2003); A. Ganjanapan, *Local Control of Land and Forest: Cultural Dimensions of Resource Management in Northern Thailand* (Regional Centre for Social Science and Sustainable Development 2000) details some of these customary laws in English and S. Chamarik and Y. Santasombat, *Community Forestry in Thailand: Development Perspectives* (Local Development Institute, Bangkok 1993) (in Thai).

16 In Thailand some of the most useful and recent references include (in English) include Santasombat, n. 15; Ganjanapan n. 15; and E. Anderson, *Plants and People of the Golden Triangle: Ethnobotany of the Hill Tribes of Northern Thailand* (Portland OR: Dioscorides 1993).

17 The term 'ethnic tribal groups' should be the preferred general term of reference of the Karen, Hmong, Lua, Lisu, Akha and other minority groups of northern Thailand due to the potential negative connotations some authors have noted associated with the term 'hill tribes'.

allowing cultural erosion or the effects of the market and globalisation to simply take their course would be highly irresponsible. Rather it is important to recognise that these groups have a limited voice for the assertion of their rights as individuals and as communities. A first step in the promotion of their traditional knowledge has to include means for these communities to actively politically engage, and represent themselves on how their customs, practices and culture should continue and evolve. This should have direct impacts on the knowledge and innovations systems that such groups continually develop. The provision of some basic rights to communities, for example the right of traditional local and ethnic communities to access (often traditionally utilised) forest lands, would be an instrumental step towards ensuring the continuity of these interlinked customs and knowledge systems.

Table 6.2 Threats to local practices and traditional knowledge of the ethnic tribal groups in northern Thailand[18]

Threat	Description
Some interventionist government policies	The Thai government has sought to intervene with increasing intensity since the 1950s in the affairs of the 'hill tribe' peoples for a number of reasons. These are: increasing concern about slash and burn agriculture in watershed areas; the cultivation of opium poppies, which was outlawed in the 1950s; national security and border protection with the Laos and Burmese borders; and assimilation with the dominant Thai population.
Tourism	Tourism has introduced a range of outside influences to local communities and has diverted them from local activities into market oriented activities like the sale of handicrafts and even tours.
Land shortages	Land shortages have been caused by an increasing population due to Western health care, immigration and natural increase. Also caused by encroachment of lowland agriculture into higher areas, logging and the sale of land to businesses and outsiders. This has had obvious effects on the ability to conduct shifting rotational cultivation and thus there is more pressure to clear new areas.
Land rights	The legal owner of most of the mountainous land of the north is the state, as administered by the Royal Forestry Department and the new Department of National Parks, Wildlife and Plant Varieties. Thus most tribal people do not own the land on which they farm and dwell and the securing of land rights, though often promised by government officials, is infrequent and sometimes impossibly expensive because of bureaucratic 'delays.' In other cases people are excluded from their traditional homes for the establishment of protected areas or development projects such as large dams or tourist developments.

---

18 Sources: adapted by the author with extracts from Anderson, n. 16, and Santasombat, n. 16.

Lack of citizenship	Many tribal peoples are legally entitled to citizenship, but often obstacles are created to deny them this coveted status. Two requirements are official house registration documents, which only half the tribal people have and individual registration documents (ID cards), which slightly more than a third of them possess. Frequently the local people cannot obtain these documents because, perhaps, they cannot prove where they were born, their birth was not registered soon after the event or they cannot prove how long they have lived in Thailand. Citizenship may even be blocked by officials who demand exorbitant payments for completing the process.
Poverty	The economy is shifting among the ethnic tribal people from a subsistence economy to a cash economy in which people are becoming more dependent upon the lowland Thai markets and travelling merchants.
Social dominance	Many dominant cultures are ethnocentric. This attitude leads to various forms of discrimination between competing cultures. This problem exists in Thailand where many Thai consider themselves to be more culturally advanced than the tribal people whom they feel are inferior subjects of Thailand. The clash of cultures may be particularly severe because the different groups are competing for limited land and resources.
Education and language	Most tribal children now have the opportunity of a Thai education as schools are constructed throughout the mountains of northern Thailand and Thai teachers sent to teach at them. This provides an opportunity by which young tribal people may integrate into the dominant Thai society; it also means better chances of technical training, better paying jobs and improved health. Yet this is also one of the most severe challenges to the perpetuation of tribal cultures and traditional ways. For example, school uniforms are usually required instead of tribal clothes, and students are instructed in Thai language, rather than their own, which was a great unifying factor among the tribes.
Loss of biodiversity	The main problem has historically been logging and illegal cutting operations in protected zones, as well as movement of lowland Thais to higher altitudes. This has been slowed significantly by greater government control.

If countries are serious about protecting TK for *all* of the roles discussed, and not just a static version of it that has been documented for the benefit of a few, then these day-to-day threats need to be addressed urgently. Due to the relative strength of civil society (people's movements, farmers' networks, academics and NGOs) in Thailand, there have been a number of legal developments for traditional knowledge protection and promotion as well as a sustained movement towards greater recognition of community rights.

6. Relevant Laws in Thailand

One consequence of the jasmine rice case has been that Thailand is now a proponent of extended Geographical Indications (GI) protection for products other than wines and spirits in TRIPS discussions and has considered amending its GI Act[19] to reflect this. During FTA negotiations with the US they have indicated such preferences, with the US responding that Thailand should instead utilise trade mark protection. GI protection of course only provides protection of the product name related to a geographic region of origin and the US negotiators have allegedly argued that jasmine rice covers too broad a geographic region to warrant protection. The Thai negotiators have indicated that jasmine rice is distinctly Thai and that trade marks would provide insufficient coverage for the breadth of jasmine rice producers and companies.[20]

In its Patent Act[21] Thailand has opted to exclude from patentability: naturally existing micro-organisms and their components, animals, plants or animal and plant extracts. They have therefore developed a sui generis Plant Variety Protection (PVP) Act[22] to comply with TRIPS requirements.

The PVP Act has built-in mechanisms for TK protection, PIC and ABS. The most pertinent section is Chapter 4 on local plant varieties. The provisions allow registration of plant varieties that can only be found in a particular locality in the Kingdom. It is designed so that a legal person, residing, commonly inheriting and passing over culture continually, who takes part in the conservation or development of the plant variety, may register as a community. The community must register the jointly conserved plant variety, with information about the methods of conservation, the names of community members, and a map clearly demarcating community areas. By registering, communities are essentially provided a prior informed consent mechanism which operates through the Department of Agriculture. A fund is also established for profit sharing in cases where people seek access to such varieties for commercialisation and there are any profits derived from the varieties. It might be assumed that the registration of such varieties including information on conservation methods and crop protection mechanisms may have some implicit protection of associated traditional agricultural knowledge as well as the plant variety by placing it broadly in the public domain. Some academics, NGOs and farmers group advocates are less convinced that the provision provides sufficient coverage for the knowledge extending beyond the explicit plant variety.[23]

Where varieties are not registered as local, they may still fall under the Act's umbrella for general domestic and wild plant varieties. Access to such varieties and benefit sharing arrangements are also required for these. In these cases prior informed consent becomes more problematic because of the broad range of potential custodians.

---

19 Act on Protection of Geographical Indications B.E. 2546 (2003).

20 Due to the confidential nature of the FTA negotiations, some sources cannot be disclosed; however, leaks of the negotiations are frequently reported in the *Bangkok Post* and the Nation newspaper in Thailand.

21 Patents Act B.E. 2522 (1979, as amended 1992 and 1999).

22 Plant Variety Protection Act, B.E. 2542 (1999).

23 For example: S. Vanakorod, interview by the author, 5 July 2005; D. Siripat, interview by the author, 29 April, 2005.

The Act on Protection and Promotion of Traditional Thai Medicinal Intelligence (1999)[24] was developed at the same time as the PVP Act to cover corresponding concerns in relation to traditional medicinal knowledge. It has various means for the protection of the different forms of traditional medicinal knowledge including the protection of formulas and texts on Thai drugs – essentially linked to copyright protection; provisions allowing the patenting of medicines; and complicated provisions for the protection of herbs and associated traditional herbal knowledge. Conservation of these herbs may be established under a Controlled Herb Management plan via the Act, which requires PIC for access to such herbs and herbal knowledge, but controversially the Act also provides for potential exclusion of people, including locals, from herb conservation areas. The Traditional and Alternative Medicines Institute has indicated that its policy is to be actively involved in discussions with local communities on such occasions with the possibility of co-management of the resource. This is an important policy because the disclosure of the medicinal effects of such herbs would not be known in the first place if it was not for the experimentation of such local communities. The Department of Health is currently trying to articulate this policy into the ministerial regulations associated with the Act. A fund established by the Act is also being developed in the regulations so that there are benefits shared with local custodian communities. At present the fund operates at the Department's discretion; however, no commercialisation and profit sharing arrangements have arisen since the development of the Act.

These pieces of legislation provide coverage for the protection of biological resources and associated traditional knowledge, whether it is medicinal, agricultural or ecological. The Acts are still relatively untested but have generally been well received by most stakeholders. There have however been some comments from NGOs, academics and local farmers' networks indicating that they are too focused on the business transaction aspects of benefit sharing and do not go far enough to adequately respect, protect and especially to *promote* traditional knowledge for its local social and environmental (roles one and two) rather than potential commercial benefits.[25]

7. Targeting Legal Treatment of TK and Biological Materials

An important point to note here is that there have been very few direct cases whereby foreign bioprospectors have sought access to *in situ* Thai genetic resources and associated knowledge in the past ten years. Due to much of the political controversy and the already established gene banks and research institutes around the globe, bioprospecting appears to have gone out of fashion as a means of research for biotechnology, especially for commercial purposes. Most relevant Thai government officials that were interviewed noted that recently there have been only a few bioprospecting contracts sought with the relevant authorities and these were

---

24 Act on Protection and Promotion of Traditional Thai Medicinal Intelligence BE 2542 (1999).

25 J. Compeerapap, unpublished interview, 30 June 2005; U. Yuwaa, unpublished interview, May 2005.

primarily for academic research purposes.[26] Indeed most of the 'biopiracy' cases that have been clearly documented in Thailand came about through the use of biological materials and TK that was already passed to gene banks or research centres and, some would argue, are already in the public domain. Thus we have to question to what extent the laws and related international provisions for disclosure and ABS are really adequately targeted, and what potential benefit they may in fact have for local communities, at least economically. It would seem in the case of Thailand that economic benefits would most likely to go to Thai universities, research centres and government bodies unless a community had already registered under one of the aforementioned Acts. Obviously it is not possible to generalise about all groups, but the extent to which TK holders in Thailand are interested in benefit sharing arrangements based on commercialisation of their knowledge or resources seems few. Even fewer actually believe that it is likely to happen to them.

What is being discussed internationally that may be of greater practical consequence to indigenous and local TK holders would be a mechanism for PIC. Such a mechanism, at least in theory, informs them, provides a means for these groups to make their own decisions, and gives them the right to consent or decline the use of their resources or knowledge. This, in essence, provides a form of empowerment that indigenous and local TK holders would not otherwise have and pays respect to their knowledge systems. Due to the lack of *in situ* bioprospecting being undertaken and with the more prevalent sourcing of GRs or TK from research institutes and government gene banks, PIC must necessarily be two-tiered. This means that consent must be sought from the national authority governing such resources as well as the original local custodians of the GRs or TK.[27]

Interestingly in Thailand, it appears that in the cases of jasmine rice, kwao krua and the marine fungi that some form of consent for the transfer of materials and knowledge may have actually been obtained; however, it is likely that the intended use and potential patent application on the materials or knowledge was not adequately *informed*, or contracts were insufficiently clear or transparent. It also seems that locals and TK-holders were relatively 'voiceless' and received little consultation in the original extraction and subsequent transactions. However the PIC requirement, although apparently useful for the respect of TK, is not necessarily easy to implement at least in an international agreement as has been pursued in TRIPS and the CBD. Exactly who is the provider may be unclear, for example in the jasmine rice case, where the genetic resource is widespread. There is some argument here for material transfer agreements in preference to a broader PIC requirement for mere practical reasons. These are becoming the norm for agricultural genetic resources, but it is yet to be seen if and how they could effectively work for related traditional knowledge and other forms of genetic resources such as medicinal biological resources.

---

26 These included interviews with officials from the Royal Forestry Department, the national biotechnology body (Biotec), the Biodiversity Research and Training Fund Project, The Department of Agriculture and the Department of Public Health, Thailand.

27 This has been clarified in the COP of the CBD, with some Member States initially questioning whether PIC only had to be sought with national authorities.

These suggestions about the moral and economic implications of TK protection seem to be broadly consistent with the findings of a questionnaire on TK and folklore (FL). The questionnaire was given to experts, academics, government officials and representatives of local ethnic groups at a strategic TK-FL meeting in April 2005 in Bangkok. The survey had a limited sample size of 25, but nonetheless it was attended by many of the key-thinkers on TK in Thailand. The survey found that TK-FL protection should be primarily aimed at preventing people from inappropriately taking advantage of TK-FL, followed by the 'restoration and promotion of TK-FL', and the 'preservation of TK-FL for broader social benefits'. Economic reasons factored in further down the list. One would then assume that these experts and representatives were less concerned with mechanisms such as ABS and more concerned with disclosure requirements and means to promote TK-FL.

The survey also indicated that the majority of respondents were concerned about the use of IPRs to protect TK (most thought that IPRs were insufficient for TK-FL protection), but where it is used they predominantly indicated that it should be to stop exploitation or use without permission and to protect personal or community rights that have created and preserved the TK-FL.

Protection mechanisms favoured a sui generis mechanism as the most accepted means of TK-FL protection and this was broadly defined. This was followed by databases, and then a few respondents agreed with contracts on access and benefit sharing.

In the comments section of the survey the experts and representatives also indicated that in cases where some form of TK-FL protection has been provided the rights owner should be the creator, developer or author (where it can be proved) as well as communities (where it is shared knowledge). In other words, there should be ways for entire communities to seek sui generis protection. There were also some responses indicating there should be overlapping systems of rights such as those provided by the Promotion of Traditional Thai Medicinal Intellgience Act which has some rights allocated to individuals, some to communities, and some to the state.

Overall these results suggest that a potentially broad range of mechanisms should be sought, with potential support for a disclosure mechanism, but also the need for unique non-IP TK-FL promotion instruments that recognise both the rights of individuals and communities as TK-FL holders.

8. Community Rights and Traditional Knowledge

Outside the options put forward in mainstream international discussions, Thailand has been developing other initiatives that promote TK, the most important being in relation to community rights. Broadly, community rights can be defined as 'group specific claims to a benefit that should be recognised and upheld by an authority (usually the state)'.[28] In Thailand the assertion of community rights relating to

---

28 C. Johnson and T. Forsyth, 'In the Eyes of the State: Negotiating a "Rights-Based Approach" to Forest Conservation in Thailand' (2002) 30(9) *World Development* 1591.

traditional knowledge and biodiversity conservation was enshrined in the 1997 'People's Constitution', section 46, which states that:

> Persons so assembled as to be a traditional community shall have the right to conserve or restore their customs, local knowledge, arts or good culture of their community and of the nation and participate in the management, maintenance, preservation and exploitation of natural resources and the environment in a balanced fashion and persistently as provided by law.[29]

Section 46 was regularly cited by local communities and supportive academics, NGOs and government officials as a source of protection for traditional knowledge and community rights. It provided an important and forceful means for greater involvement of communities in conservation and a whole range of other broader activities. Yet with the abrogation of this constitution under the current military administration, the maintenance of community rights is less clear. Sections 72, 79(6), 84(6)(7) of the new 2007 constitution all deal with the maintenance of natural resources, culture and folk knowledge, yet it is generally phrased in the 'national' context. Interestingly, Section 85 (2) indicates:

> The state shall promote invention or innovation, preserve and develop folk wisdoms, and protect intellectual property.

The Chairman of the National Human Rights Commission, Professor Saneh Chamarik, however, notes that the constitution does not provide a ready-made respect for community rights and people must struggle for its realisation.[30] The concept of community rights has been discussed by Thai academics for some time and is still being articulated and considered for more effective realisation. In other countries and regions, community knowledge/intelligence and broader community rights are also being articulated for the means of protection of the knowledge systems and local practices that provide the framework for traditional local innovations and TK.

In Thailand, the Community Forests Act (CFA)[31] assumes the primary means through which the collective rights of communities may be recognised and put into practical daily implementation. The Act represents an important opportunity for Thailand to balance desires for forest and watershed conservation areas, and the maintenance of the culture and livelihood of indigenous minority groups and local communities in situ. The primary emphasis of the CFA and its associated Community Forest Management Plans is on co-management of forest and agro-forest areas. It is an attempt to reconcile the differences between western scientific knowledge systems for conservation, and the traditional methods employed by local communities. It is true that TK can exist in various forms and environments beyond some stereotypical notion of the 'village'. Indeed, modern Thai farmers

---

29 Constitution of the Kingdom of Thailand, B.E. 2540 (1997).

30 Chamarik, 'The Community Right in Thailand' in *Right Angle*, Vol 1, 1 (Bangkok: National Human Rights Commission of Thailand, 2002).

31 The Act finally passed in November 2007: see J. Fernquest 'Community Forest Act Passed: Will it Really Solve the Problem?' *Bangkok Post*, 27 November 2007.

often utilise both modern and traditional methods of, for example, crop protection or fertilisation. However, community forest areas of Thailand are typically hotspots for non-scientific experimentation, innovation and traditional knowledge generation and preservation due to its linkage to local customs, rituals and practices, and a more holistic interaction with the surrounding environment. According to some of its original drafters, one of the main intentions of this Act is to allow the continuation of local customs, rituals and practices that generate and preserve such TK, and sustainably use and preserve biodiversity. The CFA in theory allows for communal land rights, the non-isolation of communities, co-management of natural resources with the state and appears to have also had a subsequent effect on the broader societal recognition of the importance of TK nationally and locally.

The Community Forests Act, however, went through more than 12 drafts with conflicting opinions over the conservation capacity of the communities, the over-romanticisation of TK, and the rights of individuals and communities that would otherwise have to be relocated. During these consecutive drafts, the community rights provisions contained in the Act have been continually diminished. Many community groups have been developing forest management plans in collaboration with forestry department officials in the interim. Although the CFA has now passed, the strength of community rights in Thailand still rests with the actions of communities to assert themselves as rightful custodians of their local environments, rather than through legislative means.

There have been a number of discursive attempts to link the need for recognition of community rights and broader traditional knowledge protection and promotion to work in the Sub-Commission on the Promotion and Protection of Human Rights as well as the Working Group on Indigenous Populations of the UN High Commission for Human Rights.[32] The sub-commissions have stressed the need for adequate protection of the traditional knowledge and cultural values of indigenous peoples, in particular, for adequate protection against 'biopiracy' and the reduction of indigenous communities' control over their own genetic and natural resources and cultural values. To date, parties meeting in the main international fora dealing with intellectual property have been hesitant to extend their work and negotiations to deal substantially with human rights. Furthermore, some local groups and Thai academics have indicated that any development of a broader community rights framework in Thailand would need to be much more grounded, asserting local values, customs and jurisprudence, than can be served by an international treaty of some form.

Thus articulating an argument for collective or community rights on the basis of inconsistencies between intellectual property and indigenous or human rights frameworks remain a challenge for those advocates in Thailand, the developing world, and indigenous communities. To date the most direct discursive link for the protection of local practices remains Article 8(j) of the CBD, and a PIC mechanism remains the primary 'rights-based' tool under consideration in IP and trade fora.

---

32 G. Dutfield, 'IPR Rules and Human Rights: is there a Conflict?' in *Science and Development Network Policy Brief* (2001, revised Dec 2002).

9. Other Mechanisms

Thailand also has other mechanisms for protection from biopiracy including several prior art registries or databases, administered by a number of government departments and research institutes in universities. These, however, are not always coherently organised and accessible. Some are little more than libraries and files of documents.

Members of the public have been urged to register traditional knowledge with a database in the Department of Intellectual Property; however, only 3750 have been listed since 2002 compared with more than 130,000 in similar databases in India.[33] Department officials have noted that this database has primarily received registrations relating to designs, handicrafts and folklore, rather than relating to genetic resources. The Department of Agriculture and Department of Public Health have databases on plant varieties, medicinal herbs, but it is unclear to what extent ethno-botanical information or related TK has been included in these. Databases and registries have also been regularly criticised for only capturing a static version of traditional knowledge in any case.

One Tambon One Product (OTOP) refers to a recently developed government initiative to promote local small to medium enterprises with somewhat of an emphasis on local culture. Essentially, as in the title, it seeks to focus the production of a tambon (local administrative sub-district) on one or a few specific products, cultural items or innovations that the area specialises in. The initiative has considerable merit, providing incentives and marketing for local products and consequently promoting local heritage and traditional products. One outspoken farmers' group leader noted that one primary reason for the loss of local agricultural plant varieties and associated TK has been its unattractiveness to consumers under the increasingly market-based system.[34] Another commentator, however, has warned that there has been a trend toward the production of trinkets targeting tourists, with little or no real 'traditional' or 'heritage' value. Furthermore it might be said that a focus on the promotion of products at a tambon scale, may in effect cause the diversion of production away from products unique to specific villages at the smaller scale.

The OTOP project has implications for the protection of folklore and handicrafts that may be associated with local culture, but has only to a small extent promoted traditional knowledge that relates to natural resources (although there are arguably a few cases whereby food products and herbal remedies have been listed as OTOP products). There is considerable scope for further investigation of the impact of OTOP on the preservation of traditional practices, local culture and folklore.

10. Thinking Strategically About Traditional Knowledge

There are many ways of supporting knowledge and innovation, the system that has emerged under the international intellectual property rights being just one. The failure of the modern IP system to incorporate limitations, exceptions, and development-

---

33 W. Ruamraksa, cited by *Bangkok Post*, 26 May 2005.
34 U. Yuwaa, interview, May 2005.

friendly provisions to date has been noted. Members are currently scaling back their ambitions for progress on Doha Round agenda items such as a disclosure requirement and ABS and PIC mechanisms. As the WTO Director General Pascal Lamy notes there is insufficient convergence among Member States for negotiating groups to put together 'full modalities' and requiring a 'recalibration' of expectations.[35] As has been repeatedly noted by representatives of developing countries, indigenous and local communities, the IP system may not be appropriate or compatible with their own, more holistic knowledge systems. It is confusing then that discussions continue to be centred around amendments to the IP system when other options are surfacing.

Much of the focus on the legal treatment of TK and GRs has arisen due to the misappropriation of these resources and knowledge. Biopiracy arguably does not directly erode TK, but rather has important secondary impacts causing disrespect, moral outrage, a sense of injustice and inequity. In consideration of the erosion of TK and the ongoing threats posed, it would appear there needs to be a more concerted effort towards TK promotion, particularly at the *national* level. The provision of some basic rights, such as participation in the conservation and sustainable use of natural resources, the ability to continue, conserve or restore customs and local knowledge, as well as rights to communal land tenure are a crucial part of this.

In Thailand the Constitution, the Community Forests Act, and associated community forest management plans provide the early stages of a framework to ensure traditional knowledge is respected, protected and promoted such that it endures. The potential importance of these initiatives is not to be understated because of the impact that they may have on continued traditional practices, innovation and experimentation, especially in 'TK hot-spots' such as agro-forestry areas.

Other instruments such as a disclosure requirement and an ABS mechanism also have important objectives. However, these should be recognised as having a limited focus on the implications of biopiracy or are based on a discourse that indigenous and local communities will ultimately benefit from the commercialisation of their knowledge and resources. This assumption is somewhat problematic and despite a number of emerging case studies, there remains a vague definition of what exactly 'biopiracy' means, what exactly needs to be protected, and whether communities are indeed interested in allowing the commercialisation of their knowledge and resources. Thus countries such as Thailand need to consider a policy model with multiple means and options for TK protection, promotion and respect. Internationally, community rights are currently an undervalued and ill-considered, but also a poorly articulated option, potentially due to the lack of policy space in the various international fora and likely due to a host of broader social, cultural and postcolonial factors at the national level. The role of academics and advocacy organisations is not to be understated here for their often uncritical focus on the pedantics of 'sexier' issues of disclosure and ABS in trade fora. PIC requirements should, however, be raised in terms of priority and judging by the host of voices representing indigenous and local groups, arguably the most important aspect for the respect of indigenous and local communities.

35　ICTSD, 'Members "Recalibrating" Expectations for Hong Kong and Beyond', *Bridges Weekly Trade News Digest*, 16 November 2005.

Chapter 7

Plant Genetic Resources and the Associated Traditional Knowledge: Does the Distinction between Higher and Lower Life Forms Matter?

Chika B. Onwuekwe

1. Introduction

The claim that patent, a form of intellectual property (IP) right, is a reward for invention appears untenable in the twenty-first century because of the thin line that currently exists between invention and discovery in pharmaceutical, medical and agricultural biotechnology. Currently, cell lines (plants and animals), genes, and seeds that were naturally occurring (existed in nature) are now patentable. Under this arrangement, inventive step – one of the fundamental bases for patent claim – is usually absent. Although invention is not synonymous with discovery, advances in modern biotechnology poses great challenges to the existing IP reward regime. A quick fix that appealed to most actors was an expansionist interpretation of local IP laws, especially patents, to accommodate this development. The United States was the first to blaze this expansionist trail with the passing of the Plant Patent Act (PPA) in 1930.[1] Initially, the PPA was unpopular because it created proprietary interest on something that was assumed to belong to no person. This has long changed. Both new and distinct asexually reproduced plants are currently patentable under the PPA. The case of *Diamond v. Chakraberty*[2] was the icing on the cake on this issue. This was the first case in which the US Supreme Court held that a living organism – a GM strain of bacteria – was patentable. For purposes of completeness, the United States congress enacted the Plant Variety Protection Act (PVPA) in 1970[3] for the protection of sexually reproduced plants.

The above developments make any justification of patents (or generally IP) on John Locke's labour theory of property a sham. Patents are now extended to biological discoveries (erroneously referred to as 'biological inventions') without any changes to most countries' patent laws. Part of the reason is the pressure 'to keep

---

1 35 U.S.C.A. § 161.
2 447 US 303 (1980).
3 7 U.S.C.A § 2321.

pace with developments'[4] in the biotechnology sector. Additionally, countries want to ensure they remain competitive in biotechnology development. The 2002 slight majority (five-to-four) decision of the Canadian Supreme Court in *Harvard College v Commissioner of Patents*[5] (otherwise referred to as the *Harvard Onco-Mouse*) rattled the biotechnology industry. The court held that animals are not patentable because they do not qualify as 'patentable subject matter' and for that purpose an invention under the Canadian Patent Act. While the dust on what to make out of this decision was yet to settle, the same court in 2004 by another five-to-four majority reversed itself in *Monsanto Canada v Schmeiser*. Here the court held, notwithstanding the non-patentability of plants in Canada, that a patent on a plant cell or a modified gene in a cell gives the patent owner the right to control what others can do with the whole plant. The court's reasoning is based on the fact that each cell line in the plant contains the modified gene. In other words, the value of the whole is in the part argument hitherto rejected by the same court in *Harvard Onco-Mouse* became the pillar in this subsequent matter. While the debate over the proprietary nature of PGRs and the associated traditional knowledge for patent purposes is ongoing, the distinction between 'higher' and 'lower' life forms for patent purposes compounds the issues.

It is on this basis that this chapter discusses the implications of the *Harvard Onco-Mouse* distinction between 'higher' and 'lower' life forms for developing countries, especially with the proliferation of biotechnology and genetic engineering patents. The chapter reviews the extension of patents in Western countries, notably United States and Canada, to life forms against the persistent refusal to extend patent protection to plant genetic resources (PGRs) and the associated traditional knowledge (TK) on the basis that both PGRs and TK on their uses are part of the common heritage of humankind. This is notwithstanding that ascribing the commons concept to these resources is contrary to Article 8(j) of the UN Convention of Biological Diversity (CBD), which recognises source countries' proprietary interest over them. The chapter contends that if the definition of patentable subject-matter could change to include items and things of discovery that already exist in nature and also 'life' forms, there is no legally justifiable basis for excluding a community controlled and improved resources, such as PGRs and the related TK, from proprietary protection. Since IP rights are a social construct, at least TK on PGRs qualifies as the type of knowledge known to a particular society similar to Eurocentric knowledge known to, and patented by a corporation. The chapter concludes that denial of patent or other equivalent sui generis IP protection to PGRs and the associated TK is not only inequitable, but also inconsistent with the rhetoric on diversity. It indeed makes the notion of building an inclusive rather than a divisive world a pipe-dream.

---

4 See CBAC 'Bringing Patent Law in Line with Biotechnology' (2004) 1(3) *Biotech Watch* 4.

5 [2002] 4 S.C.R. 45.

2. The Foundation of Property Right

John Locke was of the view that the main reason why people agree to unite and form a society is to safeguard against violation of their property.[6] In other words, preservation of property is the primary focus of any modern society – national or international. Citizens are eager to protect their property against internal or foreign aggression. As such, they willingly transfer some of their powers (mainly freedom, independence and equality) to an acceptable authority in return for protection of their lives and property.[7] If persons entrusted with governance are incapable of fulfilling this obligation, there is no moral basis to request obedience from citizens. In fact, Locke argues that such abdication or incapacity is one of the bases for dissolution of government.[8] Locke's labour theory of property is perceived as the foundation to modern property rights. Although Locke's theory was in relation to real property, it has been used to discuss proprietary interests that relate to intellectual property. For instance, an inventive step, which is one of the criteria for patent, fits with Locke's labour theory of property.[9] This is because, an inventor or the patent owner, would have spent some labour (including money) to bring the product to fruition. What Locke and those who rely on his theory misses is the fact that individual (or corporate-sponsored) labour over which a patent protection ensures is as good as those of a community. Moreover, the fact that a person has laboured over something does not *ipso facto* bestow on him the proprietary interest in the resulting product.

But it should be noted that Locke's labour theory of property presupposes a state of nature in which most things desired by humans are in the commons.[10] However, the notion of the commons in Locke's state of nature is virtually non-existent in modern political societies. Things that still exist in the commons today have been carefully delineated as such by sovereign states through appropriate treaties. Access to those items is supposed to be in accordance with the applicable treaty. The international regulation of the Deep Seabed[11] together with the Moon treaty[12]

---

6 C.B. Macpherson, *John Locke: Second Treatise of Government* (Indianapolis, IN: Hackett, 1980), 42–51.

7 Ibid, 52–3.

8 Ibid, 107–18.

9 Ibid, 18–19.

10 For detailed discussions around the 'commons concept': see C. Onwuekwe, 'The Commons Concept and Intellectual Property Rights Regime: Whither Plant Genetic Resources and Traditional Knowledge?' (2004) 2 *Pierce Law Review* 65.

11 See the UN Convention on the Law of the Sea (UNCLOS) and the Agreement Relating to the Implementation of Part XI of the Convention. A portion of the preamble that is interesting for this chapter reads, '*Desiring* by this Convention to develop the principles embodied in resolution 2749 (XXV) of 17 December 1970 in which the General Assembly of the United Nations solemnly declared *inter alia* that the area of the seabed and ocean floor and the subsoil thereof, beyond the limits of national jurisdiction, as well as its resources, are the common heritage of mankind, the exploration and exploitation of which shall be carried out for the benefit of mankind as a whole, irrespective of the geographical location of States'.

12 See the Treaty on Principles Governing the Activities of States in the Exploration and Use of Outer Space, including the Moon and Other Celestial Bodies, 610 U.N.T.S. 205.

are examples of international legal instruments crafted to protect items considered valuable to all humans over which no individual state should exercise ultimate and exclusive control.

Upon review of the two theoretical pillars of property propounded respectively by Locke[13] and Hegel[14] as a basis for a general understanding of American (real) property institutions, Justin Hughes[15] submits that these two theoretical perspectives also provide a justification for intellectual property.[16] He argues that intellectual property institutionalises proprietary interest over talent through a reward system enjoyed by the owner (or holder of the talent) for a limited period. With respect to ideas or talents, recognition of a person's property interest neither devalues the 'common' from where it was obtained nor breaches the non-waste conditions.[17]

While this chapter is not about the justification for patents, it must be pointed out that property rights is a social construct. In any society and in every generation, what is property and therefore subject to ownership has never been static. It changes with the development, understanding and willingness of the society to accept other property-owning structures. Changes in the nature of property rights are also driven by developments in technology. Hence, Nikolas Roos uses its public utility character to rationalise the basis for patents as legal monopolies.[18] Interestingly, Roos' explanation focuses on the acceptance by the society to 'grant temporary monopolies to investors' on grounds that it is proper.[19] Lastly, he acknowledges that this 'temporariness' makes patents an exception to the concept of property as originally formulated.[20] What this suggests is that property remains a power-relation supported by the institution of government.

3. Politics of the Global Patent System

The World Trade Organisation (WTO) is the international institution responsible for enforcing the global minimum standard of intellectual property established under the Agreement on Trade-Related Aspects of Intellectual Property Rights

---

13 Locke's property theory is based on what is commonly known as the Lockean 'labour theory.'

14 Hegel describes property as an 'expression of self' and his justification for propertisation is known as the 'personality theory.'

15 J. Hughes, 'The Philosophy of Intellectual Property' (1988) 77 *Georgetown Law Journal* 287.

16 Ibid.

17 Ibid, 300.

18 N. Roos, 'On Property Without Properties: An Inquiry into the Metaphysical Foundations and the Coherence of Property Law' in G van Maanen and A. van der Walt (eds), *Property Law on the Threshold of the 21st Century: Proceedings of an International Colloquium* (Antwerpen: Maklu 1996), 161, 170.

19 Ibid, 170.

20 For a detailed analyses of the English Statutes of Monopolies, 1623, with respect to patents in Australia and New Zealand: see J. Smillie, 'Patentability in Australia and New Zealand Under the Statute of Monopolies' in C. Rickett and G. Austin, *International Intellectual Property and the Common Law World* (Oxford: Hart 2000), 211.

(TRIPs Agreement).[21] The Agreement requires each WTO Member State to bring its IPR laws and regulation within the TRIPs minimum standard. It also empowered nations desirous of setting higher standards of IP to do so. Due to its history,[22] the agreement became a magic wand for the promotion of the North's hegemony on knowledge-based innovations. In contrast, developing countries became the obvious losers under the TRIPs system. Promises of technology transfer under the regime were not fulfilled and the core of most biotechnology development, such as PGRs and the associated TK, found in developing countries were excluded as patentable subject matters. It is no longer in doubt that PGRs and the associated TK are of great importance to modern biotechnology. Unlike the source countries of these resources, biotechnology-rich countries of the North were aware of the value in PGRs and TK on their uses prior to the negotiation of the TRIPs Agreement.[23] The choice to continuously attribute the notions of the common heritage concept to these resources is deliberate and directed at impoverishing centres of PGRs and TK despite the provisions of the CBD.

At the peak of the controversy over the proprietary nature of PGRs and the associated TK for patent purposes, paragraph 19 of the Doha Declaration was issued at the end of the WTO Ministerial meeting in Doha, Qatar.[24] The declaration directs the Council for TRIPS responsible for reviewing Article 27(3)(b) of the TRIPS Agreement[25] to 'examine *inter alia*, the relationship between the TRIPS Agreement and the Convention on Biological Diversity; the protection of traditional knowledge and folklore; and other relevant new developments raised by members pursuant to Article 71.1 of TRIPS.'[26]

The above declaration resembles a compromise by the North to subject Article 27(3)(b) to some review and in the process address the disaffection of WTO members from developing countries on the IP regime under TRIPs. Objection to Article 27(3)(b), particularly by the Africa Group, is because it left to the discretion of each country the choice of whether or not to exclude plants and animals from patentability. Furthermore, these countries object to the murky distinction in Article 27(3)(b) between plants and animals and 'essentially biological processes' for which they may exclude from patentability and micro-organisms and microbiological processes over which they are obliged to extend patents. Some other grounds of objection over this TRIPs provision that allows for life patenting (plants and animals) include economic, religious (playing god syndrome), moral, ethical and social biases.[27]

---

21 TRIPs came into force in January 1994, following a long and protracted WTO multilateral trade negotiation known as the Uruguay Round.

22 See P. Drahos, 'Developing Countries and International Intellectual Property Standard-Setting' (2002) 5 *Journal of World Intellectual Property* 765.

23 Jack Ralph Kloppenburg, *First the Seed: The Political Economy of Plant Biotechnology, 1492–2000* (Cambridge and New York: Cambridge University Press, 1988).

24 The conference was held between 9 and 14 November 2001.

25 The sub-Article deals with issues on patenting or otherwise of genetic resources.

26 Article 71(1) is on Review and Amendment of the TRIPS Agreement.

27 See J. Menikoff, *Law and Bioethics: An Introduction* (Washington, DC: Georgetown University Press 2001). However, the political reasons for this objection are often missed. There is a marked fear of bio-colonialism by developing countries, which may not be unfounded or

4. Criteria for Determining Patentable Subject Matter

The TRIPS Agreement provides the minimum guidelines for determining whether an invention qualifies for patent protection.[28] An invention is a patentable subject matter if it meets the three conditions for patentability set out in Article 27(1) of the TRIPs Agreement. Specifically, Article 27(1) requires that patents be provided for 'any inventions whether products or processes, in all fields of technology, provided that they are *new, involve an inventive step and are capable of industrial application*'.[29] Article 27(2) permits the denial of patents to certain innovation judged to be morally unacceptable by countries. In other words, the provision allows WTO members to 'exclude from patentability inventions, the prevention within their territory of the commercial exploitation of which is necessary *to protect* ordre public *or morality, including to protect human, animal or plant life or health or to avoid serious prejudice to the environment...*'[30]

Article 27(2) helps WTO members decide, in accordance with their culture and morality, what is patentable in their respective jurisdictions. The provision assumes that all members are economically equal and capable of prohibiting certain kinds of inventions from patent protection. The European Patent Convention (EPC), like patent laws of some countries, excludes morally unacceptable inventions from patentability.[31] In countries with Article 27.2 kind of provision, the Patent Commissioner exercises a fair amount of discretion on what qualifies for patent protection by making value judgments on each patent application. For instance, in dealing with contentious patent applications, the European Patent Office (EPO) applies the morality limitation in Article 53 of the EPC. It makes this determination through three tests. These are the balancing interests, unacceptability and public abhorrence tests.[32] In contrast, the patent laws of both the United States and Canada have no moral limitations on what is patentable. In fact, the United States law and approach supports the patenting of any thing under the sun and made by man. In the absence of such provision, the Supreme Court of Canada pointed out in the *Harvard Onco-Mouse* case, 'that the Commissioner of Patents was given *no discretion* to refuse a patent on the grounds of morality, public interest, public order, or any other ground if the statutory criteria are met.'[33]

---

far-fetched. *cf.* the minority judgment in *Harvard College v. Canada (Commissioner of Patents)* [2002] 4 S.C.R. 45; see also Canadian Biotechnology Advisory Committee, 'Patenting of Higher Life Forms and Related Issues' (June 2002): http://cbac-cccb.ca/epic/internet/incbac-cccb.nsf/vwGeneratedInterE/ah00188e.html (last visited on 1 August 2007).

28 See Articles 27(1) and (2).

29 Emphasis added.

30 Article 27(2) of TRIP Agreement [emphasis added].

31 See Article 53(a) of the European Patent Convention.

32 For a detailed discussion of this tests and their application by the EPO; see M. Bagley 'Patent First, Ask Questions Later: Morality and Biotechnology in Patent Law' (2003) 45 *William and Mary Law Review* 469, 519–25.

33 *Harvard College v Canada (Commissioner of Patents),* [2002] 4 S.C.R. 45, per Binnie J, (dissenting), par. 11 [emphasis added].

Confusion on whether life forms are patentable subject matters was the crux of the *Harvard Onco-Mouse* case that came before the Canadian Supreme Court. In this case, the Harvard medical college claimed a Canadian patent for an 'onco-mouse' entitled 'transgenic animals'. The patent was for a mouse genetically engineered by Harvard to carry a cancer-causing gene. The application sought protection for both 'the process by which the oncomice are produced and the end product of the process.' In other words, the claim was for the founder mice and the offspring whose cells are affected by the oncogene. It should be quickly pointed out here that Harvard had already obtained this same patent in both the United States and European patent offices. The Canadian Patent Commissioner allowed the process claim but rejected Harvard's patent application on the product claim. The reason provided was that the product claim is 'outside the scope of the definition of 'invention' in section 2 of the (Canadian) Patent Act.[34]

In *Harvard Onco-Mouse*, the Canadian Supreme Court shocked other biotechnology-rich countries in December 2002 when it held that the meaning of 'manufacture' and 'composition of matter' under the country's Patent Act did not include *higher life forms*. By a five–four majority, the court stated:

> the best reading of the words of the Act supports the conclusion that *higher life forms are not patentable*. ... I do not believe that a higher life form such as the oncomouse is easily understood as either a 'manufacture' or a 'composition of matter' ... I am *not* satisfied that the definition of 'invention' in the Patent Act is sufficiently broad to include higher life forms...[35]

By this judgment, the Canadian Supreme Court took a more welcoming approach to developing countries on life patenting debate. Indeed, the decision set Canada apart from its biotechnology competing countries in the North. The court acknowledged that while expansive interpretation may be plausible, it is not for it (as a court) to engage in rule making when the words of the Patent Act was clear on the meaning of 'manufacture' and 'composition of matter'. The court further pointed out that despite suggestions (including from the minority of the Supreme Court justices in this case) that the Canadian Parliament may want to encourage biomedical inventions, it does not appear that they would do so without proper consideration of the implications. According to the court:

> Even if a higher life form could, scientifically, be regarded as a 'composition of matter', the scheme of the Act indicates that the patentability of higher life forms was not contemplated by Parliament. Owing to the fact that the patenting of higher life forms is a highly contentious and complex matter that raises serious practical, ethical and environmental concerns that the Act does not contemplate, I conclude that the Commissioner was correct to reject the patent application. This is a policy issue that raises questions of great

---

34 Harvard appealed the Commissioner's decision to the Federal Court, Trial Division, and the court dismissed their appeal. Its further appeal to the Federal Court of Appeal was allowed by a majority of two-to-one. The Commissioner of Patents subsequently appealed the Court of Appeal decision to the Supreme Court.

35 *Harvard College v Canada (Commissioner of Patents)* [2002] 4 S.C.R. 45, par. 155, per Bastarache, J. (who delivered the majority judgment) [emphasis added].

significance and importance and that would appear to require a dramatic expansion of the traditional patent regime. Absent explicit legislative direction, the Court should not order the Commissioner to grant a patent on a higher life form.[36]

The sensitive mature of the *Harvard Onco-Mouse* case may have influenced the Supreme Court of Canada's cautious approach. The court toed a narrow rather than an expansive interpretation approach on what is patentable subject matter under section 2 of the Canadian Patent Act. This is contrary to the approach adopted on this issue by its close biotechnology competitors – the United States and the European Union – where the onco-mouse patent had been granted. Unfortunately, the above judgment of the Canadian Supreme Court was short-lived as a precedent on life patenting debate. This is because the court reversed itself by implication when it had another bite at the cherry two years later in *Monsanto Canada Inc. v Schmeiser*.[37]

In the *Schmeiser* case, Monsanto was the owner and licensee of the patent that discloses the invention of chimeric genes. These genes were tolerant to glyphosate herbicides such as Roundup and cells containing those genes. Monsanto markets a special kind of canola containing the patented genes and cells under the trade name Roundup Ready Canola. On the other hand, Percy Schmeiser grows canola commercially in Bruno, Saskatchewan. Mr Schmeiser neither purchased Roundup Ready Canola nor obtained a licence to plant it. Following a suspicion of infringement of its kind of Canola, Monsanto tested and found that over 95–98 per cent of Mr Schmeiser's canola was Roundup Ready Canola. Monsanto sued Schmeiser for patent infringement. At trial, the judge found the patent to be valid and allowed the action, concluding that the appellants knew or ought to have known that they saved and planted seed containing the patented gene and cell in addition to selling the resulting crop that contains the patented gene and cell. On appeal, the Federal Court of Appeal affirmed the decision but made no finding on patent validity. Upon further appeal to the Supreme Court of Canada, the court held by a split of *five–four* decisions, that Monsanto's patent (on a higher life form) was valid. According to the court:

> The respondents did not claim protection for the genetically modified plant itself, *but rather for the genes and the modified cells that make up the plant.* A purposive construction of the patent claims recognizes that *the invention will be practised in plants regenerated from the patented cells, whether the plants are located inside or outside a laboratory.* Whether or not patent protection for the gene and the cell extends to activities involving the plant is not relevant to the patent's validity.[38]

The above decision clearly validated gene and cell patenting of higher or lower life forms.[39] After all, as the Court earlier noted in *Harvard Onco-Mouse* case 'the Patent Act 'does not distinguish ... between subject matter that is less complex

---

36 Ibid.

37 *Monsanto Canada Inc. v. Schmeiser* [2004] 1 S.C.R. 902.

38 Ibid, 903 (emphasis provided).

39 Prior to this case, patenting of 'lower life forms' was not an issue as the Patent Commissioner would issue such patent application if it meets the criteria for patents.

('lower life forms') and subject matter that is more complex ('higher life forms').'[40] Since cells are patentable subject matter, it follows that direct products *or progenies* of such patented cells would automatically be infringed upon if used without the consent of the patent owner. It does not matter that the end product, such as plants, was not originally part of the patent claim. According to the court, '[A] purposive construction of the patent claims recognizes that the invention will be practised in plants regenerated from the patented cells, whether the plants are located inside or outside a laboratory.'[41]

It is important to note that the Supreme Court's reasoning in *Schmeiser* appears to have been influenced by Binnie, J.'s dissenting opinion in *Harvard Onco-Mouse* as follows:

> What it did (that is the oncogene patent) was to modify the genome of the oncomouse so that every cell in its body contained a modified gene. It is not like adding a new and useful propeller to a ship. The oncogene is everywhere in the genetically modified oncomouse, and it is this important modification that is said to give the oncomouse its commercial value, which is what interests the Patent Act.[42]

Although Justice Binnie's opinion did not persuade the majority of the Supreme Court in *Harvard Onco-Mouse*, it did in *Schmeiser*. On the same issues and similar arguments, the court reversed itself and held as valid a claim on whole plants that contained a patented gene. The court's approach in *Schmeiser* was expansive rather than narrow.

Unlike *Schmeiser*'s, the Supreme Court was critical in the earlier *Harvard Onco-Mouse* case of the expansive approach adopted by the United States regarding the meaning of patentable subject matter. Disapproving such a method even in the earlier US case of *Diamond v. Chakrabarty*,[43] where 'the majority attributed the widest meaning possible to the phrases "composition of matter" and "manufacture" for the reason that inventions are, necessarily, unanticipated and unforeseeable.'[44] The Supreme Court rejected a broad interpretation of invention under the Canadian Patent Act in a manner adopted in *Chakrabarty* or suggested in the *Harvard Onco-Mouse* patents by other competing jurisdictions – US and EU. Consequently, the court held that animals (including a mouse that was genetically modified to make it susceptible to cancer), seeds and plants were unpatentable higher life forms. This is why the *Schmeiser* case is perceived, and rightly so, as a huge somersault by the court.

In view of the forgoing and the proliferation of innovation in biotechnology, it appears that the three criteria for patents are no longer the core basis for patent protection. Extending patents to processes and products of biotechnology despite the ability of various life forms to self-reproduce makes mockery of the distinction in

---

40 Minority in *Harvard College v Canada (Commissioner of Patents)* [2002] 4 S.C.R. 45, par 47.

41 *Monsanto Canada Inc. v. Schmeiser,* [2004] 1 S.C.R. 902, par 19.

42 *Harvard College v Canada (Commissioner of Patents)* [2002] 4 S.C.R. 45, par. 68.

43 447 U.S. 303 (1980).

44 *Harvard College v Canada (Commissioner of Patents)* [2002] 4 S.C.R. 45, par. 157.

patent law between invention (or 'inventive step') and discovery. Both the European Patent Convention (EPC) and the Canadian Patent Act[45] clearly provide that patent may only be granted for invention and nothing else. The recent increase in the patenting of genes, mainly discovered or isolated from their natural surroundings, has changed this equation.[46] Fowler queries the basis for this development:

> Has the plant breeder who finds a mutation in the field (perhaps a flower with a new colour) discovered a new plant or invented one? Is the new plant patentable or is it simply a product of nature? What, then, is the nature of the inventive process associated with living things?[47]

While the author support each country's capacity to determine what is patentable in its jurisdiction within the framework of Articles 27(1) and 27(2) of the TRIPs Agreement, it is submitted that such a capacity will be of no value if powerful countries can influence what ends up as patentable subject matter in less powerful ones. For instance, the persistent opinion by commentators and policy makers from most industrialised countries that state-occurring PGRs and the associated TK are part of the common heritages of humankind is deliberate. There is no existing international legal instrument to support this bogus common heritage claim. It can safely be asserted that if PGRs and their associated TK are not useful to the powerful biotechnology countries in the North, the controversy this one-sided 'categorization' has generated will not arise. It is on this basis that this chapter calls for a better understanding of the different cultures, Eurocentric and indigenous epistemological knowledge respectively, without attempt by one to eclipse the other. The chapter urges biotechnology-rich countries to embrace diversity because it is more inclusive than imposing Eurocentric positions and cultures on developing countries through an international institution like the WTO. PGRs occurring within the territorial threshold of nation states and the related traditional knowledge do not fit into the commons paradigm.

---

45 The earlier (Canadian) Patent Act contained the word 'discovery' but this was removed by subsequent amendments to the Act. See Act respecting Patents of Invention, S.C. 1869, c. 11, s. 6. Cf. s. 2 of the Patent Act, R.S.C. 1985, c. P-4, which defines invention without 'discovery' as follows: '"invention" means any new and useful art, process, machine, manufacture or composition of matter, or any new and useful improvement in any art, process, machine, manufacture or composition of matter…'.

46 See for instance the US cases of *Diamond v. Chakrabarty*, 447 U.S. 303 (1980) and *Moore v. Regents of the University of California*, 51 Cal.3d 120 (1990). See also the Canadian cases of *Pioneer Hi-Bred Ltd. v. Canada (Commissioner of Patents)* [1989] 1 S.C.R. 1623; *Monsanto Co. v. Commissioner of Patents* [1979] 2 S.C.R. 1108 and *Re Application of Abitibi Co.* [1982] C.P.R. LEXIS 587. In *Re Abitibi*, the Patent Appeal Board held that 'patentable subject-matter includes microorganisms, yeast, moulds, fungi, bacteria, actinomycetes, unicellular algae, cell lines and viruses or protozoa.'

47 C. Fowler, *Unnatural Selection: Technology, Politics, and Plant Evolution* (Switzerland: Gordon & Breach, 1994), 226–7.

5. Plant Genetic Resources and the Associated Traditional Knowledge

Through its leading biotechnology countries, the North – mainly United States, European Union, and Canada – has signified its intentions to extend patents to life forms. The approach complies with Article 27.3, which makes optional the exclusion of animals and plants from patentability. What is surprising is the inability of developing countries to effectively utilise Articles 27.1 and 27.2 to elevate PGRs and TK on their uses to patentable subject matters in their respective jurisdictions. Rather, what these countries have done without success has been to call 'for the establishment of a new category in TRIPs that would protect their traditional-knowledge assets. Developing countries and LDCs also sought to restrict and even prohibit the patenting of plant and animals (life-patenting).'[48]

The incapacity to achieve any of these objectives reiterates the weak structural power of developing countries to at least protect existing and future TK about PGRs with IP, especially patent. It is more worrying that without the support of the biotechnology countries no such 'radical' extension may occur. Until there is a change, PGRS and their related TK are robbed of their proprietary quality because of the persistent notion in industrialised countries that they are common heritages of humankind. As argued elsewhere,[49] there is no legal basis for extending the commons concept to either state-occurring PGRs or their associated TK. This attitude compels source communities to freely make available their PGRs and TK about these resources contrary to Article 8(j) of the CBD. One would have thought that with the informal redefinition of the criteria for patents in the North where items that essentially existed in nature, such as isolated genes,[50] are now patentable, the controversy over the patentability of PGRs and TK would have ceased. Unfortunately, this has not been the case. Rather, developing countries have continued to scramble on the appropriate benefit sharing mechanism with which to enjoy plant germplasm continuously nurtured by their local knowledge.

The CBD was the first international treaty to effectively recognise the role of traditional communities in the conservation of biodiversity.[51] It created a regime that will facilitate access to PGRs in developing counties to biotechnology-rich North on mutually acceptable terms. By this development, the convention attempts to guarantee compensation to owners of PGRs on one hand, and ensuring uninterrupted access to those who need it, on the other hand. The preamble to the convention

---

48 M. Pugatch, *The International Political Economy of Intellectual Property Rights* (Cheltenham: Edward Elgar 2004), 165.

49 Onwuekwe n. 10.

50 See the European Patent Convention, which excludes objects of 'discoveries' from the patent regime. Also in *Funk Bros. Seed Co v Kale Inoculant Co*, 333 US 127 (1948). the US court rejected a patent on the basis that 'it was a discovery of a phenomenon of nature. Cited in Crucible II Group, *Seeding Solutions: Options for National Laws Governing Control over Genetic Resources and Biological Innovations*, vol. 2 (Ottawa & Rome: IDRC & IPGRI, 2001).

51 See G. Dutfield, 'Indigenous Peoples, Bioprospecting, and the TRIPS Agreement: Threats and Opportunities' in P. Drahos and M. Blakeney (eds), *IP in Biodiversity and Agriculture: Regulating the Biosphere* (London: Sweet and Maxwell 2001), 135, 136.

confirms that states 'have sovereign rights over their own biological resources.' The CBD's overall goal remains the pursuit of global equity. As noted by Dutfield:

> The CBD is the only international treaty that specifically acknowledges the role of traditional knowledge, innovations, and practices in biodiversity conservation and sustainable development, as well as the need to guarantee their protection, whether through IPRs or other means.[52]

The convention's two main objectives can be gleaned from its Article 1. The first is to conserve and promote a sustainable use of biological resources and the second, to provide for a fair and equitable sharing of the benefits arising from the utilization of these resources.[53] Article 3 rubberstamps the Charter of the United Nations and the principles of international law on sovereign rights of states to control and exploit their resources, albeit genetic resources, in accordance with their own environmental policies.

Article 8(j) recognises indigenous knowledge, innovations and practices in biodiversity conservation and demands respect from contracting parties as they access, exploit and use them. This provision is the embodiment of 'the dynamic and living character of traditional knowledge.'[54] Specifically, the Article requires signatory parties to:

> [R]espect, preserve and maintain knowledge, innovations and practices of indigenous and local communities embodying traditional lifestyles relevant for the conservation and sustainable use of biological diversity and promote the wider application with the approval and involvement of the holders of such knowledge, innovations and practices and encourage the equitable sharing of the benefits arising from the utilization of such knowledge, innovation and practices.[55]

Article 15 guarantees sovereign rights to source countries over their biodiversity. It acknowledges these countries' authority to grant access to genetic resources located within their territories.[56] It also requires the granting of access to these resources only on mutually agreed terms[57] and through a prior informed consent of sovereign

---

52 G. Dutfield, 'TRIPS-Related Aspects of Traditional Knowledge' (2001) 33 *Case Western Reserve Journal of International Law* 233, 260–1.

53 This objective can also be gleaned from the preamble to the CBD. Part of it reads, '[a]ware that conservation and sustainable use of biological diversity is of critical importance for meeting the food, health and other needs of the growing population, for which purpose access to and sharing of both genetic resources and technologies are essential'.

54 I. Mgbeoji, 'Patents and Plant Resources-Related Knowledge: Towards a Regime of Communal Patents for Plant Resources-Related Knowledge' in N. Islam *et al.* (eds), *Environmental Law in Developing Countries: Selected Issues* (Cambridge: IUCN, 2001), 81, 100.

55 Article 8(j) of the Convention on Biological Diversity.

56 Article 15(1).

57 Article 15(4).

proprietary owners.[58] In their analysis of the import of this Article 15, Utkarsh and Dasgupta stated:

> In conjunction with other articles, these provisions [that is article 15] require the recipient agencies to inform the national governments about the likely developments from the proposed research and provide for reasonable remuneration, transfer of technology on concessional terms, involvement of donor country scientists, locating R&D units preferentially in the germplasm donor countries.[59]

The underpinning of the CBD is the recognition of the (proprietary) rights of communities and source states as relevant to the protection of biological resources.[60] The convention realises that notwithstanding that it has placed an obligation on national governments to safeguard the rights and entitlements of their people to their traditional knowledge and germplasm, these governments still require the co-operation and support of advanced countries and their multinational biotechnology corporations to succeed in carrying out this responsibility. Accordingly, Article 10(c) of the CBD places a strong obligation on contracting parties by requiring them to 'protect and encourage customary use of biological resources in accordance with traditional cultural practices that are compatible with conservation or sustainable use requirements.'

Despite the CBD, the false notion in the North that PGRs and the TK about their uses are common heritages of humankind[61] has affected the proprietary status of these resources and associated knowledge. The erroneous attribution of the commons concept to these resources reduces them to a *res nullius*. It further makes them freely accessible and incapable of private ownership.[62] Lastly, the notion takes away exclusive control or ownership over PGRs and the related TK from local communities and places it in the commons.[63] The implication is a blatant disregard

---

58 Article 15(5).

59 G. Utkarsh *et al.*, *Protecting People's Knowledge in the Emerging Regime of Intellectual Property Rights (IPRs)* (Bangalore: Centre for Ecological Sciences, Indian Institute of Science).

60 Gaia Foundation and Genetic Resources Action International, 'Global Trade and Biodiversity in Conflict' (1999) 19 *Synthesis/Regeneration*: http://www.greens.org/s-r/19/19-10.html (accessed 1 August 2007).

61 Kindred *et al.* refers to this concept as 'a new legal category of territory': see H. Kindred *et al.*, *International Law: Chiefly as Interpreted and Applied in Canada* (6th ed., Toronto: Emond Montgomery, 2000), 398.

62 A. Low, 'The Third Revolution: Plant Genetic Resources in Developing Countries and China: Global Village or Global Pillage?' in J. Kinsler *et al.* (eds), *International Trade and Business Law Annual* (Newport: Cavendish 2001), 323, 330-331. Kindred *et al.*, n. 61, asserts that '[A]part from an unclaimed portion of Antarctica, there is no area of the planet earth which can today be characterized as *res nullius*' (at 397). With respect to discussions on the proprietary quality of traditional knowledge: see M. Battiste and J. Henderson, *Protecting Indigenous Knowledge and Heritage: A Global Challenge* (Saskatoon: Purich, 2000).

63 See S. Bragdon 'Recent Intellectual Property Rights Controversies and Issues at the CGIAR' in V. Santaniello, *et al.* (eds), *Agriculture and Intellectual Property Rights:*

for past and present labour of indigenous or local communities in conserving bio-diversity deemed essential for the maintenance of their PGRs.[64]

Source countries and indigenous communities reject the commons concept attached to their PGRs and allied TK on the basis that they have proprietary interest in them. They describe their interests in these resources as communal in accordance with communal proprietary structure practiced in centres of origin.[65] The structure endorses communal property right with the same bundle of rights implications as private proprietary interest in the North. On the possibility of community property right in TK, Gopalakrishnan argues:

> It is also evident that, wherever possible, it must be identified with the community, treating the members thereof as the holders of such knowledge if it is confined to the community. It is the notion of collective enjoyment of property by the members of the community that is reflected in these norms. The concern is to recognize it and to take measures to ensure that communities are involved in the preservation and development of it and that proper benefits are given to them in case of commercial exploitation by others.[66]

Considering that the diverse nature of the world necessitates the existence of different proprietary structures, the author supports a formal binding institutionalisation of the proprietary rights of source communities or states over their PGRs and associated TK within the TRIPs regime. The institutionalisation should contain an enforcement mechanism similar to that under the TRIPs Agreement in order to cure the present limitations of the CBD in this regard. It is indeed ironic and inequitable that the so called 'elite' products developed from PGRs and TK could be subject to private ownership when neither 'raw' or 'locally improved' PGRs, nor the TK about their uses, enjoy a similar proprietary protection. Besides epistemological differences, which the CBD attempts to address, there is no justification for this dichotomy. This is why I view the controversy as a clash between the liberal concept of property promoted by the North, and the communal property concept, widely accepted in most developing countries.[67] I concur with Dutfield that if developing countries could accept the Western-oriented system of patents, which is now institutionalised in the TRIPs Agreement of the WTO, there is no reason why their

---

Economic, Institutional and Implementation Issues in Biotechnology (Oxford & New York: CABI, 2000), 77.

64 V. Shiva, *Biopiracy: The Plunder of Nature and Knowledge* (Toronto: Between the Lines, 1997).

65 Communal property right is different from communitarian rights, which is one of the conceptual foundations of IP policies. For a detailed explanation on the evolution of communitarian rights and other two conceptual foundations of IP policies, see L. Cohen and R. Noll, 'Intellectual Property, Antitrust and the New Economy' (2001) 62 *University of Pittsburgh Law Review* 453, 453–63.

66 N. Gopalakrishnan, 'Protection of Traditional Knowledge: The Need for a *Sui Generis* Law in India' (2002) 5 *Journal of World Intellectual Property* 725, 729.

67 See generally W. Lesser, 'An Economic Approach to Identifying an Effective "*Sui Generis* System" for Plant Variety Protection Under TRIPs' in V. Santaniello, *et al.*; see also J. Watal, *Intellectual Property Rights in the WTO and Developing Countries* (The Hague: Kluwer International, 2001).

own concept of communal property rights to their traditional knowledge and PGRs should not be accorded equal treatment.[68]

Formally institutionalising the proprietary interest of source communities over their PGRs and TK will only provide legal teeth to what already exists. Its potency lies in the fact that source communities either on their own or through their governments can regulate uses through proper enforceable arrangements similar to the technical use agreement applicable for seed patents. When it becomes available, each country will determine how to realise the full benefits of any changes to the persistent notion that state-occurring PGRs and the associated TK are part of the commons.

Within the classical property concept, the insistence by the industrialised capitalist countries of the North that PGRs and TK are common heritages of humankind undermines the international law concept of sovereignty of nations and inviolability of territorial integrity. It is absurd that sovereignty of states over natural resources found within their territory is still extant in international law yet plant genetic resources occurring within states are treated differently. The attitude appears discriminatory and largely imperialist. This is particularly because the North's attitude is against the specific provisions of the CBD and the 2001 International Treaty on Plant Genetic Resources for Food and Agriculture (the Global Seed Treaty). Both instruments recognise the labour of source communities in the conservation of biodiversity through traditional knowledge and practices.

The non-propertization of PGRs as property capable of patent protection presents different problems to the various stakeholders[69] in biotechnology development.[70] For instance, one of the key debates on this issue revolves around the purported difficulty in attaching economic value to PGRs.[71] David Wood argues that lack of unanimity on the compensation to pay source countries for the use of their germplasm is because there is no 'workable mechanism for valuing germplasm'. He contends rightly that 'failure to define such a mechanism could lead to long drawn-out bargaining over access to germplasm'.[72] However, Wood failed to discuss how such a mechanism could be fashioned in view of the existing mutual suspicion between the North and South on this issue. The persistent denial of IP protection to PGRs and related TK occurs despite the treatment of these resources by multinational corporations (MNCs), governments and others as a property with some commercial value.[73] Indeed, the economic utility of TK was underscored in the recent report to the Canadian government:

---

68 Dutfield n. 51, 142.

69 These include multinational seed companies, farmers, indigenous and local communities, governments (developed and industrial countries) and environmental non-governmental organisations.

70 See the report of the World Intellectual Property Organisation (WIPO), 'Intellectual Property and Genetic Resources, Traditional Knowledge, and Folklore, available online: <http://www.wipo.int/globalissues/tk/index.html> (accessed 1 August 2007).

71 See D. Wood, 'Crop Germplasm: Common Heritage or Farmers' Heritage' in J. Kloppenburg, *Seeds and Sovereignty: The Use and Control of Genetic Resources* (Durham & London: Duke University Press, 1988), 274, 285.

72 Ibid.

73 See Battiste and Henderson n. 62, 242.

The commercialization of products derived from genetic resources revealed to researchers by holders of traditional knowledge has made it clear that traditional knowledge is an asset that could be of significant economic value to the community of which the knowledge holders are a part.[74]

It is therefore contended that the politicization of ownership of plant germplasm has shown that rather than allow market forces to determine the worth of these resources, the powerful industrialised states have shielded their multinational seed and pharmaceutical corporations from adverse market impacts that may arise from the propertisation of PGRs. After all, as Kloppenburg noted, 'the utility of plant genetic resources for the maintenance and improvement of the elite commercial cultivars of the industrial North is not mere theoretical proposition, it is historical fact.'[75]

Consequently, the effort by some indigenous communities to establish their own system for protecting traditional knowledge[76] is commendable but at the moment the various declarations lack extra-territorial effect until institutionalised by a binding international treaty. This chapter submits that even though the social (including the aesthetic and spiritual) utilities of traditional knowledge and PGRs are important to these communities they are nevertheless entitled to some form of compensation for the utilisation of their resources in biotechnology research and development. A compensatory regime in economic terms will largely be in compliance with the CBD's benefit-sharing provision. It will not diminish the aesthetic and spiritual connections of source communities to some of these resources. Besides providing a level-playing platform for access to these resources, source communities are under no obligation to accept any compensation for sharing their knowledge of PGRs with scientists and biotechnology companies. In fact, this solution provides traditional communities with an option in contrast to the current position under which neither their communal labour in conserving and improving PGRs nor their usable knowledge of these resources are rewarded.

---

74 Canadian Biotechnology Advisory Committee, 'Patenting of Higher Life Forms and Related Issues: Report to the Government of Canada' (June 2002), 20: http://cbac-cccb.ca/epic/internet/incbac-cccb.nsf/vwapj/E980_IC_IntelProp_e.pdf/$FILE/E980_IC_IntelProp_e.pdf (accessed 1 August 2007).

75 J. Kloppenburg, *First the Seed: The Political Economy of Plant Biotechnology, 1492–2000* (Cambridge University Press 1988), 167; see also S. Pinel and M. Evans, 'Tribal Sovereignty and the Control of Knowledge' in T. Greaves (ed.), *Intellectual Property Rights for Indigenous Peoples: A Sourcebook* (Oklahoma: Society for Applied Anthropology 1994), 43–55.

76 See for instance, The Mataatua Declaration on Cultural and Intellectual Property Rights of Indigenous Peoples, 1993; Charter of the Indigenous – Tribal Peoples of the Tropical Forests, signed at Penang, Malaysia; Kari–Oca Declaration and the Indigenous Peoples' Earth Charter, 1992; UN Draft Declaration on the Rights of Indigenous Peoples, (E/CN.4/Sub.2/1994/2/Add.1) (1994); Declaration of Principles of the World Council of Indigenous Peoples ratified by the IV General Assembly of the Council at Panama, September 23–30, 1984 and reproduced as Appendices 3–7 in D. Posey and G. Dutfield, *Beyond Intellectual Property: Towards Traditional Resource Rights for Indigenous Peoples and Local Communities* (Ottawa: IDRC, 1996), 179–208.

Denial of proprietary interest to PGRs and the associated TK for purposes of patent protection has led to accusations of biopiracy. The patents granted by the United States Patent and Trademark Office (USPTO) to W.R. Grace on the *Indian neem tree*;[77] to the University of Mississippi on *Use of Turmeric in Wound Healing*;[78] and to Larry Proctor of POD-NERS on *Enola (Mexican) Bean*[79] are some classical examples of the race for bioprospecting and the subsequent appropriation of TK and resources without recompense, acknowledgement or recognition by profit-seeking institutions and biotechnology multinational corporations.[80] As earlier noted, this development has been branded biopiracy.[81] The term 'biopiracy' is similar to what Karl Marx called 'primitive accumulation' which refers to old fashioned theft, expropriation, looting, enslaving, privatising the commons – without any substantial addition of value through labour or investment.[82] It also provides the underlying principle why developing countries are questioning the basis for patents, particularly on life forms and things for which prior art already exists in source communities.[83]

6. Conclusion

This chapter argues that in *Harvard Onco-Mouse*, the Canadian Supreme Court introduced into the Canadian patent lexicon the idea of 'higher life' forms. This presupposes that there is a lower life form. In modern biotechnology, the distinction between higher and lower life forms may be meagre. What bothers developing countries and other states sympathetic to their cause was the speed with which the subsequent case of *Monsanto v. Schmeiser* overruled the earlier Canadian position on life patenting. As it is, the Canadian parliament has no immediate need to amend the Canadian Patent Act as earlier suggested by the court in *Harvard Onco-Mouse*. In other words, the court's subsequent somersault enabled it to do what it avoided in the earlier 2002 case, which is approval of a patent claim over a higher life form.

The implications of these two Canadian cases go beyond the country's borders. While *Harvard Onco-Mouse* appeared to alienate the country's biotechnology sector, the subsequent *Schmeiser* case cemented the country's place in the league

---

77 See G. Dutfield, 'Protecting and Revitalising Traditional Ecological Knowledge: Intellectual Property Rights and Community Knowledge Databases in India' in M. Blakeney (ed.), *Intellectual Property Aspects of Ethnobiology* (London: Sweet & Maxwell 1999), 103. It should also be noted that the European Patent Office (EPO) granted W.R. Grace & Co. patent for the fungicidal effects of the neem oil (ibid, 112).

78 Ibid, 111.

79 See details in M. Blakeney, 'Intellectual Property Aspects of Traditional Knowledge' in P. Drahos and M. Blakeney (eds), *IP in Biodiversity and Agriculture*, 31, 37.

80 See the BBC report, 'Neem Tree Patent Revoked', Thursday 11 May 2000, http://news.bbc.co.uk/1/hi/sci/tech/745028.stm (accessed 1 August 2007); see also C. Raghavan 'Neem Patent Revoked by European Patent Office' (2000) *Third World Network*, available online: http://www.twnside.org.sg/title/revoked.htm (accessed 1 August 2007).

81 Shiva, n. 64.

82 See K. Marx, *The Grundrisse* (ed. David McLellan) (New York: Harper & Row 1971); see also K. Marx and F. Engels, *Selected Works* (Moscow: Foreign Languages, 1958).

83 Dutfield, n. 51, 142 (emphasis in the original).

of biotechnology nations. In contrast, developing countries lost an important ally in Canada as the voice of reason, strength, and support in their opposition to the optional life patenting provision in the TRIPs Agreement. This is even worse as the Canadian parliament may not be debating the issue any more. From all indications, the law-making institution feels comfortable hiding under the court's decision in *Schmeiser* on patenting life form.

The extension of patents to life forms in the North has increased the suspicion and tension over patentable subject-matter between the two sides – technology-rich countries in the North and PGRs-rich countries of the South. It will further open up opportunities to narrow the line on what aspects of life forms, organs, or any other parts of the human body are patentable if deemed commercially viable. With both the *Harvard Onco-Mouse* and *Schmeiser* cases in Canada, it may be only a matter of time before life patenting extends to humans and their progenies. Of grave concern to developing countries is the 1998 European Union Biotech Directive issued by the European Parliament. The directive advised that life patents, is proper except in relation to patents pertaining to the human body.[84] The combined effects of the Directive, the Canadian cases and the US liberal approach of patenting everything under sun suggest that developing countries are in the minority in rejecting life patenting of any form. At this rate, it may not after all matter whether the patent is sought for a 'higher' or 'lower' life form.

Despite these implications and concerns, the controversy over the patentability of PGRs and TK about their uses should be seen differently from life patenting. This is the approach developing countries must adopt at any future multilateral negotiating arrangement on these issues. Developing countries deserve not only recognition of their proprietary interest in PGRs found within their borders but also compensation for prospecting those resources. In addition, since the existing and evolving TK on the medicinal, agricultural and ecological uses of these resources are with the local communities where these resources are found, they also deserve recognition and compensation. The basis of that compensation could be fashioned within the existing IP rights regime or a mutually agreeable sui generis property right. As Matthews pointed out, 'because rights to indigenous knowledge are not explicitly protected in the TRIPs Agreement, the complaint has been that patents allow global corporate actors to appropriate medicinal treatments used widely in developing countries.'[85]

Knowledge, and indeed TK on the uses of PGRs, is no longer a public good.[86] Hopefully, developing countries are able to use the platform provided by the ongoing review of Article 27(3)(b) of the TRIPs agreement, ignited by Doha Declaration, to obtain a favourable bargain. The combined intentions of the CBD and the FAO *International Treaty on Plant Genetic Resources for Food and Agriculture* on

---

84 See the Directive 98/44/EC of the European Parliament and of the Council of 6 July 1998 on the legal protection of biotechnological inventions, art. 5(1), (2), 6.

85 D. Matthews, *Globalising Intellectual Property Rights: The TRIPs Agreement* (London & New York: Routledge 2002), 116.

86 L. Mytelka, 'Knowledge and Structural Power in the International Political Economy' in T. Lawton *et al.* (eds), *Strange Power: Shaping the Parameters of International Relations and International Political Economy* (Aldershot: Ashgate, 2000), 39, 43.

the proprietary status of PGRs and associated TK should strengthen developing countries' case as they seek to preserve their property right on these resources. If this were achieved within the umbrella of the TRIPs-WTO, developing countries would be better for it. Up till now, these countries have relied on non-legally binding instruments, conventions, or undertakings rather than on well-articulated international binding legal instruments for the protection of PGRS and the associated TK. The increased co-operation amongst developing countries (including indigenous communities that are geographically located in the North) to resolve this issue through the WTO mechanism is a good step.

PART 5
Agriculture

Chapter 8

Analysis of Farmers' Willingness to Pay for Agrobiodiversity Conservation in Nepal

Diwakar Poudel and Fred H. Johnsen

1. Introduction

Nepal is rich in diversity of crop genetic resources (CGRs); it contains more than 2000 rice landraces including wild relatives.[1] Conservation of such crop genetic resources has high priority on the conservationist's agenda. The Convention on Biological Diversity (CBD) has also emphasised the need for conservation of such genetic resources.[2] Although priority is given to conservation *ex situ* at national level, *in situ* conservation of such genetic diversity has been initiated to strengthen the so-called '*de facto* conservation' through the national and international agencies.[3] The *de facto* conservation is governed by the apparent attributes of the CGRs. The important attributes of crop genetic resources are the production, consumption, ecological adaptability, social, cultural, and economical diversity.[4] However, how long the *de facto* conservation will be continued is uncertain due to the land conversion and invasion of exotic species.[5] The present importance (the use value), and the existence or future values (the non-use values) of the genetic diversity are among the parameters affecting the *de facto* conservation of crop genetic resources *in situ*. Considering this, many efforts have been made to conserve these crop genetic resources either *in situ* or *ex situ*. The conservation of biodiversity particularly CGRs

---

1 S. Gupta *et al.*, 'Status of Plant Genetic Resources of Nepal' (1996) 19th Summer Crop Workshop, RARS Parwanipur, Nepal; D. Gauchan, 'Economic Valuation of Rice Landraces Diversity: a Case Study of Bara Ecosite, Terai, Nepal' in B. Sthapit *et al.*, (eds), *A Scientific Basis of* in Situ *Conservation of Agrobiodiversity on Farm: Nepal's Contribution to Global Project* (Rome: IPGRI 2003).

2 UNEP, Convention on Biological Diversity: Text and Annexes UNEP/ CBD/94/1. The Interim Secretariat for the Convention on Biological Diversity, Geneva (1994).

3 D. Jarvis *et al.*, *Conserving Agriculture Biodiversity* in Situ*: A Scientific Basis for Sustainable Agriculture* (Rome: IPGRI 2000).

4 S. Brush 'The Issue of *in situ* Conservation of Crop Genetic Resources' in S. Brush (ed.), *Genes in the Field: On Farm Conservation of Crop Diversity* (Canada: IDRC 2000).

5 J. Turpie, 'The Existence Value of Biodiversity in South Africa: How Interest, Experience, Knowledge, Income and Perceived Level of Threat Influence Local Willingness to Pay' (2003) 46(2) *Ecological Economics* 199.

could be possible in different approaches such as *ex situ*, *in situ* (household level) and community gene bank.[6] The conservation strategy could be designed based on the people's preferences for the different conservation methods and the value they assign to the genetic resources.

The value that individuals and societies place on the conservation is measured by their willingness to forgo the benefits of the alternative uses of the same resources. This can be reflected by a measure of their willingness to pay to acquire benefits or satisfaction from the resources.[7] Measuring the people's willingness to pay for genetic resources is difficult because no market exists for such resources. Economists generally choose one of two methods, either to use surrogate market, the revealed preferences, such as travel cost method (TCM), or to use the simulated market, the stated preferences such as contingent valuation method (CVM) to value the 'public goods' such as biodiversity.[8] The reasons for using the CVM are non-existence of surrogate market and the opinion that non-use values have to be valuated, which may elicit these non-use values.[9] The CVM tries to solve this problem by creating a hypothetical market. In the hypothetical market, consumers can express their preferences in monetary terms.[10] By deriving willingness to pay (WTP) values for the different conservation approaches and types of resources, these can be compared to provide information for policy makers on the relative values of the genetic resources to the societies.[11]

The study uses the contingent valuation method to assess the willingness to pay (WTP) for conservation of CGRs particularly rice landraces in three different conservation approaches. The study investigates and analyses how the people's WTP differs with the importance of the landraces, the perceived threat of extinction of the

---

6 M. Worede, 'Ethiopia: A Gene Bank Working with Farmers' in D. Cooper *et al.* (eds.), *Growing Diversity: Genetic Resources and Local Food Security* (Intermediate Technology 1992); UNEP, *Global Biodiversity Assessment* (Cambridge University Press 1995); D. Rijal, 'Concerning the Biodiversity Conservation, the Concept of Community Seed Banking: Process and Constraints' (Pokhara: Adarsha Samaj 2002); K. Hammer *et al* '*In situ* and On-farm Management of Plant Genetic Resources' (2003) 19(4) *European Journal of Agronomy*, 509; R. Rana *et al.*, 'Strengthening Community Based Organizations for Effective On-farm Conservation: Some Lessons and Issues from the *in Situ* Project Nepal' in B. Sthapit *et al.*, (ed.), *On Farm Management of Agricultural Biodiversity in Nepal* (Rome: IPGRI 2003); B. Jarvis and D. Jarvis, 'Implementation of on Farm Conservation in Nepal' in D. Gauchan *et al.*, (eds), *Agrobiodiversity Conservation on Farm: Nepal's Contribution to Scientific Basis for National Policy Recommendation* (Rome: IPGRI 2003).

7 UNEP, n. 6.

8 Ibid.

9 P. Nunes and J. Van den Bergh, 'Economic Valuation of Biodiversity: Sense or Nonsense?' (2001) 39(2) *Ecological Economics* 203; OECD. *Handbook of Biodiversity Valuation: A Guide for Policy Makers* (Paris: OECD 2003); I. Bräuer, 'Money as an Indicator: To Make Use of Economic Evaluation for Biodiversity Conservation' (2003) 98 *Agriculture, Ecosystems and Environment* 483.

10 R. Mitchell and R. Carson, *Using Surveys to Value Public Goods: The Contingent Valuation Method* (Washington: RFF Press 1989*)*; UNEP, n. 6.

11 P. White *et al.*, 'The Use of Willingness to Pay Approaches in Mammal Conservation' (2001) 31(2) *Mammal Review* 151.

landraces and different methods of conservation. The main purpose is to provide a basis for designing conservation strategies for crop genetic resources.

2. Material and Methods

The Contingent Valuation Method

The contingent valuation is a method of valuing environmental goods for which no market prices exist. This method involves setting up a hypothetical market, obtaining bids, estimating mean WTP, constructing bid curves, aggregating data and evaluating the CVM exercise.[12] The CVM has been extensively used to value environmental and natural resources in developing countries.[13] Therefore, CVM was employed to value CGRs in this study. While using the CVM, the recommendations by the National Oceanic and Atmospheric Administration (NOAA) panel[14] were followed wherever possible in designing and implementing the survey. In setting the hypothetical market for CVM, the evaluated programme was clear in its aims and consequences and the valued goods (CGRs) were well known and of interest to the people. Although the current trend in contingent valuation (CV) survey is towards the referendum formats using dichotomous choice[15] bidding game approach is also used for bid collection.[16] This study used open ended bidding game approach to elicit willingness for contribution. Two main reasons for using the open ended question are: first, the dichotomous choice question tends to give higher estimates compared with the open ended[17] especially for studies conducted in low income countries. Secondly, the sample required for the dichotomous choice method for statistical reliability is higher[18] which was restricted in the present study due to time and resource constraints. The form and frequency of payment was clearly explained

---

12 N. Hanley and C. Spash, *Cost Benefit Analysis and the Environment* (United Kingdom: Edward Elgar 1993).

13 S. Navrud and E. Mungatana, 'Environmental Valuation in Developing Countries: The Recreational Value of Wildlife Viewing' (1994) 11 *Ecological Economics* 135; J. Mbelwa, 'Improving Beach Management: An Analysis of the Role of the Government and Local Community in the Management of the Beach Areas in Dar es Salaam' (2002 MSc thesis, University of Norway, Ås).

14 K. Arrow *et al.*, 'Report of the NOAA Panel on Contingent Valuation' (1993) 58 *Federal Register* 4601.

15 Ibid; D. Whittington 'Improving the Performance of Contingent Valuation Studies in Developing Countries' (2002) 22 *Environmental & Resource Economics* 323.

16 Mitchell and Carson; Mbelwa; H. Dong *et al.*, 'A Comparison of the Reliability of the Take-it-or-Leave-it and the Bidding Game Approaches to Estimating Willingness to Pay in a Rural Population in West Africa' (2003) 56 *Social Science and Medicine* 2181.

17 I. Bateman *et al.*, 'Elicitation and Truncation Effects in Contingent Valuation Studies' (1995) 12 *Ecological Economics* 161; P. White and J. Lovett, 'Public Preferences and Willingness to Pay for Nature Conservation in the North York Moors National Park, UK' (1999) 55 *Journal of Environmental Management* 1.

18 Mitchell and Carson n. 10; White and Lovett n. 17; OECD n. 9.

to the respondents. The payment vehicle in the study was an annual contribution for the conservation programme.

The CVM is always accompanied with doubts about its viability because of various potential biases such as hypothetical bias, information bias, strategic bias, design bias (bid vehicle, starting point) as well as embedding bias.[19] This study was designed to reduce such potential biases as far as possible. Efforts were made to deliver clear and equal information to all the respondents, payment vehicle was clear, pre-tested questionnaire used and four different local enumerators were employed to reduce the biases. To test the response validity, the questionnaire was designed to generate information on demographic and social background and embedded biodiversity knowledge of the respondents.

The Study Area

The study area is one of the *in situ* conservation project sites implemented by Nepal Agriculture Research Council (NARC), Local Initiatives for Biodiversity, Research and Development (LIBIRD) and International Plant Genetic Resource Institute (IPGRI). It is situated in Kaski district in the mid-hill region (800m to 1500m) of Nepal. The topography of the region is ancient lake and river terraces in moderate to steep slopes. The area experiences high rainfall (>3900 mm/per annum) with warm temperate to subtropical climate. Mean daily minimum temperature of the coldest month is 7°C and the mean daily maximum of the hottest month is 30.5°C with annual mean of 20.9°C.[20]

The area is reported to be a hot spot in terms of crop diversity.[21] The major crop is rice, almost all the farmers grow this crop for which the farmers are maintaining 63 local landraces.[22] Nepal is the centre of origin for rice. Therefore, the study used rice landraces as an example of crop genetic resources.

Population, Sample and Sampling

The study population was selected from 12 hamlets[23] of the project area. Proportionate random sampling was done to draw the samples by stratifying the hamlets and the socio-economic status of the people.[24] The total samples were 20 per cent constituting

19 Mitchell and Carson n. 10; Hanley and Spash n. 12; J. Hausman, *Contingent Valuation – A Critical Assessment* (Amsterdam: North Holland 1993); Mbelwa n. 13.

20 R. Rana *et al.*, In situ *Crop Conservation: Findings of Agro-ecological, Crop Diversity and Socio-Economic Baseline Survey of Begnas Eco-site* (NP working paper No. 2/2000. NARC/LIBIRD) (Rome: IPGRI).

21 D. Rijal *et al.*, *Strengthening the Scientific Basis of in situ Conservation of Agrobiodiversity: Finding of Site Selection Kaski, Nepal* (Nepal: Lalitpur 1998).

22 Ibid; R. Rana *et al.*, 'Cultural and Socio-Economic Factors Influencing Farmer Management of Local Crop Diversity: Experience from Nepal' in B. Sthapit *et al.*, (eds), *A Scientific Basis*.

23 Hamlets are smaller villages or are parts of the bigger village, also called *Tol*.

24 P. Nichols, *Social Survey Methods: A Field Guide for Development Workers* (Oxford: Oxfam 2000).

107 households drawn proportionally from three socio-economic strata.[25] As each household represented a sampling unit, one of the household members taking the decisions in agriculture was selected for the survey.

The Survey and the Questionnaire

The instrument used for the study was a survey questionnaire. Local experienced enumerators were trained and employed to conduct the household survey. The open ended structured questionnaire was pre-tested with eight respondents outside the sample frame and revised before the administration. The questionnaire consisted of three sections. The first section addressed the household and the respondents' demographic and socio-economic information. The second section elicited the information regarding the resources (land, genetic diversity) and the perception towards general knowledge on biodiversity and particularly on agrobiodiversity and rice landraces. The third section consisted of the explanation of the study hypothesis and elicited the WTP for landraces conservation. An explanation of the subject matter was given before asking WTP questions. The respondents were briefed on the need of conservation using hypothetical market value of the landraces and asked whether they were willing to contribute for landraces conservation.

Three different methods of conservation (*in situ* household level, community gene bank, and *ex situ or* gene bank) were presented and discussed. Different modes of questions were used to assess the willingness to pay for different methods of conservation. The modes of payment were: growing landraces instead of high yielding variety (HYV) in one's own farm, indirect payment or contribution to a community gene bank, and direct cash payment for conserving their landraces in a gene bank (*ex situ*). The question modes were:

- *Mode 1*: Are you willing to grow local landraces for the sake of conservation instead of growing your preferred variety? If yes, state the area (*ropani*),[26] and expected yield of those conserved varieties (n=6) in your own land. Please provide the productivity and market price of your preferred landrace or variety.
- *Mode 2*: Are you willing to contribute in cash or kind if you are asked for conservation of landraces in community seed bank or gene bank? If yes,

---

25 The socio-economic strata (rich, medium and poor) were identified using farmers' own criteria. The main parameters for the categorisation were food self-sufficiency of households, landholdings, government services, business, house and homestead properties, possessing house and/ or land in major cities (Rana *et al*., n. 22). People who had more than 0.75 ha of land, were almost food self-sufficient, had permanent monthly income sources or remittances, had land and house in cities, were considered socio-economically 'rich'. Similarly, people having 0.25 to 0.75 ha of land, more than six months' food self-sufficiency, and off-farm income sources were considered 'medium category' and people with less than 0.25 ha of land, less than six months' food self-sufficiency, and working as casual labourers were categorised as 'poor'.

26 A local unit for the area measurement (20 *ropani* = 1 hectare).

state the amount of labour (man-days), area (*ropani*), and inputs (chemical fertilisers, pesticides, manure or seed).

- *Mode 3*: Are you willing to pay cash, if you are asked to pay for government or NGOs, to conserve local landraces in an *ex situ* /gene bank? If yes, how much will you be willing to pay monthly? Rs 70, 60, 50 40 30 25 20 15 10 …

WTP bids were then calculated from the willingness for contribution using specific procedures for the respective methods of conservation.

WTP Bids Calculation, Data Analysis and Model Specification

The data were entered in the Excel worksheet and WTP bids were calculated. The individuals' WTP bids for conservation of landraces *in situ* at household level were calculated using the following equation. During data analysis, 14 protest bids were omitted from the data set. These bids contained negative values due to higher expected market price of the said landraces.

$$WTP = \Sigma(AiYiPi) - \sum_{i=1}^{N} (aiyipi) \tag{1}$$

Where, WTP = total willingness to pay for *in situ* conservation of landraces, Ai = total area for conservation = $a_1 + a_2 \ldots a_n$, Yi = yield of preferred variety, Pi = price of the preferred variety, ai = area for conservation of landraces i (I = 1 to n where, n = 6), yi = expected yield of landrace i, and pi = price for the landrace i.

The individuals' WTP bids for conservation of landraces in community gene bank were calculated using equation 2. None of the WTP bids were protest bids and all were used in the analysis.

$$WTP = [L*Pl + A *Pa + F + P + M* Pm + S* Ps] \tag{2}$$

Where, L = labour contribution in man-days, A = area contribution in hectare, F = chemical fertiliser contribution in cash, P = chemical pesticides contribution in cash, M = manure contribution (*doko*[27]), S = seed contribution in kg, Pl = labour price, Pa = price of land renting, Pm = price of manure, and Ps = price of seed.

In case of cash contribution for the *ex situ*, the WTP bids were calculated using equation 3. None of the WTP bids were protest bids and all the bids were used in the analysis.

$$WTP = [\sum_{i=1}^{N} (Xi) / N] *12 \tag{3}$$

---

27 A basket-like structure, which is locally used to carry the manure from the farm to the field. One *doko* costs about Rs 20 (USD 1 = Rs 73).

Where, WTP = Average willingness to pay per landrace per year, Xi = amount paid to conserve landrace i (i = 1 to n), n = number of landraces (max 6), N = total number of landraces considered for conservation.

The WTP bids were then transferred to Minitab statistical software for analysis.[28] Mean WTP, standard deviation, confidence interval (CI), and the relationship between WTP and categorical variables were analysed using descriptive statistics, 2-sample t-test and ANOVA. The WTP bids were also regressed with various explanatory variables. The bid function was arrived at using general regression analysis, starting from all the potential explanatory variables, removing the non-significant, re-estimating the model and so on until all remaining variables were significant at 95 per cent level.[29]

The WTP function is:

$$WTP = \beta_0 + \beta_1 X_1 + \beta_2 X_2 + \beta_3 X_3 + \ldots + \beta_n X_n + \varepsilon_i \qquad (4)$$

Where, WTP = farmers willingness to contribute for landraces conservation, β_0 = constant, $\beta_1 - \beta_n$ = coefficients, $X_1 - X_n$ =variables contributing in WTP, and εi = random error $\sim N$ (0, 1).

3. Results and Discussion

Sample Characteristics

The demographic data obtained from the 107 households were proportionately stratified within socio-economic status as presented in Table 8.1. The mean age of the respondents was 45 years and the respondents were nearly evenly divided between males and females. Almost 46 per cent of the respondents were either illiterate or had no schooling knowledge and less than 5 per cent had attended university-level education. The average household size was 6.5 which is higher than the national average at 5.44,[30] but exactly the same as reported by Rana *et al.*[31] The mean household income was US $1156 in the study area, which is slightly lower than the national level.[32] The average land capital of the respondents was 0.90 ha which is almost equal to the national average 0.96 ha (p>0.05).[33] The average number land parcels was 7.75 in the study area, which is very high compared to the national average 4.0 (p<0.01).[34] The average food self-sufficiency was 9.95 months. It was found that 25 per cent of the households produced food for ≤6 months, whereas 25

28 MINITAB statistical software, MINITAB Inc.

29 B. Horton, 'Evaluating Non-user Willingness to Pay for a Large-scale Conservation Programme in Amazonia: a UK/Italian Contingent Valuation Study' (2003) 30(2) *Environmental Conservation* 139.

30 Central Bureau of Statistics, *Statistical Year Book of Nepal* (Kathmandu: 2003).

31 Rana *et al.*, n. 22.

32 Central Bureau of Statistics n. 29.

33 Central Bureau of Statistics n. 29; Rana n. 20.

34 Central Bureau of Statistics n. 29; Rana n. 20.

Patenting Lives

per cent produced food sufficient for ≥12 months. The average number of landraces (excluding modern varieties) grown was 3.2.

The findings indicate that the land holdings, annual income, literacy rate and food sufficiency months are greater with the resource rich people than the poor in the study site. The number of landraces grown by richer people is higher as compared to the poor people.

The sample data are almost representative of the study area with respect to the gender, household size, the educational status of people, the annual income and landholdings of the people, although the average diversity of landraces is higher than in *terai* and high hills of the country.[35]

Table 8.1 Characteristics of respondents by socio-economic strata (n=107)

Characteristics	Rich	Medium	Poor	Total
Age (years; mean)	49	41	45	45
Gender (no; %)				
Male	22 (20.5)	23 (21.5)	8(7.5)	53 (49.5)
Female	19 (17.8)	17 (15.9)	18(16.8)	54 (50.5)
Education of the respondents (number, %)				
Illiterates	4 (3.7)	3 (2.8)	9 (8.5)	16 (15)
Literates	10 (9.3)	12 (11.3)	11 (10.4)	33 (31)
Primary	8 (7.5)	6 (5.6)	2 (1.9)	16 (15)
Secondary	10 (9.3)	14 (13.0)	4 (3.7)	28 (26)
Higher secondary	7 (6.5)	3 (2.5)	0 (0)	10 (9)
University	2 (2)	2 (2)	0 (0)	4 (4)
Household size (mean)	7.3	5.8	6.3	6.5
Household income US$ (mean)	1341	1193	820	1156
Landholdings (ha) (mean)	1.29	0.81	0.42	0.90
Parcels of land (mean)	10.1	7.79	4.23	7.75
Food self-sufficiency months (mean)	12.51	9.91	6.19	9.95
Number of varieties grown (mean)	4.02	2.9	2.5	3.2
Knowledge on agrobiodiversity (number, %)				
Yes	31 (29)	30 (28)	11 (10.3)	72 (67.3)
No	10 (9.3)	10 (9.3)	15 (14.1)	35 (32.7)

35 C. Paudel *et al.*, 'Agro-ecosystem Factors for *in Situ* Conservation of Agrobiodiversity in Different Eco-zones of Nepal' in B. Sthapit *et al.*, (eds), *A Scientific Basis*; Rana *et al.*, n. 22.

Farmers' Knowledge of Biodiversity

Since the study was conducted in the *in situ* conservation project area the farmers of the study area have been found very much informed by the project on the need for conservation. They were familiar with the term 'agrobiodiversity' and different methods of biodiversity conservation. The majority (67 per cent) of the farmers were familiar with the concept of agrobiodiversity. Most of the farmers explained the use value of the rice landraces relating to conservation. Although some farmers (12 per cent) perceived that landraces must be conserved for the future generations need (intrinsic value), most of them acknowledged the need of the conservation due to ecological, direct use and option use values of landraces. This resembles the findings of Rana *et al.* regarding the factors influencing the conservation and maintenance of landraces on farm. Farmers have been very enthusiastic to explain the need for landraces conservation and all the respondents participated in explaining why the local rice landraces should be conserved. The farmers' perceived knowledge on the 'need for rice landraces conservation' is presented in Table 8.2.

Table 8.2 Farmers' reasons for conservation of rice landraces in Kaski Nepal

Need for landraces conservation	Responses (n = 107)	
	n	%
Diverse adaptability	64	59.8
Local varieties have diverse taste, use, straw need and importance	57	53.3
Possibility of extinction from the habitat	33	30.8
Medicinal values	27	25.2
Possesses cultural value	23	21.5
These have yield stability over years	13	12.1
Security for future	12	11.2
Improved variety have no guarantee of yield	10	9.3
Local landraces are suitable in adverse climatic conditions such as epidemic etc	8	7.5
Need for choice in seed in future	7	6.5
For improvement of new varieties	6	5.6
The basis for subsistence are landraces	2	1.8
These should be conserved because of international or global importance	1	0.9
These are being grown from ancient time	1	0.9

Willingness to Pay for Conservation

The people's WTP for conservation of crop genetic diversity is analysed with regards to the importance of the landraces to the farmers, the possible threat of extinction of the landraces/genetic diversity and the different methods of conservation. Since the genetic diversity, in the Nepalese context, is considered as a public good (neither having rivalry in consumption nor excludability), the analysis presents what is the interest of the people for the conservation of these public goods, how they prefer to conserve and which genetic resources they wish to conserve.

Importance of Landraces

Grain quality, market price, yield attributes, and ecological adaptability of crop landraces determine the people's participation in conservation[36] and thereby influence willingness to contribute. The direct use value of landraces is the main influences on farmers' willingness to pay. The reasons behind the different levels of willingness to contribute for the crop landraces are their socio-cultural importance, the agro-ecological diversity and the direct consumption values.[37] The people's WTP has been analysed for the grain quality as one of the important attributes of the rice landraces.

The landraces were categorised in three different grain qualities based on the farmers' preferences. The basis of categorisation was the grain size, cooking quality, grain stickiness and the market price. The fine grain landraces are those that have very good cooking quality, high price and preferably aromatic in quality. The medium quality grains have medium cooking quality, medium price and no aroma, while the coarse grain quality has relatively poor cooking quality and a low market price. The different landraces categorised based on the above criteria are listed in Table 8.3.

Table 8.3 The major rice landraces under different types of grain quality

Types of landraces		
Fine grain quality	Medium grain quality	Coarse grain quality
Jethobudo	Ekle	Sanomadhise
Anadi	Gurdi	Madhise
Panhele	Jarneli	Manamuri
Bayarni	Gauriya	Ramsali
Jhinuwa	Flyankote	Jhauri
	Lame	Mansara

The analysis shows that the WTP for different grain quality rice landraces was different for both *in situ* and *ex situ* conservation. The mean willingness for contribution of land for *in situ* conservation of fine and medium grain quality landraces was significantly higher than the coarse grain (p<0.01), and for *ex situ* conservation the mean willingness to pay for fine and medium quality landraces was also higher than for the coarse grain types (p<0.01) (Table 8.4).

---

36 Brush n. 4.
37 Rana *et al.*, n. 22.

Table 8.4 The mean contribution of land (ha) for in situ conservation and mean willingness to pay (USD) for ex situ conservation to different grain quality landraces

	Fine grain type landraces		Medium grain type landraces		Coarse grain type landraces	
	Contribution of land for *in situ* (ha)	Cash ($) payment for *ex situ*	Contribution of land for *in situ* (ha)	Cash ($) payment for *ex situ*	Contribution of land for *in situ* (ha)	Cash ($) payment for *ex situ*
Mean	0.01275	2.337	0.01088	2.22	0.003776	1.796
95% CI	0.0096–0.016	2.1–2.6	0.0085–0.0132	2.0–2.4	0.0027–0.0049	1.5–2.1
No.	107	102	107	103	107	82

The willingness to pay for the different grain quality landraces was also affected by the socio-economic status of the people (Table 8.5). The contribution of land for conservation was significantly lower for fine grain landraces by poor people than for medium and rich people, whereas the poor's cash contribution was significantly less for medium grain landraces than that of the medium and rich. For coarse grain both rich and poor people expressed significantly lower willingness to pay compared to the medium income group. The reason is that poor people cannot afford to grow low yielding fine grain quality and, therefore, they are less willing to contribute land compared to the rich people. Similarly, the richer people have more land to grow fine grain rice and they do not prefer the coarse grain, therefore their contribution is less. On the other hand the poor people also consider the fine grain rice landrace important and, therefore, they are willing to conserve them in a gene bank. Interestingly, the poor people do not contribute more cash for conservation in gene banks because this conservation occurs *in situ*, growing in their own field.

Table 8.5 Mean willingness to pay for different grain quality of rice landraces by different socio-economic status of the people for in situ and ex situ conservation

	Fine grain type landraces		Medium grain type landraces		Coarse grain type landraces	
	Contribution of land for *in situ* (ha)	Cash ($) payment for *ex situ*	Contribution of land for *in situ* (ha)	Cash ($) payment for *ex situ*	Contribution of land for *in situ* (ha)	Cash ($) payment for *ex situ*
Rich	0.01810	2.471	0.01187	2.448	0.004479	1.808***
Medium	0.01103	2.388	0.01174	2.298	0.003907	2.915
Poor	0.00697**	2.035	0.00799	1.763**	0.002686	1.125***

** P<0.05, and *** p<0.01

Perceived Threats of Extinction

Analysis was conducted to learn whether the perceived threat of extinction of the genetic resources influences the farmers' WTP. The landraces of rice were categorised in four cells based on the area for cultivation and number of farmers cultivating the landraces in the community[38] as shown in Table 8.6. The landraces grown by many people in large or small areas, or grown by few farmers in large areas, are identified as abundant landraces and these are not threatened by extinction but the landraces grown by 'few farmers in small area' are under threat of extinction, which requires prompt action for conservation.

Table 8.6 The landraces identified as abundant and threatened in the community based on the four cell analysis suggested by Jarvis et al.[39] and Bajracharya et al.[40]

Growing area	Number of households	
	Many farmers (>11)	Few farmers (<11)
Large (>1.2 ha)	*Abundance* Ekle, Madhise Jethobudo, Mansara Panhele, Gurdi	*Abundance* Sano madhise
Small (< 1.2 ha)	*Abundance* Anadi, Bayarni, Jarneli	*Threatened* Gauriya, Flyankote, Lame Manamuri, Ramsali, Jhauri, Jhinuwa

Farmers' willingness to pay for the conservation of rice landraces in a gene bank (*ex situ*) showed no significant difference ($p>0.10$), whether the landraces are abundant (grown by many farmers or few farmers in large area) or rare and almost extinct (grown by few farmers in small area). However, the contribution of area for conservation *in situ* differs significantly ($p<0.01$). The area contribution was higher for those landraces, which are presently grown by many farmers in a larger area than for the other three categories (Table 8.7).

---

38 Jarvis *et al*. n. 3; J. Bajracharya 'Assessment of Local Crop Genetic Diversity in Nepal' in D. Gauchan *et al*.

39 Jarvis *et al*. n. 3.

40 Bajracharya *et al*. n. 37.

**Table 8.7 The mean contribution of land (ha) for in situ conservation
and mean willingness to pay (USD) for ex situ conservation
for abundant and threatened rice landraces in the community**

	Many farmers (>11)		Few farmers (<11)	
	Area (ha) for *in situ*	Cash ($) for *ex situ*	Area (ha) for *in situ*	Cash ($) for *ex situ*
Large area (>1.2 ha)				
Mean	0.01783	2.30	0.007	2.00
95% CI	0.0138–0.0219	2.07–2.52	0.005–0.009	1.77–2.24
N	94	98	85	85
Small area (< 1.2 ha)				
Mean	0.00407	2.13	0.00643	2.01
95% CI	0.0033–0.0048	1.89–2.38	0.0037–0.009	1.65–2.37
N	94	99	42	40

The analysis shows that farmers are not willing to contribute to conserve CGRs which are rare and prone to extinction, but the strategy of farmers for contribution is more influenced by the importance of CGRs' use values (cultural, social, ecological) than their non-use or option (intrinsic or existence) values.

Methods of Conservation

The different methods of conservation have influenced the people's willingness to pay for crop genetic resources. Three different methods of conservation (*community gene bank, in situ* at household level and *ex situ*) were discussed with farmers and they were asked for their contribution for conservation.

Mean WTP per annum: The mean willingness for contribution to conserve the genetic resources particularly the rice landraces in three different methods of conservation was significantly different (p<0.05). The highest WTP was for conservation in a community bank, where all the farmers enthusiastically agreed to participate and provide land, labour or cash, or all three. The mean WTP for community conservation was four times higher than *in situ* household level conservation and eight times higher than the *ex situ* conservation (Table 8.8). This means that farmers perceived the community gene bank conservation as the appropriate method for CGRs conservation. Through the *in situ* community conservation, farmers not only conserve, but also utilise and have access to and control over, all the CGRs.

Table 8.8 Mean WTP per annum per household for landrace conservation in three different methods

	In situ at household level	Community gene bank	*Ex situ* or gene bank
Mean	US$ 4.181	USD 16.75	USD 2.195
95% CI	US$ 2.832–5.530	USD 13.74–19.75	USD 1.994–2.396
N	93	107	107

Factors influencing the contribution: Table 8.9 shows household size is significantly associated with the WTP bids for *ex situ* conservation. The larger households are willing to contribute less, which is consistent with the economic theory as the higher number of people the more cash that is needed for running the household, which decreases the capacity for expending in conservation or for similar purposes. These households might not be willing to contribute for *ex situ* conservation of landraces, but instead they could contribute more to *in situ* conservation. Age of respondent was only associated with the *in situ* community gene bank conservation, where elderly people are willing to contribute more than the younger. Household income and food sufficiency status of the family were not significantly associated with the WTP bids. Although this differs from what one would expect based on economic theory, the empirical result by the World Bank on WTP for quality water supply also does not depend on income. Similarly it has been found by Aldy *et al.*[41] that the low income population is at disproportionately higher environmental risk compared to the wealthy or high income population. The conservation of landraces is therefore more important for those who depend on agriculture and have a low income. This might be the reason that income and food sufficiency have no effect on the WTP for landraces conservation. Larger landholdings are associated with higher WTP bids, which is theoretically acceptable because people having more land are richer and have more need of such landraces in the future when they expect to change their varieties or landraces in their diverse lands.[42] Although more land parcels require a higher number of landraces,[43] the willingness to pay was not associated with the number of land parcels. Number of landraces grown was negatively associated with the WTP bids. An increase in the number of landraces grown decreased farmers' contribution for conservation, which is theoretically acceptable because when they already have a large number of landraces in their farm they will not be interested in paying for conservation of the same landraces.

---

41 J. Aldy *et al.*, 'Environmental Equity and Conservation of Unique Ecosystems: An Analysis of the Distribution of the Benefits for Protecting Southern Applachian Spruce-fir Forests' (1999) 12 *Society and Natural Resources* 93.

42 Rana *et al.*, n. 22.

43 Ibid.

Table 8.9 Full and best regression models of explanatory variables determining WTP for in situ at household level, community gene bank and ex situ conservation of rice landraces

Explanatory variables	All variables included in the model			Best fitting model		
	In situ at household level	Community bank	*Ex situ*	*In situ* at household level	Community bank	*Ex situ*
Constant	0.321	−5.26	2.47***	−0.63	2.20	2.254***
Household size	0.403	−0.924	−0.069*	–	−1.17**	−0.093***
Respondent age	−0.079	0.324**	−0.005	–	0.256**	–
Education level	0.867*	1.337	−0.109	1.01**	–	–
Household income (USD)	-1.2×10^{-4}	6.4×10^{-4}	9×10^{-5}	–	–	–
Food sufficiency	0.620**	0.395	0.043	0.63***	–	–
Landholding	0.569	10.4***	0.566**	–	11.73***	0.616***
Land parcels	−0.046	−0.416	0.019	–	–	–
Number of landraces grown	−1.04**	1.337	−0.116*	1.06***	–	–
R^2	0.28	0.29	0.22	0.25	0.26	0.16
N	93	107	107	93	107	107

* $p < 0.10$, ** $p < 0.05$ and *** $p < 0.01$

The mean willingness to pay was higher for male respondents, the richer households and the people with previous knowledge on biodiversity (Table 8.10). The mean WTP was significantly higher for male respondents for *in situ* conservation methods, but not for *ex situ conservation*. The mean WTP for the resource rich people was significantly higher than the resource poor people for all methods of conservation.

Table 8.10 The categorical variables influencing the farmers' willingness to contribute (USD) for rice landraces conservation in Kaski Nepal

Influencing variables	Mean willingness-to-contribution for rice landraces conservation		
	In situ at household level	Community bank	*Ex situ*
Sex of the respondents			
Male	5.711**	20.48**	2.328
Female	2.618	13.08	2.064
Socioeconomic status			
Resource rich	6.158***	20.44***	2.317*
Resource medium	6.079	19.20	2.330
Resource poor	0.827	7.15	1.794
Knowledge on biodiversity			
Rich knowledge	5.331**	18.18	2.289
Poor knowledge	1.644	13.81	2.002

* p<0.10, ** p<0.05 and ***p<0.01

4. Concluding Remarks

The mean willingness to contribute for conservation either *in situ* or *ex situ* for important crop genetic resources such as rice landraces was higher than the less important ones. Mainly the use values of the concerned genetic resources were paid more than non-use values because the grain quality at present is more important than the resistance gene for future. Similarly, the willingness to contribute to conservation of the crop genetic resources that are threatened by extinction was lower than for the abundant landraces. The conservation of landraces that are considered by farmers to be less important should therefore be conserved *ex situ* or in gene bank, but the CGRs that farmers consider to be important should be conserved *in situ*.

The mean WTP for community conservation was higher than *in situ* at household level and *ex situ* conservation. The difference was mainly because such goods are also public goods[44] having neither rivalry in consumption nor excludability. However, this significant difference of WTP for different methods of conservation does not mean that farmers have valued the resources differently but they have elicited the best method for conservation. This willingness to pay denotes that at least some amount of the conservation costs could be covered by the farmers who are the genetic resource users. How to fund the conservation of genetic resources is, however, a political rather than a scientific question.

The better conservation approach for landraces that are highly valued by farmers seems to be the *in situ* conservation and even best is the *in situ* community

---

44 Bräuer n. 9.

conservation. This is not to argue that the contingent valuation method is a panacea in solving the problem of decision-making concerning genetic resources conservation but contingent valuation should be considered as a crude guide while implementing the conservation strategies. Such studies conducted in valuation of agro-biodiversity open the door for further research and valuation of the agricultural resources including the horticultural and floricultural crops.

Chapter 9

Is More Less?
An Evolutionary Economics Critique of the Economics of Plant Breeds' Rights

Dwijen Rangnekar

1. Introduction

The chapter explores the relationship between the standards of intellectual property protection, the nature of technical advance and the wider selection environment within which technical change occurs. This focus of the exploration is plant breeders' rights (PBRs); thus, our attention is devoted to the conditions for grant of protection: distinctness, uniformity, stability and (commercial) novelty. The epistemological position adopted is that of a neo-Schumpeterian study of technology, christened here as evolutionary economics. Our broader concern is the rhetoric in the economics literature that, focussing on PBRs counts, rationalises its introduction, strengthening and global harmonisation on the grounds that more is better. This suggests that an increase in the number of PBRs is welfare enhancing in some technological sense. Elsewhere economists themselves have critiqued and rejected patent counts as an adequate indicator of inventive activity on recognising that sectors differ in their propensities to patent and acknowledging the underbelly of patents in their strategic use to stall the diffusion of inventions. However, economists studying PBRs have neglected such epistemological considerations on the adequacy of PBRs counts as an indicator of inventive activity. Picking up this challenge, the chapter poses two questions. First it queries how 'inventiveness' is theoretically conceptualised and empirically assessed by economists. Second, it unpacks the standards of protection in PBRs law. There being no presumption that the legal definition based on the standards of protection is unambiguously adequate for economic considerations. Tying these two questions together, the primary query concerns the role of standards of protection in PBRs as a nexus between a technological trajectory and a selection environment.

The chapter begins with elaborating the core features of an evolutionary economics approach to the study of technology. Here, attention is primarily devoted to the notion of selection mechanisms and how they act as a nexus in protecting a particular technological trajectory. This discussion is followed by an overview of the economics literature on PBRs where the focus on PBRs counts is detailed. Critical questions are posed to this literature to exhibit its methodological weakness. This weakness is elaborated in the subsequent section through a demonstration of how a focus on PBRs counts obfuscates an underlying dynamic in plant breeding: an increasing rate of varietal turnover captured in a shortening life span of varieties (i.e., planned obsolescence). The final section draws out the political expediency in delinking the construction of the standards of protection from issues of inventive step.

2. A Framework to Study Technology

Many critiques of how economists study technology exist. These, with varying emphasis, argue for incorporating a historical and sociological dimension and urge recognition of the role of institutions and actors in enabling and hindering technical change. If there is an exception to these criticisms of economics then it would apply to the strands of the neo-Schumpeterian approach, here termed evolutionary economics. Its foundational precepts can be located in the early contributions of Dosi[1], Freeman[2] and Nelson and Winter.[3] This section briefly maps out some of the central tenets whilst highlighting the efficacy of the selection mechanism in relation to the continuing dynamics of a particular technological trajectory. This focus relates to the primary motivation of the chapter: exploring the role of the standards of protection in PBRs with respect to a particular form of technical change in plant breeding. Evolutionary economics is deeply empirical in its origins and its motivation. It can be understood as an effort to explain the reality of (continuous) incremental technical change and the observation of cumulativeness in technical change (the persistence of productivity/profit differentials).[4] Picking a particularly Schumpeterian theme with respect to the corporate location and organisation of innovation, scholars have argued that accumulated skills provide a 'familiar rhythm' to the activity of innovating.[5] This does not suggest that uncertainty is completely resolved; rather, that innovations occur in the 'civilised regions of established routines'.[6] As such, recognising that much of innovation is a highly routinised activity.

As a heuristic development, Dosi modifying a Kuhnian metaphor proposes the organising analytical category of technology paradigms:[7] '... we shall define

---

1 G. Dosi, *Technical Change and Industrial Transformation: The Theory and an Application to the Semiconductor Industry* (London: Macmillan 1984); and G. Dosi, 'Sources, Procedures, and Microeconomic Effects of Innovation' (1988) 26(3) *Journal of Economic Literature* 1120.

2 C. Freeman, *The Economics of Industrial Innovation* (London: Pinter 1982).

3 R. Nelson and S. Winter, 'In Search of Useful Theory of Innovation' (1977) 6(1) *Research Policy* 6; R. Nelson and S. Winter, *An Evolutionary Theory of Economic Change* (Cambridge: Harvard 1982).

4 G. Dosi, 'Technological Paradigms and Technological Trajectories: A Suggested Interpretation of the Determinants and Directions of Technical Change' (1982) 11(3) *Research Policy* 147, 158–61.

5 Nelson and Winter, *An Evolutionary Theory*, 75.

6 Ibid, 131.

7 Nomenclature problems exist in evolutionary economics with the increased and varied contributions over time. For example, some prefer the term 'regimes': R. Boyer 'Formalizing Growth Regimes. Technical Change and Economic Theory' in G. Dosi *et al.* (eds), *Technical Change and Economic Theory* (London and New York: Pinter Publishers 1988), 608; while others use 'technology systems' – see C. Freeman and L. Soete, *The Economics of Industrial*

a "technological paradigm" as "model" and a "pattern" of solution of *selected* technological problems, based on *selected* principles derived from natural sciences and on *selected* material technologies'.[8] There are many similarities between Kuhn's scientific paradigms and Dosi's technology paradigms: the 'puzzle solving' activity of scientific paradigms are transparent in the focus on artefact development and modification within technology paradigms; while scientific paradigms are realised in normal science, technology paradigms are realised in their trajectories of development chartered through normal problem-solving activity.

There is a strong *focusing* element in the way that paradigms are conceptualised by evolutionary economists that begins with the abiding feature of 'selected' problems, principles and technologies. This is also apparent in the notion of the exemplar which is best understood as the artefact that is to be developed or improved; thus, providing the 'technological guideposts' in terms of specific technoeconomic problems.[9] There is a Lancastrian sense of 'bundles' of characteristics being implied here.[10] The desired techno-economic characteristics being targeted act as 'focusing devices' for the members of the shared paradigm.[11] For example, in the development of aircraft technology, the focus for long has been on reducing the cost per seat mile so as to exploit the scale economies existing in long hauls and larger capacity; thus, resulting in each new generation of commercial aircraft being larger bodied vehicles.[12] For sociologists, this approach is promising but does not adequately explore the cognitive dimension of how shared perceptions of progress amongst practitioners emerge and get entrenched.[13] To be fair, as will be noted later, the technology paradigm approach does justice to notions of the shared cognitive frames and demands for strong commitment amongst adherents to the paradigm.

Technology paradigms manifest themselves in the empirical tracing of the trajectory of technical development, i.e. the map of the techno-economic pay-offs exercised through the process of technical change.[14] Here, the observations indicate towards specific clusters of techno-economic characteristics and their narrow, bounded trajectories of development.[15] This clustering is empirically apparent in 'innovation avenues'. For example, technical progress in aircraft technology is

---

Innovation (2nd Ed, London: Pinter 1997). Given the variety of notions, there is a need for terminological standardisation (M. Cimoli and G. Dosi, 'Technological Paradigms, Patterns of Learning and Development: An Introductory Roadmap' (1995) 5(3) *Journal of Evolutionary Economics* 243, 245.

8 Dosi, n. 4, 152 (emphasis in original).

9 D. Sahal, 'Technological Guideposts and Innovation Avenues' in C. Freeman and V. Brookfield, *The Economics of Innovation: International Library of Critical Writings in Economics*, No. 2 (Aldershot: Edward Elgar 2000), 442.

10 Dosi (1988), n. 1, 1127.

11 N. Rosenberg, *Perspectives on Technology* (Cambridge University Press: 1976).

12 Ibid; Nelson and Winter (1977), n. 3.

13 W. Bijker *et al.*, *The Social Construction of Technological Systems: New Directions in the Sociology and History of Technology* (Cambridge: MIT Press 1987).

14 Nelson and Winter (1977), n. 3.

15 Dosi, n. 4; Cimoli and Dosi, n. 7; J. Metcalfe 'Technology Systems and Technology Policy in an Evolutionary Framework' (1995) 19(1) *Cambridge Journal of Economics* 25.

characterised by the ordered trade-offs between horsepower, gross take-off weight, cruise speed, wing loading and cruise range.[16] In microelectronics the trajectory is mapped by the closely clustered relationship between density of the chip, speed of computation and the cost per bit of information.[17] As technologies develop along particular paths, the competences, organisational routines, intraproject heuristics, cumulative features of the learning process, and technological opportunities and complementarities increasingly entrench the direction of technical change.[18] Further, attributes of technical change such as path dependency,[19] lock-in effects,[20] scale economies and irreversibility, reinforce the clustering.

It is here that evolutionary economists mark their difference from the dominant epistemology of economics by emphasising the general weakness of the market in the *ex ante* selection of technological direction, especially at the initial stages of its establishment.[21] In earlier formulations this independence from the market has even been christened 'natural'.[22] If technologies were mere 'recipes', pieces of malleable information, that could be simply added and utilised to meet diverse consumer tastes (i.e. the market) then 'this would lead toward the exploration of the entire characteristic space of final products, machine tools, components, etc.'[23] Simply put, there are no smooth and continuous technology indifference curves upon which one could optionally place oneself.

There remains the question concerning the emergence and entrenchment of technology paradigms. Some transform the question: 'The interesting question may be rather how certain technological achievements (such as the DC – 3) come to be recognised as exemplary or paradigmatic'.[24] Building on the work of evolutionary economists, they suggest that 'new paradigms must of necessity be protected against the myopia of natural selection'.[25] This resonates well with Dosi, who argues that 'the technological imaginations of engineers and of the organisations they are in are focussed in rather precise direction while they are, so to speak, "blind" with respect to other technological possibilities.'[26] This protection or blindness, it appears, is performed by a variety of social institutions that result in a nexus between the

---

16 Nelson and Winter (1977), n. 3; Sahal, n. 9.

17 Dosi (1984), n. 1.

18 Nelson and Winter (1977), n. 3; Nelson and Winter (1982), n. 3; Dosi (1984) n, 1; Dosi, n. 4.

19 P. David, 'Clio and the Economics of QWERTY' (1985) 75(2) *American Economic Review* 332.

20 B. Arthur, 'Competing Technologies, Increasing Returns, and Lock-ins by Historical Small Events' (1989) 99 *Economic Journal* 116.

21 Dosi, n. 4.

22 Nelson and Winter (1977), n. 3, 56.

23 Dosi (1988), n. 1, 1129.

24 H. van den Belt and A. Rip, 'The Nelson-Winter-Dosi Model and Synthetic Dye Chemistry' in W. Bijker *et al.* (eds), *The Social Construction of Technological Systems: New Directions in the Sociology and History of Technology* (Cambridge: The MIT Press 1994), 135, 141.

25 Ibid.

26 Dosi n. 4.

technological trajectory and the selection environment for competing technologies. Others have developed the idea in promising directions either in terms of 'selection mechanisms',[27] 'bridging institutions',[28] and 'lobbies'.[29] It is through such institutional entities that technologies get developed, accepted, normalised and entrenched.

An example makes the significance of selection mechanism clear.[30] The synthetic dye industry emerged with the discovery of aniline purple in 1856 by William Henry Perkin and took off a few years later with the 'invention' of aniline red. Over time, with the stabilisation of this emergent paradigm, it can be said that an azo dye regime was constituted (around the year 1877). This coincides with the passage of the German Patent Law. The emergent paradigm of azo dyes presented serious problems of patentability, such as whether it qualified as a 'particular process' and whether it satisfied the standards of inventiveness. In particular, while novelty in terms of colours could be claimed it was not immediately clear if inventiveness was demonstrated. The practice of granting (and, often rejecting) patents itself left many in doubt as to what standards were being established. It is here that the Congo Red decision of 1889 marks a crucial point. The original patent for Congo Red was acquired by Agfa in 1884. Bayer, exploiting a loophole in the patent, developed a similar dye (Benzopurpurin). Though Agfa challenged Bayer, the two sought a compromise to fight another, but smaller, competitor, Ewer & Pick. The case was eventually heard in the highest court, the Reichsgericht. Carlo Duisberg, then a young scientist at Bayer, spoke to the court emphasising the commercial significance of the process and the product, Congo Red. In taking in Duisberg's exposition, the court formulated the doctrine of new technical effect. This doctrine ensured the validity of the Congo Red patent on the grounds that the industrial applicability and technical and commercial value of the product more than compensates for a lack of inventiveness. The doctrine of new technical effect was central in safeguarding the technology paradigm of azo dye and equally in providing juridical legitimation for routinised innovation activity in the industry; thus establishing a nexus between the trajectory and the selection environment.

3. The Focus on Numbers

A central premise rationalising IPRs is the inappropriability of knowledge.[31] While Nelson[32] notes that firms with economies of scale can overcome this problem, the popular characterisation of inappropriability prevails. Inappropriability follows from the public good characteristics of knowledge: uncertainty in predicting the

---

27 Nelson and Winter (1982) n. 3.

28 Freeman n. 2.

29 Ibid, esp. ch 16.

30 This paragraph is based on van den Belt and Rip n. 24.

31 R. Nelson, 'The Simple Economics of Basic Scientific Research' (1959) 67 *Journal of Political Economy* 297; K. Arrow, 'Economic Welfare and the Allocation of Resources for Invention' in R. Nelson (ed.), *The Rate and Direction of Inventive Activity: Economic and Social Factors* (New Jersey: Princeton University Press 1962), 609.

32 Ibid.

returns, non-excludability (of benefits) and non-rivalry (in consumption). Owners of information are unable to maintain their monopoly position on information as any purchaser can simply reproduce it at little (or no) cost.[33] Thus, to the extent that property rights are difficult to establish and enforce there will be an under-investment in investments in research.[34] Inappropriability is compounded, it has been argued, in the case of plant breeding by features of the technology and the product.[35] Technical change is embodied and the artefact, the seed, can be recycled, re-used and multiplied; thus, presenting the real possibility of secondary competition.

This characterisation of the inappropriability problem is *prima facie* valid. The public good properties of knowledge have been critiqued and diminished by economists and sociologists. For instance, neoclassical critiques of Arrow's approach notwithstanding,[36] sociologists draw attention to the tacit, local and cumulative nature of knowledge that disallows its easy transmission.[37] Distinguishing between the free availability of information and the costs associated with the techno-economic application of the same, evolutionary economists suggest recognising these spillovers as 'untraded interdependencies' between firms and sectors that do not correspond to commodity flows.[38] In the case of plants there are further complications to this characterisation of public goods. To begin, the heritability of genetic characteristics differs across species, where for example natural out-crossing in cross-pollinated species leading to loss of genetic purity. Further, genetic information is only economically useful to the extent that the technological mix of complementary inputs is also available. Independent of IPRs, there are organisational solutions (e.g. horizontal integration), technological solutions aimed at discontinuous heritability (e.g. F1-hybrids and terminator technology) and planned obsolescence.[39]

These considerations aside, the popular construction of IPRs as resolving the inappropriability of knowledge (and seeds) has prevailed; thus, the focus on the relationship between IPRs and R&D. Promoting private investments in research remains a primary policy objective for IPRs. In the case of patents, economists have developed sophisticated models that assess this incentive effect.[40] These models

---

33 Ibid.

34 P. Dasgupta and P. David, 'Toward a New Economics of Science' (1994) 23(5) *Research Policy* 487.

35 S. Jaffee and J. Srivastava, *Seed System Development: The Appropriate Roles of the Private and Public Sector* (Washington DC: World Bank 1992); P-W. Lim, *The Privatisation of Species: An Economic History of Biotechnology and Intellectual Property Rights in Living Organisms* (Stanford University 1993).

36 H. Demsetz, 'Information and Efficiency: Another Viewpoint' (1969) 12(1) *Journal of Law and Economics* 1.

37 M. Callon, 'Is Science a Public Good?' (1994) 19(4) *Science, Technology, and Human Values* 395.

38 Dosi (1988), n. 1.

39 D. Rangnekar, 'R&D Appropriability and Planned Obsolescence: Empirical Evidence from Wheat Breeding in the UK (1960–95)' (2002) 11(5) *Industrial and Corporate Change* 1011.

40 I. Reinganum 'General Theory of Diffusion and Innovation' (1981) 25(4) *Journal of Economic Theory*; J. Bound *et al.*, 'Who does R&D and Who Patents?' in Z. Griliches

have been complemented by empirical contributions.[41] Evolutionary economists have contributed to the debate by drawing attention to sectoral peculiarities in the relationship between patents and technical advance[42] and variations in appropriation strategies.[43]

Disturbingly, little of these theoretical preoccupations have filtered into the research on PBRs (and by extension on the general research on plant breeding R&D). It would have been quite easy to translate the view that sectors exhibit idiosyncratic differences into the area of PBRs through conceptualising the specie-based differences in the innovation/appropriation relationship. In the absence of this and other nuances, it is generally felt that the literature is remarkable for its limited theoretical sophistication or sound methodology.[44] In its empirical research, the literature focuses on the 'impact' of IPRs in terms of a 'before' and 'after' approach; thereby suggesting that evidence identified is causally linked to the event (introduction of IPRs).

At the other end of the pipeline are the new varieties released. Focus on the number of varieties protected has generated a popular claim: 'the availability of PBRs has increased the number of private sector breeders, as well as the number of varieties released and planted'.[45] For that matter, evidence for the US indicates that the number of varieties released in the 1990s is higher than that in the 1980s.[46] A study on PBRs in Canada reported increased breeding activity and release of new varieties.[47] A study of the impact of PBRs in Spain found a positive incentive effect

---

(ed.), *Patents, R&D and Productivity* (Chicago IL: University of Chicago Press, 1984), 21; Z. Griliches 'Patent Statistics as Economic Indicators: A Survey' (1990) 28(4) *Journal of Economic Literature* 1661; M. Schankerman and J. Lanjouw 'Stylized Facts of Patent Legislation: Value, Scope and Ownership' (STICERD, London School of Economics Discussion Papers Series EI 20) (1998), 41.

41 E. Mansfield *et al.*, 'Imitation Costs and Patents: An Empirical Study' (1981) 91 *Economic Journal* 907; E. Mansfield, 'R&D and Innovation: Some Empirical Findings' in Z. Griliches, 127; E. Mansfield, 'Patents and Innovation: An Empirical Study' (1986) 32(2) *Management Studies* 173.

42 R. Merges and R. Nelson, 'On the Complex Economics of Patent Scope' (1990) 90 *Columbia Law Review* 839.

43 R. Levin *et al.*, 'Appropriating the Returns from Industrial-Research and Development' (1987) (3) *Brookings Papers on Economic Activity* 783; A. Klevorick *et al.*, 'On the Sources and Significance of Interindustry Differences in Technological Opportunities' 24(2) *Research Policy* 185.

44 D. Godden, 'Plant Variety Rights: Framework for Evaluating Recent Research and Continuing Issues' 3(3) *Journal of Rural Studies* 255; J. Kennedy and D. Godden, 'Plant Variety Rights and the Incentive to Innovate' (1993) 21(2) *Oxford Agrarian Studies* 105.

45 W. Lesser, 'Sector Issues II: Seeds and Plants' in W. Siebeck *et al.*, *Strengthening Protection of Intellectual Property in Developing Countries* (Washington DC, World Bank 1990), 59, 60.

46 K. Fuglie *et al.*, *Agricultural Research and Development: Public and Private Investments Under Alternative Markets and Institutions* (Washington DC, Economic Research Service, U.S. Department of Agriculture 1996), 36.

47 Canada Food Inspection Agency, 2001.

on private breeding activity that saw international firms enter the Spanish market.[48] At an apparent level this has been accepted by well-known critics, though noting the high incidence of cosmetic breeding.[49] Beyond sceptics, even corporate breeders acknowledge the pervasive presence of cosmetic breeding; thus, raising a disturbing question regarding the focus on the number of varieties:

> USA farmers have many more soybean varieties available to them today ...
> unfortunately, many of these commercial soybean varieties are very close relatives, if not essentially identical ...[50]

This focus on the number of varieties takes on an entirely different turn in the hands of the International Union for the Protection of New Varieties of Plants (UPOV) – the multilateral organisation dedicated to improving and strengthening PBRs. A recent study[51] is evidence of this focus on the number of varieties protected.[52] Kamal Idris, Secretary-General of UPOV, in his foreword, suggested that this 'systematic study' demonstrates 'remarkable and substantial benefits' of plant variety protection consistent with the UPOV Convention.[53] The President of the UPOV Council, Molina Macías, in her foreword was convinced that 'the study has shown how effective plant variety protection can be in encouraging the development of new varieties of plants'.[54] The study adopts a rather simplistic methodology of comparing the number of varieties released and/or protected around two key events: the enacted of PBRs legislation and accession to UPOV. By way of example, here is the evidence and explanation for Argentina.[55] PBRs were initially introduced in Argentina through the Law of Seed and Phytogenetic Creations[56] and the first varieties to be protected were in 1981/82. In 1991, a Regulatory Decree[57] introduced core elements of the 1978 Act of UPOV. Finally, in 1994 the 1978 Act was fully incorporated into national law. Using these legislative events, the study examines the number of varieties protected

48 M. Diez, 'The Impact of Plant Varieties Rights on Research: The Case of Spain' (2002) 27(2) *Food Policy* 171.

49 P. Mooney 'The Law of the Seed: Another Development and Plant Genetic Resources.' (1983) (1–2) *Development Dialogue* 1, 150–4.

50 D. Duvick, 'Plant Germplasm Resources and Agribusiness' *Background Paper for the Keystone Dialogue on Plant Genetic Resources*, Madras, India; quoted in C. Pray and M. Knudson 'Impact of Intellectual Property Rights on Genetic Diversity: The Case of US Wheat' (1994) 12(1) *Contemporary Economic Policy* 102.

51 UPOV undertook to study the impacts of PBRs in a select number of countries (Argentina, China, Kenya, Poland, and Korea) and brought evidence of changes in a range of indicators that include the number of varieties protected, foreign and domestic investments in plant breeding, agricultural exports, and the structure of the seed and plant breeding industry.

52 International Union for the Protection of New Varieties of Plants (UPOV) (2005). UPOV, *Report on the Impact of Plant Variety Protection. Geneva, International Union for the Protection of New Varieties of Plants*, 98.

53 Ibid, 3.

54 Ibid, 5.

55 Ibid, 35–43.

56 Law No. 20.247/73 of 30 March 1973.

57 Regulatory Decree 2183/91.

in a 'pre-UPOV' period (1982–91) and a 'post-UPOV' period (1992–2000): 26 varieties were protected in the former period and 70 varieties in the latter. This is a rather simplistic methodological approach to the issue. To begin, its fails to adequately reflect on the historical rate of introduction of new plant varieties. More importantly, to establish proof of a causal relationship to a single event requires a robust empirical test of the relationship where other interfacing influences are identified and their impact isolated. At issue is the following question of causality: 'do innovations cause the increase in PBRs or is it the other way around?'[58]

Few scholars have taken on this difficult challenge. One such study reviews historical rates of varietal release for select UK crops across 1930–90 and then queries these in light of the passage of the Plant Varieties and Seeds Act, 1964.[59] The conclusions are mixed: after the passage of the legislation in 1964, the rate of release of new varieties increased for apples, was marginally different for French beans, and exhibited negligible changes for strawberries. Da Rocha proceeds to examine a range of factors that influence the annual rate of varietal release. These factors include biological factors and economics, such as the timing and cost of breeding, the life-cycle and turnover of the crops and natural barriers to propagation. Similar reflections exist in a study of vegetables and fruit plant breeding in the US where focus is on the juvenile period of the species and the exclusion costs to stall 'piracy'.[60]

4. The Merit in Numbers

It does seem far fetched that society would simply be interested in increases in PBRs counts, the annual number of varieties protected.[61] A wider set of concerns underpin the socio-political and economic bargain of granting IPRs which would include social well-being, industrial efficiency, techno-economic progress and equity. Even accepting a narrow frame of 'inventive activity', one can question the adequacy of using PBRs counts as a reliable indicator. It has been suggested that the 'disclosure' of new plant varieties, such as through a successful application for PBRs, is representative of inventive activity.[62] The presumption being that meeting the conditions for grant of protection is an adequate demonstration of inventiveness.

---

58 The more troubling question that queries this undiminished faith in PBRs counts is pursued in the subsequent section.

59 A. da Rocha, *An Analysis of the Impact of Plant Breeders' Rights Legislation on the Introduction of New Varieties in UK Horticulture* (Wye College, University of London, 1994).

60 J. Stallman, 'Impacts of the 1930 Plant Patent Act on Private Fruit Breeding Investment' (dissertation, Michigan State University 1986).

61 This criticism of the focus on annual number of varieties protected should not be taken to suggest that a number of the studies on PBRs do not consider a wide set of issues that include industrial concentration, restructuring of the industry and agronomic factors. However, little of these concerns have filtered into the focus on PBR counts, which is the point being made.

62 da Rocha n. 58, 46–9.

There is circularity to this argument as the conditions for grant of protection do not assess inventiveness. In particular, all that a variety must demonstrate is distinctness, uniformity and stability. Methodologically, every new variety could be ranked using a composite criterion mixing agronomic, such as yield or disease resistance, and/or techno-economic, such as market share or duration of protection, factors. A qualified PBRs count would be one useful step towards constructing an indicator that is more representative of inventive activity.

To elaborate on the fallacy of focusing on PBRs counts we draw attention to how such counts mask a deeper reality. In the absence of a test for merit or inventiveness, breeders face a relatively low threshold for securing protection. In the search for profitability and continuing uptake by farmers, breeders have incentives to reduce the durability of varieties so that, ideally, farmers purchase a fresh stock of seeds every year.[63] Recognising this implies a regular dynamic of entry/exit of varieties. Thus, rather than simply focusing on the annual PBRs counts, it would be more useful to focus on the net varieties in the market.

There is another implication of the low threshold for securing PBRs protection. Concern regarding agronomic and techno-economic aspects of new varieties has led to the introduction of regulatory systems of field trials and requirements for achieving some norm before commercialisation is permitted. This field trial system exists with varying emphasis in different jurisdictions. For example, in Europe there is a Common Catalogue where varieties are entered into National Lists based on agronomic field trials. There is a clear, and painfully reiterated, regulatory separation between PBRs and the National List system. Yet, all varieties to be marketed must meet the standards of the National List – and it is a very rare occurrence, if at all, that a variety on the National List has not already been protected by PBRs.

One of the consequences of this apparent regulatory separation is that breeders have tended to submit a large number of varieties for field trial. This allows them to monitor agronomic performance of their varieties as well as those of their competitors. Thus, through subsequent field trials, commercial decisions are taken on whether to maintain a particular variety for next year's field trial and also whether to continue with the application for PBRs protection. Where protection has been secured, the issue is whether to pay the renewal fee or to terminate the right. It is from this 'pool of varieties' that PBRs emerge, withdraw and/or terminate. Evidence of this 'pool of varieties' and how a dwindling proportion is maintained through subsequent field

---

63 J. Berlan and R. Lewontin 'Breeders' Rights and Patenting Life Forms.' (1986) 322 *Nature* 785, 786–87). Economists predict that oligopolists producing a durable good would seek to reduce the economic durability of the good so as to induce customers into regular replacement purchases: R. Coase 'The Problem of Social Costs' (1960) 3 *Journal of Law and Economics* 1; J. Bulow 'An Economic Theory of Planned Obsolescence.' (1986) 101 *Quarterly Journal of Economics* 729; M. Waldman 'A New Perspective on Planned Obsolescence' (1993) 108 *Quarterly Journal of Economics* 273. For example, textbook publishers not only regularly introduces new edition but also seek to modify the new edition so as to 'kill off' the market for old editions (Waldman, ibid). It has been suggested that a level of planned obsolescence is a necessary condition for technical progress (A. Fishman *et al.*, 'Planned Obsolescence as an Engine of Technological Progress' (1993) 41 *Journal of Industrial Economics* 361).

trial stages has been commented upon.[64] A relatively small share, less than 10 per cent for any one company, ever achieve the status of 'General Recommendation'. This reasserts that the focus on PBRs counts obfuscates the underlying dynamics of commercial breeding. A more representative indicator would take account of the total number of PBRs applications (i.e., the pool) and the number of successful applications. Such an indicator, the rate of success, would represent the number of grants as a proportion of the pool (i.e., total number of applications). This can be calculated for a single company or aggregated across all companies. Thus, even if PBRs counts increase, the rate of success would reflect this only if the number of grants increase faster than the number of applications.

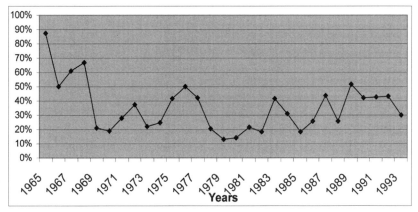

Figure 9.1 The rate of success using UK data of PBRs granted in wheat (1965–1993)

Figure 9.1 shows the rate of success using UK data of PBRs granted in wheat (1965–90). During this period there were 1002 applications for PBRs of which 62 per cent were withdrawn before a decision on the application was taken. In fact, during the early period from 1965 to 1980s, the rate of success actually falls. It is only from the mid-1980s that the rate of success increases. Even while accommodating for the 'pool effect', there is need to consider the dynamic of planned obsolescence. Figure 9.2 brings together data on annual PBRs counts and annual net grants. Net grants are the difference between the number of grants issued in a year (PBRs count) and the number of grants that 'exit' either because they have been surrendered, terminated or have expired in that year. The two graphs exhibit a remarkable difference with a generally secular increase in PBRs counts and substantial fluctuation for Net Grants. The fact that Net Grants are systematically less than PBR counts validates the suspicion of a regular trend of varieties 'exiting'. Often, Net Grants are negative which implies more grants 'exit' rather than enter the market. Exit of grants can occur for a number of different reasons but essentially relate to a corporate marketing

---

64 S. McGuire, *Privatisation of Agricultural Research: A Case Study of Winter Wheat in the United Kingdom* (School of Development Studies, University of East Anglia 1996).

decision reflecting relatively weaker agronomic performance compared to existing competition.

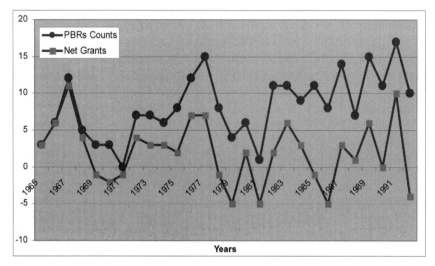

Figure 9.2 PBR counts and Net Grants (UK wheat PBRs, 1965–1993)

These wider dynamics around the breeding effort and PBRs corroborate the suggestion that firms producing a durable good tend to adopt appropriation strategies that reduce the durability of the good. This occurs through a duality of focussing on incremental productivity improvements (e.g. yield increases) and simultaneously breeding reduced durability (e.g. narrow disease resistance).[65] Rangnekar[66] provides empirical evidence of planned obsolescence in the case of wheat breeding in the UK. The limited disease resistance of newer vintages along with incremental yield increases have been pursued to promote regular adoption of the contemporary vintage. This is captured by the substantial fall in the average life-span of varieties which has fallen from 13 years in the 1960s to 5.5 years in the 1990s.

5. The Selection Mechanism: Delinking Merit from Protection

PBRs are granted to varieties that are distinct, uniform, and stable in their essential characteristics:[67]

Distinctness: Article 7 of UPOV require that the variety must be 'clearly distinguishable from any other variety whose existence is a matter of common knowledge' at the time when protection is applied for. This requirement ensures inter-varietal identification.

---

65 Rangnekar, n. 39.
66 Ibid.
67 This is with reference to the UPOV's 1991 Act.

Uniformity: Article 8 place the condition that the variety must be sufficiently uniform in its distinguishing characteristics, such that different individuals of the same variety are reasonably similar. This requirement ensures intra-varietal uniformity.

Stability: Article 9 states that a variety must be stable in its distinguishing characteristics, i.e. it remains 'unchanged after repeated propagation or, in the case of a particular cycle of propagation, at the end of each such cycle'. This requirement addresses temporal varietal identification.

Finally, the plant variety must be novel in that the propagating material or harvested material has not been offered for sale by or with the consent of the breeder, either earlier than one year in the jurisdiction of application or four years in jurisdictions of contracting members.[68] These four requirements has been criticised for being strikingly liberal compared to patents and setting a very low threshold for intellectual property protection.[69] Yet, at the time of framing the standards of protection in the early 1960s, breeders involved in the negotiations recognised that the requirement for distinctness, uniformity, and stability provided a 'sound legal basis' for identification and legal protection.[70] The retention of distinctive characteristics, which some critique as a 'snap-shot' requirement,[71] is further entrenched by establishing grounds for cancelling or nullifying a grant.[72]

A hint at the treatment of inventiveness and merit in the standards of PBRs can be gathered from how 'discoveries' are handled. Most PBRs laws, if not all, grant protection for varieties that have been discovered. For the Plant Patent Act (1930) in the US this was formally reiterated in the 1954 amendment.[73] In the UK, the Committee on Transactions in Seeds (CTS), the body that the government established to review the introduction of PBRs, the granting of rights in acts of discovery was rationalised in terms of promoting individuals to 'keep a sharp look out for useful variants which otherwise might escape notice'.[74] For that matter, UPOV's 1991 Act, in Article 1, incorporates discoveries through its definition of a breeder as being 'the person who bred, or discovered and developed, a variety'. This is remarkably different from patents where demonstrating industrial utility has been designed to patents being granted in discoveries. The doctrine of enablement has been elaborated to achieve this distinction.[75] In keeping discoveries beyond the ambit of patents there is a philosophical recognition that discoveries relate to the mere recognition of what

---

68 cf. Article 6.

69 J. Byrne, *Analysis of the Basic Proposal for a New Act of the International Convention for the Protection of New Varieties of Plants* (London, CLIP 1991).

70 S. Fejer, 'The Problem of Plant Breeders, Rights' (1966) 4(3) *Agricultural Science Review* 1, 5.

71 S. Bent *et al.*, *Intellectual Property Rights in Biotechnology Worldwide* (New York: Stockton Press 1987).

72 cf. Articles 21 and 22.

73 Stallman n. 59, 16–18; Lim n. 35, 184–5.

74 Committee on Transactions in Seeds, *Plant Breeders' Rights: Report of the Committee on Transactions in Seeds* (HMSO 1960) Cmnd 1092, 62.

75 Merges and Nelson n. 42.

already exists; whereas inventions entails developing a solution to a problem through some technical means.

The particular architecture of the PBRs standards relate to the historical legacy of UPOV's origin in 1961. In the 1950s when breeders were seeking legal measures for protection suspicion was raised regarding the inventive step in breeding plant varieties. The incremental nature of development in plant breeding fell short of the inventive step requirement of patent grant.[76] Novelty in plant breeding largely resided in the choice of material being crossed. Patent lawyers, through the International Association for the Protection of Industrial Property (AIPPI), in the 1930s through into the 1950s, consistently rejected proposals for translating the permissive definition of industrial property of the Paris Convention (i.e. Article 1(3)) into an explicit inclusion of plant varieties.[77] Eventually, breeders organised through the International Association of Plant Breeders for the Protection of Plant Varieties (ASSINSEL), decided to proceed for developing a *sui generis* system dedicated to protecting plant varieties. This activist route is best reflected in the words of the first secretary of UPOV:

> It is for the agronomists to say what it is they consider should be protected, and to indicate the conditions under which protection should be granted, in order for it to be made effective and legitimate.[78]

It is from here that the specific standards of distinctness, uniformity and stability with (commercial) novelty were scripted. Two particular solutions were designed. First, is exclusion of any element of 'inventive step' in the standards of protection. Second, is the remarkably liberal notion of commercial novelty.

The translation of the delinking of a requirement for inventiveness from the standards of protection into national practice is telling. In the US, breeders not only opposed the role of the government in adjudicating 'merit', an activity undertaken until the 1950s,[79] but also contested the statutory link between protection and merit.[80] Consequently, merit tests became a voluntary requirement depending on the fancy of the breeder.[81]

---

76 D.I.F. Wuesthoff and D.F. Wuesthoff, *Protection of New Varieties of Cultivated Plants* (1952).

77 F. Beier *et al.*, *Biotechnology and Patent Protection: An International Review* (Paris: OECD 1985), 27; A. Heitz, *The History of Plant Variety Protection. The First Twenty-Five Years of the International Convention for the Protection of New Varieties of Plants* (Geneva: UPOV 1987), 53.

78 B. Laclaviere 'The Convention of Paris of December 2, 1961, for the Protection of New Varieties of Plants and the International Union for the Protection of New Varieties of Plants' (1965) 10 *Industrial Property* 224.

79 J. Kloppenburg Jr, *First the Seed: The Political Economy of Plant Biotechnology* (Cambridge University Press 1988), 135–9.

80 Lim, n. 35, 198–9.

81 G. Bugos and D Kevles, 'Plants as Intellectual Property: American Practice, Law, and Policy in World Context' (1992) 7 *Osiris* 75, 94–5.

In the UK, the political decision went through a trialling process. The Committee on Transactions in Seeds[82] recommended the introduction PBRs as a means to revitalise the ailing domestic breeding industry.[83] In its submission, the National Farmers Union[84] gave principled acceptance to the introduction of PBRs; but wanted 'merit' to be included either in the standards of protection or, at least, as a condition for marketing. On the other hand, breeders opposed any consideration of merit. Responding to these different positions, the Committee closely followed construction of the standards that were being elaborated at UPOV; thus sticking to the requirements of distinctness, uniformity and stability and rejecting any link with merit or inventiveness. This is not surprising as the Committee prepared their recommendations in close co-operation with those involved in establishing UPOV.[85] Interestingly, in the Parliamentary debate on the Bill, there was strong favour for the construction of standards proposed by the National Farmers Union.[86] However, it is also through the Parliamentary debate that this position is rejected. Even while recognising the possibility of pioneering legislation in this area, Lord Oswald states that the including merit requirements would conflicts with the country's emergent obligations to UPOV.[87]

However, the concern for ensuring that good quality varieties reach the farmers remained. Here, faith was reposed in the functioning of the market and statutory field trials without the need for legislating on merit:

[G]rowers should remain free to determine the commercial success or failure of varieties provided that they are given adequate information about them and were not confused by different names ... use of improved varieties could be promoted more readily by short recommended lists of the best in performance trials than by legislation restricting the sale of seeds to varieties which were equal to those in current use.[88]

It took the UK's joining the European Common Market in 1972 for merit to become a statutory requirement for entry into a Recommended List and for marketing. This occurred through an amendment to the Plant Variety and Seeds Act

---

82 Committee on Transactions in Seeds, n. 72, 20–6.

83 The UK cereal market was dominated by continental varieties (Ibid, 14–16; P. Palladino, 'Science, Technology, and the Economy: Plant Breeding in Great Britain, 1920–1970' (1996) 49 *Economic History Review* 116, 129). For example in wheat, market shares of continental varieties rose from 15 per cent in 1935 to 50 per cent in 1947, reaching 78 per cent in 1956.

84 NFU's submission to CTS (1960) titled 'Note on PBRs' (Document no. CTS/PBR/51, dated 27 January, 1958, at the Public Records Office, file MAF/370/65).

85 G. Dworkin, 'Plant Breeders' Rights: The Scope of United Kingdom Protection' (1982) 4 *European Intellectual Property Review* 11, 11; A. Bould and A Kelly 'Plant Breeders' Rights in the UK' (1992) 5 *Plant Varieties and Seeds* 143, 143–4.

86 Lord Balerno, House of Lords (November 26, 1963).

87 House of Lords, November 26, 1963. UK signed the UPOV 1961 Act in November 1962.

88 P. Wellington, 'Crop Varieties: Their Testing, Commercial Exploitation and Statutory Control' (1974) 135 *Journal of the Royal Agricultural Society of England* 84, 100.

1964 to bring itself into conformity with respect to the requirements of the Common Catalogue.[89]

6. Conclusion

The construction of the standards of protection in PBRs, like in other areas of IPRs, should be seen as acts of socio-political accomplishment, contested as they may be. Not only have breeders and seed merchants achieved a *sui generis* multilateral treaty for the protection of new varieties in UPOV; but, more importantly, have translated this architecture into national jurisdictions. A key focus of the chapter was the delinking of issues of merit and inventive step from the standards of protection for PBRs. The standards for protection require a demonstration of distinctness, uniformity, stability and (commercial) novelty; thus, presenting a relatively low threshold for protection. This low threshold has enabled a particular trajectory of technical change in plant breeding. Firms produce new varieties as a routinised activity and use the regulatory system of field trials to sift out their varieties from the competition. This is evident in the low rates of success that were reported. More significant is the empirical evidence of an active dynamic of entry/exit of varieties reflected in the fluctuations in the number of Net Grants in contrast to the generally secular increase in PBRs Counts. Further, this quickening of the turnover rate of varieties is evidence of strategies of planned obsolescence which here is empirically captured in the fall in average age. Delinking the standards of protection from a requirement to demonstrate merit or inventive step not only enables this strategy but provides juridical legitimisation. The chapter, itself, is a critique of the economic literature where PBRs counts continue to be used as an uncontested indicator of inventive activity.

---

89 Bould and Kelly, n. 83.

Index

Page numbers in bold indicate illustrations, italics indicate tables. Headings in italics indicate legal cases or publication titles.